THE ARCHAEOLOGY OF DARKNESS

THE ARCHAEOLOGY OF DARKNESS

edited by

Marion Dowd and Robert Hensey

Oxbow Books
Oxford & Philadelphia

Published in the United Kingdom in 2016 by
OXBOW BOOKS
10 Hythe Bridge Street, Oxford OX1 2EW

and in the United States by
OXBOW BOOKS
1950 Lawrence Road, Havertown, PA 19083

© Oxbow Books and the individual contributors 2016

Paperback Edition: ISBN 978-1-78570-191-7
Digital Edition: ISBN 978-1-78570-192-4

A CIP record for this book is available from the British Library

Library of Congress Cataloging-in-Publication Data

Names: Dowd, Marion. | Hensey, Robert.
Title: The archaeology of darkness / edited by Marion Dowd and Robert Hensey.
Description: Oxford : Oxbow Books, 2016. | Papers from "Into the earth : the
  archaeology of darkness," a conference held at the Institute of Technology
  Sligo, in the north-west of Ireland, October 27, 2012. | Includes
  bibliographical references.
Identifiers: LCCN 2015049027 (print) | LCCN 2016006939 (ebook) | ISBN
  9781785701917 (paperback) | ISBN 9781785701924 (digital) | ISBN
  9781785701924 (epub) | ISBN 9781785701931 (mobi) | ISBN 9781785701948 (
  pdf)
Subjects: LCSH: Social archaeology--Congresses. |
  Ethnoarchaeology--Congresses. | Landscape archaeology--Congresses. |
  Darkness--Social aspects--History--Congresses. | Night--Social
  aspects--History--Congresses. | Caves--Social
  aspects--History--Congresses. | Passage Graves culture--Congresses. |
  Human ecology--History--Congresses.
Classification: LCC CC72.4 .A7346 2016 (print) | LCC CC72.4 (ebook) | DDC
  304.209--dc23
LC record available at http://lccn.loc.gov/2015049027

All rights reserved. No part of this book may be reproduced or transmitted in any form or by any means, electronic or mechanical including photocopying, recording or by any information storage and retrieval system, without permission from the publisher in writing.

Printed in the United Kingdom by Hobbs the Printers

For a complete list of Oxbow titles, please contact:

UNITED KINGDOM	UNITED STATES OF AMERICA
Oxbow Books	Oxbow Books
Telephone (01865) 241249, Fax (01865) 794449	Telephone (800) 791-9354, Fax (610) 853-9146
Email: oxbow@oxbowbooks.com	Email: queries@casemateacademic.com
www.oxbowbooks.com	www.casemateacademic.com/oxbow

Oxbow Books is part of the Casemate Group

Front cover: Fourknocks passage tomb chamber, Ken Williams.
Back cover: Robert Mulraney.

Contents

List of figures vii

List of plates ix

List of tables x

Background and acknowledgements xi

List of contributors xiii

1. Past dark: a short introduction to the human relationship with darkness
   over time 1
   Robert Hensey

2. Darkness visible. Shadows, art and the ritual experience of caves
   in Upper Palaeolithic Europe 11
   Paul Pettitt

3. Between symbol and senses: the role of darkness in ritual
   in prehistoric Italy 25
   Ruth D. Whitehouse

4. Experiencing darkness and light in caves: later prehistoric examples
   from Seulo in central Sardinia 39
   Robin Skeates

5. The dark side of the sky: the orientations of earlier prehistoric monuments
   in Ireland and Britain 51
   Richard Bradley

6. In search of darkness: cave use in Late Bronze Age Ireland 63
   Marion Dowd

7. Digging into the darkness: the experience of copper mining
   in the Great Orme, North Wales 75
   Sian James

8. Between realms: entering the darkness of the *hare paenga*
   in ancient Rapa Nui (Easter Island) 85
   Sue Hamilton and Colin Richards

9. Dark places and supernatural light in early Ireland 101
   John Carey

10. Enfolded by the long winter's night 107
    Charlotte Damm

11. 'The outer darkness of madness' – the Edwardian Winter Garden
    at Purdysburn public asylum for the insane 117
    Gillian Allmond

12. Descent into darkness 129
    Tim O'Connell

13. Coming in and out of the dark 139
    Gabriel Cooney

List of figures

Figure 1.1 Leipzig street-lighting scene, 1702 (Koslofsky 2011, fig. 5.4).

Figure 1.2 Pilgrim entering St. Patrick's Purgatory (Pinkerton 1856).

Figure 2.1 Hand stencil placed on stalactite, Ardales Cave, near Malaga, Spain (Pedro Cantalejo Duarte).

Figure 2.2 The 'falling horse' of Lascaux (Jean Vertut, courtesy of Paul Bahn).

Figure 3.1 Plan of Grotta di Porto Badisco, showing the different zones and groups of wall paintings (after Graziosi 1980).

Figure 3.2 Plan of Grotta Scaloria/Grotta di Occhiopinto cave complex. Stippled areas represent stalagmites; solid dots represent pottery vessels (after Tinè and Isetti 1982).

Figure 3.3 Plan of the underground complex of Pozzi della Piana. Shaded areas represent greatest concentrations of archaeological finds; small arrows indicate positions of entrances (after Passeri 1970).

Figure 3.4 Miscellany of images of Mediterranean caves (Ruth Whitehouse).

Figure 4.1 Plans of (1) Grutta 1 de Longu Fresu and (2) Grutta de is Janas (Yvonne Beadnell).

Figure 4.2 Interior of Grutta 1 de Longu Fresu (Jeff Veitch).

Figure 4.3 Upper Chamber, Grutta de is Janas (Robin Skeates).

Figure 4.4 Head of stone figurine from large Lower Chamber, Grutta de is Janas (Robin Skeates).

Figure 4.5 Speleothems, modern walkway and lighting along the middle section of the northern branch of Grutta de is Janas (Jeff Veitch).

Figure 4.6 Darkness along the middle section of the northern branch of Grutta de is Janas (Robin Skeates).

Figure 5.1 View of the midwinter sunset looking along the passage of the south-west cairn at Balnuaran of Clava (Ronnie Scott).

Figure 5.2 The entrance to the north-east passage tomb at Balnuaran of Clava at the time of the midwinter sunset (Ronnie Scott).

Figure 5.3 View of the midwinter sunset looking along the passage of the north-east cairn at Balnuaran of Clava (Ronnie Scott).

Figure 6.1 Caver Terry Casserly squeezing through the narrow passage into the third chamber of Robber's Den (Colin Bunce).

Figure 6.2 Irish caves with material of Late Bronze Age date (Thorsten Kahlert).

Figure 6.3 Metalwork hoard from the Gut in Brothers' Cave, illustrated by Colonel Richard W. Forsayeth in 1906 (Dowd and Corlett 2002).

Figure 6.4 Drystone structure in Glencurran Cave, marking the beginning of the dark zone (Peter Rees).

Figure 8.1 Distribution of *ahu* on Rapa Nui (after Lee 1992 and Martinsson-Wallin 1994).

Figure 8.2 The canoe ramp assumes a central position in the *ahu* complex at Tahai, on the west coast of Rapa Nui (Adam Stanford).

Figure 8.3 A *hare paenga* adjacent to the Akahanga section of the *ara moai*. Note the *poro* pavement extending beyond the entrance (Adam Stanford).

Figure 8.4 Entrance passage into a *hare paenga*; note the entrance passage is also paved with rounded *poro* (Adam Stanford).

Figure 8.5 Probable portable house *moai* (Mike Seager Thomas, courtesy of Museo Antropologico P. Sebastian Englert).

Figure 11.1 Exterior of male wing of the hospital showing Winter Garden roof lantern (Belfast Mental Hospital 1924: PRONI HOS32/1/9).

Figure 11.2 Photograph of architect's ground floor plan of male wing of hospital showing Winter Garden, *c.* 1910 (Gillian Allmond).

Figure 11.3 Photograph of architect's drawing, *c.* 1910, of the Winter Garden roof lantern at Purdysburn public asylum (Gillian Allmond).

Figure 11.4 Winter Garden interior dating from *c.* 1914 (Belfast District Lunatic Asylum Annual Report 1922).

Figure 12.1 The author on a caving trip in Poll na Grai, Co. Clare (Colin Bunce).

Figure 12.2 Niall Tobin and Eoghan Mullan with their caving gear, 500m deep into Krubera (Niall Tobin).

Figure 12.3 Back outside: after eleven days in the world's deepest cave (Niall Tobin).

List of plates

Plate 1 Paul Pettitt with hands positioned over a pair of hand stencils on the Panel of Hands in El Castillo Cave, Cantabria, Spain. Note the association with natural cracks in the cave ceiling, and the extension of arms in the form of shadows (Becky Harrison, courtesy of Gobierno de Cantabria).

Plate 2 The 'bison-man' column, painting and shadow, El Castillo Cave, Cantabria, Spain (Marc Groenen).

Plate 3 Greenstone axe-head from Grutta 1 de Longu Fresu, Sardinia (Jeff Veitch).

Plate 4 Inner Chamber, Grutta de is Janas, Sardinia (Robin Skeates).

Plate 5 The entrance to the south-west passage tomb at Balnuaran of Clava, Scotland at the time of the midwinter sunset (Ronnie Scott).

Plate 6 The entrance to the north-east passage tomb at Balnuaran of Clava, Scotland at the time of the midwinter sunset (Ronnie Scott).

Plate 7 Moneen Mountain with location of Moneen Cave indicated, Co. Clare, Ireland (Ken Williams).

Plate 8 Area of Glencurran Cave, Co. Clare, Ireland, where ritual offerings were deposited during the Late Bronze Age (Ken Williams).

Plate 9 The Great Orme mines, Wales, and visitor entrances in 2013 (Sian James).

Plate 10 The *ahu* platform at Nau Nau, Anekena, Rapa Nui (Easter Island) (Colin Richards).

Plate 11 Several massive hare nui overlook the *ahu* complex at Te Peu on the west coast of Rapa Nui (Easter Island) (Adam Stanford).

Plate 12 Chief's house on Rapa Nui (Easter Island) in 1872, by Pierre Loti (alias Julien Viaud 1850-1923) (after Heyerdahl and Ferdon 1961, fig. 11).

Plate 13 Extract on the theme of darkness from the fourteenth-century Book of Ballymote, RIA MS 23 P 12, folio 196v (© Royal Irish Academy. Courtesy of Irish Script on Screen).

Plate 14 Inuit woman playing a string game. The figures can be boats or sledges, but animals and humans are also popular. In some areas the game is restricted to the long dark season (Malaurie 2002, 373).

Plate 15 Descending Peter Bryant's Bullock Hole, Co. Fermanagh, Northern Ireland (Axel Hack).

List of tables

Table 3.1 Structural contrasts in Neolithic Italy.

Table 3.2 The structure of rites of passage, and how the movement into and out of darkness fits into the structure of the rites.

Table 5.1 Sources of variation among the alignments of prehistoric monuments.

Table 5.2 The principal orientations of prehistoric structures between 3700 and 800 BC, illustrated by typical examples.

Table 5.3 The dominant orientations of monuments and domestic buildings, and the relationships between them.

Background and acknowledgements

Marion Dowd and Robert Hensey

This book began with a conference entitled 'Into the Earth: the Archaeology of Darkness'. The event took place just before Halloween 2012, at the Institute of Technology Sligo, in north-west Ireland. The success of the present volume is in no small part due to the contributors to that conference; we thank them all for their insights and enthusiasm for the subject. We would like to sincerely thank those speakers who are not represented in this volume: Colmán Ó Clabaigh, Muiris O'Sullivan, Jack Santino, Ken Williams and Brian Keenan for their involvement.

Brian Keenan's powerful and moving account of his physical and mental deterioration, coping mechanisms and recovery from the four and a half years he was held hostage by Islamic Jihad in Beirut between 1986 and 1990, was for many a highlight of the conference. The impact his talk had on the other speakers is clear from several chapters in this book. Brian's meditation and reflections on darkness through his various publications (*An evil cradling*; *Turlough*; *Four quarters of light*) was an important influence on us from the conception of the conference through to the production of *The archaeology of darkness*.

Darkness is a fundamental feature of life, which we realize was not just an important and undertheorized feature of the monuments and sites we studied, megalithic tombs and caves, but a central aspect of human experience in the past and present (see Chapter 1). Certain religious practices evident in the archaeological record have, at their core, an interaction with darkness. Current research by Paul Pettitt, for instance, reveals that shadows played a significant role in the creation and appreciation of Palaeolithic art in European caves (Chapter 2). Similarly, Marion Dowd examines the use of the darkest areas of caves for ritual activities in Bronze Age Ireland (Chapter 6) while Ruth Whitehouse argues for the centrality of darkness in initiation ceremonies held deep inside caves in Neolithic and Bronze Age Italy (Chapter 3). The symbolism and interplay between light and dark are themes found in ritual landscapes, from the prehistoric monuments of Ireland and Britain as explored by Richard Bradley (Chapter 5), to the famous *hare paenga* of Easter Island re-examined in a fresh light by Sue Hamilton and Colin Richards (Chapter 8). Robin Skeates' contribution (Chapter 4) highlights a topic that is common for many of the authors: the sensory experience of physically and spiritually navigating dark underground spaces.

The living and working conditions of some people past and present also involved intense interaction with darkness, such as the Bronze Age and post-medieval miners who exploited the Great Orme copper sources in Wales as explored by Sian James

(Chapter 7). In spite of the pervasive associations between darkness and negativity, Charlotte Damm presents a refreshing account of the welcome communities north of the Arctic Circle have for the 'great darkness' (Chapter 10). In a similar vein, the received wisdom that Victorian and Edwardian asylums were grim dark places is challenged by Gillian Allmond's review of the contemporaneous literature and architecture which suggest, rather, that light and brightness were at the forefront of mental institution design (Chapter 12). Medieval Irish literature portrays darkness as a metaphor for wisdom, a theme brilliantly illuminated by John Carey (Chapter 9). Caver Tim O'Connell brings us on an enthralling journey into the darkest and deepest place in the known world (Chapter 12). As Gabriel Cooney notes (Chapter 13), the challenge in understanding how darkness was perceived in other societies is to be reflexive and aware that our interpretations are conditioned by and grounded in our own culture and experience.

The high quality of these chapters, the punctuality of the contributors in meeting deadlines, and their interest in the subject have made our work as editors pleasant and enjoyable. For help in the organization of the conference we would like to thank: Jeremy Bird, Rory Connolly, Ciarán Davis, Billy Fitzgerald, Phyl Foley, Alan Healy, Pádraig Meehan, Sam Moore, Sinead Neary, Paul Rooney and Gordon Ryan. Special thanks are due to I.T. Sligo for a grant towards the conference costs, and to the School of Geography and Archaeology NUI Galway and the Sligo Field Club who provided financial support for this publication. We are grateful to the team at Oxbow Books for their work. We would like to acknowledge all those who gave permission to include their images. For the illustration from the *Book of Ballymote* we thank Bernadette Cunningham and the Royal Irish Academy, and Anne Marie O'Brien and the Irish Script on Screen (www.isos.dias.ie). Thanks to Counterpoint Press for permission to reproduce the Wendell Berry poem 'To Know the Dark', and Craig Koslofsky and Cambridge University Press for permission to reproduce figure 1.2. We are indebted to Ken Williams and Robert Mulraney for their wonderful photographs which grace the front and back covers respectively.

This book and the opportunity it has given us to delve into the subject of darkness has been extremely rewarding. Though we have not completely gone over to the dark side (!) we are quite sure our respective archaeological work and thinking will never again be quite the same.

January 2016

Marion Dowd
Robert Hensey

Contributors

Gillian Allmond is a buildings archaeologist based at Queen's University Belfast. Having worked for several years on the Northern Ireland Environment Agency's survey of listed buildings, she is currently completing a doctoral study of colony asylums in Scotland, Ireland and Germany.

Richard Bradley taught prehistoric archaeology at the University of Reading between 1971 and 2013, and is Emeritus Professor of Archaeology there. He has a special interest in ancient landscapes and monumental architecture in Europe. In 2007 he published *The prehistory of Britain and Ireland* (Cambridge University Press).

John Carey is Professor of Early and Medieval Irish at University College Cork. The collection *The end and beyond: medieval Irish eschatology*, edited by him together with Emma Nic Cárthaigh and Caitríona Ó Dochartaigh, was published in 2014.

Gabriel Cooney is Professor of Celtic Archaeology at University College Dublin. His research interests focus on Irish prehistory, particularly the Neolithic. He is co-director of the Irish Stone Axe Project, and is currently involved in researching prehistoric quarrying on Shetland.

Charlotte Damm is Professor of Archaeology in the Department of Archaeology and Social Anthropology at the Arctic University of Norway. Her main field of research is early (Stone Age) hunter-fisher societies in the northern circumpolar region, particularly northern Scandinavia.

Marion Dowd is an archaeologist with a specialist interest in caves. She has directed excavations in many Irish caves, and has written and lectured widely on the subject. Her book *The archaeology of caves in Ireland* (Oxbow Books) was published in 2015. She is Lecturer in Prehistoric Archaeology at the Institute of Technology, Sligo.

Sue Hamilton is Professor of Prehistory at UCL Institute of Archaeology. She is interested in landscape archaeology, sensory and gendered landscapes, and late prehistoric Europe. She is co-director of the Rapa Nui (Easter Island) Landscapes of Construction Project.

Robert Hensey specializes in Neolithic Ireland and Europe with particular reference to the Irish passage tomb tradition, megalithic art and religion. He is the author of *First light: the origins of Newgrange* (2015) published by Oxbow Books.

Sian James has worked as the archaeologist on the Bronze Age copper mining site at Great Orme for over ten years. Previously researcher and lecturer in the History, Welsh History and Archaeology department at the University of Bangor she is an avid caver as well as archaeologist and is interested in the experience of working in challenging environments.

Tim O'Connell is an educator and caver. He is a founding member of the Clare Caving Club, and has been involved in numerous explorations of cave systems both new and old.

Paul Pettitt is Professor of Palaeolithic Archaeology at Durham University. He holds degrees from the universities of Birmingham, London and Cambridge; was archaeologist in the Radiocarbon Accelerator Unit at Oxford University (1995-2001), research fellow and tutor, Keble College, Oxford (1998-2003), and taught at Sheffield University (2003-2013). He researches aspects of Palaeolithic mortuary activity and art.

Colin Richards is Professor of World Prehistory at the University of Manchester. He has published widely on the Neolithic, particularly of Orkney, most recently *Building the great stone circles of the north* (2013). He is co-director of the Rapa Nui (Easter Island) Landscapes of Construction Project which has been running since 2008.

Robin Skeates is a specialist in central Mediterranean prehistory and in museum and heritage studies. His latest book is *An archaeology of the senses: prehistoric Malta* (2010). He has a long-standing interest in cave rituals, and directs two field projects (in Sardinia and central Italy) on the cultural life of caves.

Ruth D. Whitehouse is an archaeologist who specializes in Italian and west Mediterranean prehistory. She has published widely on the role of caves in ritual and religion in prehistory. She is Emeritus Professor of Archaeology at UCL Institute of Archaeology.

Chapter 1

Past dark: a short introduction to the human relationship with darkness over time

Robert Hensey

'To Know the Dark' – Wendell Berry

To go in the dark with a light is to know the light.
To know the dark, go dark. Go without sight,
and find the dark, too, blooms and sings,
and is travelled by dark feet and dark wings.

Darkness within darkness

Though comprehensive books have been penned on areas related to darkness, such as the history of the night and the increasing electrification of the world (Bowers 1998; Jonnes 2003; Dewdey 2004; Ekirch 2006; Koslofsky 2011; Bogard 2013), literature on the subject of darkness from an archaeological or historical perspective – especially as regards human interactions with ancient places and monuments – is rare, if not non-existent. Given that darkness would have had an even greater role in the past than it has today, it is unclear why this might be so.

One possible explanation is that darkness has been so much part of our lives and of the history of our species that we tend not to acknowledge it; it is too big to see, too fundamental, too pervasive. Darkness is so many things: the dark of night; the darkness of deep winter; the darkness of the subterranean world; darkness as a metaphor we live by. It is only recently as we have been able to exclude it more successfully from our lives that, conversely, we have become more aware of it, realized we may be missing something.

Another reason perhaps is that darkness, by its very nature, seems to repel objectification – to actively resist study. You cannot photograph the dark, for instance. When we see images of deep caves or megalithic recesses we can only do so because of camera flashes and other artificial means of lighting. What we are actually photographing is the temporary removal of darkness. Darkness is the opposite of 'illumination', enlightenment – and all those other light-oriented words we rely on so heavily to describe understanding (Thomas 2009); the dark is where the unseen, unformed and misunderstood things abide, that which has not been examined in the cold hard light of day. The route to 'understanding' the dark may be somewhat different than other areas of investigation. Wendell Berry's poem 'To Know the Dark' at the beginning of this piece captures something of this elusiveness.

A further factor that could explain our limited appreciation of darkness is that we may have simply lost touch with it over succeeding generations. For three hundred years we have gradually been lighting up our world, particularly over much of the last century. It is now estimated that two thirds of Europeans and Americans no longer experience real night or darkness (Bogard 2013, 9). In *Evening's empire: a history of the night in early modern Europe* (2011), Craig Koslofsky records perceptions of light and dark in European history over the course of our steady 'colonization' of the night. He details the dramatic change in the lives of European city inhabitants that came with the introduction of street lighting from the eighteenth century onwards, in particular the pacifying effect light had on cities (Fig. 1.1). People began to see the night in a more positive way; it was now safe to go out in the night, deviant behaviours had less places to hide – the threat of darkness was being driven back. This process of driving out the dark has continued to a point whereby we now have almost complete ability to exclude darkness from our everyday lives. Indeed, as Bogard (2013) has highlighted in *The end of night: searching for natural darkness in an age of artificial light*, it has become difficult to find places in our world where we can see truly dark skies anymore.

Figure 1.1: Leipzig street-lighting scene, 1702 (Koslofsky 2011, fig. 5.4).

Perhaps it is because of the naturalization and ever-presence of artificial mediums of light that darkness today can hold a certain fascination for us; it has become a novelty. Charitable road race events such as *Run in the Dark* and *Darkness into Light* have become innovative mediums for fundraising. 'Dancing in the dark' events have become popular. Restaurants in major cities all over the world now offer 'dining in the dark' experiences. Some are exclusively dark dining venues. The first of these was opened by a blind man in Zurich, Switzerland in 1999 (Dewdney 2004). He employed only blind table staff to serve diners and guide them around the restaurant, giving his customers an insight into the sightless world. One reason 'dark dining' has taken off is because diners say that with restricted sight their other senses become more heightened. One's sense of taste and smell of course is magnified, but the texture of foods becomes a more important part of the eating experience too, as does consistency and temperature. This increase in sensory experience perhaps runs counter to the sensory deprivation that we might at first tend to associate with darkness – and is something that perhaps should be considered as we interpret human engagement with dark sites and monuments in the past.

Darkness and archaeology

The role of darkness is hugely apparent in the archaeological record. Many artefacts were intentionally deposited in places that exclude light, not only caves and megalithic monuments, but also barrows, cists, pits, tree throw holes and countless other site types, or simply buried directly into the earth. Moreover, while there are certain activities we automatically think of when we consider the past – tool production, food procurement and building – other necessary activities would have taken place in the subterranean world, such as mining for stone tools and metals (e.g. Russell 2000; James this volume). Vast subterranean quarries such as Grimes Graves indicate just how much time was spent in shadowy underground tunnels sourcing materials for upperworld activities (Mercer 1981).

Our tendency is to view archaeological monuments and sites only in the bright light of day. Artificial light has an important role in archaeology too. We examine megalithic chambers with powerful torches, aiming to expose corners and niches, to reveal all in precise and measurable detail. But perhaps in doing this, by driving out shadow, we miss part of the story of these places. Is it possible that in some cases darkness was not an incidental feature of a site or place but a fundamental feature (also see Pettit this volume)? Illuminating these sites and monuments, removing artefacts from their repositories, may result in excluding a crucial foundation of the ritual that lay behind the deposition: darkness.

Chris Tilley (2008, 117), for instance, has noted that our exacting recording of megalithic art, laying bare every incision and peck mark, betrays the actual experience of entering a decorated monument where many motifs were intended to be more hidden, perhaps shrouded in darkness, whereas other designs were intended to be visible. A person in the Neolithic, not having the advantage of the catalogue of motifs we have today, would have missed many of the less prominent or badly lit carvings. Conversely, the size and/or prominent position within the monument of other designs may have meant those examples loomed larger and perhaps struck people more forcibly, leaving a more lasting impression. When we remove darkness from the equation, we remove something of the experience of place.

As noted already, most of what we investigate in archaeology has to do with people's outward activities. Because of this we rarely consider people's inward life or emotions and how that might impact on the archaeological record (Tarlow 2000). For instance, one of the persistent associations with darkness is fear. One imagines fear of darkness is very deep within our species, perhaps rooted in us at a genetic level. For so much of our evolution, a poisonous creature or a human assailant lurking in the dark could have meant injury or death. It is then somewhat understandable that fear of the dark, *achluophobia*, is suffered by children and adults alike. Fear of darkness is reflected in much folklore, mythology and religion (Ekirch 2006). In Christianity, Lucifer, the angel of light, transforms into Satan, the ultimate symbol of fear, the prince of darkness (Koslofsky 2011, chapter 2).

The dead, and various lands of the dead such as the Greek Hades, are also associated with darkness and night. Of course these places too are often associated with caves, swallow holes, and other entrances into the earth or the 'underworld' (Davies and Robb 2004). Most living things, in particular vegetation, stop at these thresholds. Connections with life and death lend darkness a theatrical power which may have been harnessed in past myth. Yet darkness can equally be protective and nourishing; the dark safe womb; the life-giving earth where seeds germinate and from whence life springs forth.

When we speak about darkness we need to be aware that there are different types or levels, or that different people may associate darkness with differing levels of visibility. For instance, there are places and monuments which seem internally very dark on first appearances but as one's eyes become accustomed, especially if prolonged time is spent inside, one realizes that actually quite a lot can be seen. To discuss this subject we may need to reclaim knowledge of, and language for, different types of darkness. It may be better not just to speak about 'darkness', but about 'opaque', 'crepuscular', 'sunless', 'inky', 'pitch-black' and other types and degrees of darkness. Terms such as these could be associated with a simple scale describing degrees of darkness in a not dissimilar way to how we use the Munsell colour chart to describe soils in archaeological excavation. Though we do not as yet have a technical scale for the degrees of darkness of the interiors of archaeological sites, one does exist to measure the darkness of the night sky. This scale, created by John Bortle in 2001, ranks the night sky from 9 to 1, from the heavily obscured inner-city skies that many of us experience today (9), to 'truly dark' locations (1) a quality of darkness that most of us have never experienced (Bogard 2013).

Newgrange is a place that we naturally tend to think of in terms of extreme light and dark, the visitation of the rays of sun on the winter solstice at the very darkest point of the year. Crowds of people visit Newgrange every December, and it is probable that the passage tomb complex was a place of gatherings in the Neolithic also (Hensey 2015). Pilgrimage is not something that we automatically associate with darkness – though those familiar with the pilgrimage site of Croagh Patrick in Co. Mayo will know that people traditionally climbed the mountain at night. It is possible that some people travelled at night to Newgrange, even if only from nearby settlements, to reach the site before sunlight entered the monument at dawn. However, due to the limited size of the chamber, very few people would actually have been able to enter the structure to witness the entry of light; most probably gathered outside the monument before dawn and waited in darkness. One could say that darkness was a key component of the winter solstice Newgrange event (and other astronomically oriented sites), yet that aspect is rarely considered.

Outer darkness and inner light

Very elderly Irish people still talk with great enthusiasm about the Rural Electrification Scheme of the 1950s and the many benefits it brought to their lives; though the philosopher and writer John Moriarty (1998) has spoken about the subtle loss of perception people experienced with this change. Yet even with considerable electrification of our lives, we spend much of our time in darkness. Sleep takes place in darkness, as do dreams. People in the past must have wondered where dreams came from, or at the connections between darkness and inner vision. In Irish folktales, night and darkness are associated with spirits, danger, and potentiality, and are sometimes a symbol for dramatic changes of fortune (Danaher 1972; 1988).

Absolute darkness could be described as the visual equivalent of silence. Records of diverse cultures in which periods of silent retreat in darkened places were undertaken are common. In the Tibetan Buddhist tradition retreats in total darkness (typically for 49 days) have been part of religious practices at least since the fifteenth century. They were known as *Yangti nagpo*, or Single Golden Syllable of the Black Quintessence (Ricard and Shabkar 1994, note 17). A famous female retreatant from that tradition, *Ayu Khandro Dorje Pendron*, born in the mid-nineteenth century, is reputed to have spent many years in dark retreat (Tsultrim 2000, 71). A visitor to her retreat house records that even in old age she could see much better in the dark than he, and she did not need the candles which he required (Norbu 1986, 146). In this religious context, one of the reasons for the dark environment was to better achieve the mental visualizations necessary to a particular meditation practice without outward visual distraction. Equally, in Christian hagiography, several saints were believed to have spent time in caves and similar retreat places pursuing spiritual goals. In this they were following the lead of the ascetics of the deserts of Syria and Egypt (Chryssavgis 2009). For willing retreatants such as these, darkness in isolation could be seen as a unique opportunity where high levels of tranquillity might be found, or perhaps where temptations could be overcome and saintly qualities developed.

Yet it would be wrong to think of solitary isolation in darkness as simply a pleasurable pursuit or a spiritual indulgence of some kind. It is notable that solitary confinement and deprivation of natural light are two of the most severe forms of punishment that have been meted out in prison systems throughout the world. Unquestionably time spent in isolation and in darkness could be a challenging ordeal and was not something for the faint-hearted. Brian Keenan's (1991) disturbing account of nine months in total darkness, the beginning of a four-year period as a hostage at the hands of Islamic Jihad, is testament to how challenging this could be.

A site famed for its fear-filled journey into darkness is the cave-like structure known as St. Patrick's purgatory which once existed on one of the pilgrimage islands at Lough Derg, Co. Donegal (Dowd 2015). The fame of this pilgrimage site spread all over Europe in the late medieval period (Fig. 1.2). It was thought to be an entry point into purgatory, a place where one could pass through the tortures awaiting one after death, whilst still in this life, and thereafter be granted heavenly visions. We know, for example, of an Italian merchant and pilgrim named Antonio Mannini who left his home at Florence, eventually ending up at St. Patrick's purgatory in the year 1411 (Seymour 1918). Whether

Figure 1.2: Pilgrim entering St. Patrick's Purgatory as imagined in the fifteenth century (Pinkerton 1856).

he experienced purgatory as envisioned in the medieval imagination we cannot say; his account – unusually for the period – is entirely devoid of references to the supernatural or the miraculous. We can say that by journeying to Ireland and Lough Derg, he left behind his family, his culture, his language, many of the supports on which he would have based his identity. Equally, prolonged time in darkness, especially in isolation, often seems to involve a dissolution of the supports upon which we base our identities and can be experienced as something catastrophic.

In Christian literature this type of spiritual and personal experience is sometimes referred to as 'the dark night of the soul', after the famous work of Spanish sixteenth-century Carmelite monk and mystic St. John of the Cross (2003). In darkness we retreat from our worldly reference points. In this outer experience vacuum, inner experience is heightened. For some that could involve a challenge to their mental stability; for others it could allow them develop greater awareness or sensitivities. In darkness memory is encouraged, as outside influences and new memories are fewer. Darkness allows time to assimilate previous experience; time that we rarely have nowadays. Darkness encourages this processing, a kind of getting back to the start. Before birth we all spend nine months in the womb in darkness: growing, changing, transforming. This might partly explain why darkness has such a profound effect. There is a great metaphorical resonance between this time before birth and what is replicated in dark and isolation.

Culture and cultural variation

So much of the dynamism and drama of theatre is dependent on lighting a dark stage, the manipulation of specific areas with light against a dark backdrop (Nicoll 1996). The use of darkness and shadow has had a key role in the development of cinema too, most notably perhaps through German Expressionism where it was used to generate atmosphere and emotion through cinematic masterpieces such as *Nosferatu* (1922), *Metropolis* (1927) and *M* (1931) (Gunning 2000). Fritz Lang, the director of the latter two films, is often referred to as the 'Master of Darkness'. The explicit manipulation of darkness in cinema continued through film noir and horror genres, via the masterful works of Orson Welles, Alfred Hitchcock and many others, and continues today through the expressionist and gothic sensibilities of directors such as Ridley Scott and Tim Burton. German Expressionism of course has a wider role in the early twentieth century and involved architecture, theatre, photography and painting, as well as cinema. In a short piece such as this it is not possible to discuss the use of light and darkness in German Expressionist painting, or in painting in general, but it would be an oversight not to at least mention the work of one painter, Caravaggio (1571–1610), whose paintings represent one of the greatest expressions of the power and potency of darkness, a wholly new world that emerged from the blackest of backgrounds (Langdon 1999). The work of Carravaggio foreshadowed much of what was yet to come in art and cinema by hundreds of years.

In the 1970s Irish town in which I grew up, there was no dedicated theatre or art gallery, and film noir had long had its day. Perhaps the most arresting example of darkness, of its drama and transformative power, was the confession box in the Catholic Church; participants persuaded that the sensation of a cleansed soul could only be achieved by entering and passing through this peculiar ritual darkness. The hard wooden kneeling bench was all there was to moderate the seeming total darkness in the confessional compartment, and the mumble of prayers and whispers of sins from the churchgoer to the priest in the opposed confessional. Darkness then held the key to direct communication with the highest power; counter-intuitively, nothing could remain hidden in darkness, no act or transgression. The dark confession box was the fail-safe valve of the Church; arguably it could not have survived through history as well as it did without the release facilitated by that dark environment.

Research comparing cultural responses to darkness highlights surprising variation in how different cultures react to darkness (see Kasof 2009 with references). For instance, it has recently been shown that in studies using artificial indoor lighting that brighter light typically improves mood in Western countries, but can have an opposite effect in Japan (Nakamura and Masato 1999; Miwa and Hanyu 2006). Joseph Kasof (2009, 80) notes Tanizaki's *In praise of shadows* (1977) as an example of Japanese art and literature that celebrates darkness, an Eastern 'propensity to seek beauty in darkness' and 'delight in shadows', that disparages Western influence for imposing 'the evils of excessive illumination'. Though Tanizaki's treatise is arguably as much a defence of traditional Japanese life and aesthetics in the face of Westernization and consumerism as it is a defence of darkness, it does exhibit a nuanced and eclectic sensitivity to the mysteries of shadow and light:

> *Whenever I see the alcove of a tastefully built Japanese room, I marvel at our comprehension of the secrets of shadows, our sensitive use of shadow and light. For the beauty of the alcove is not the work of some clever device. An empty space is marked off with plain wood and plain walls, so that the light drawn into its forms dim shadows within emptiness. There is nothing more. And yet, when we gaze into the darkness that gathers behind the crossbeam, around the flower vase, beneath the shelves, though we know perfectly well it is mere shadow, we are overcome with the feeling that in this small corner of the atmosphere there reigns complete and utter silence; that here in the darkness immutable tranquility holds sway* (Tanizaki 1977, 32–3).

For people who live in more northerly latitudes, most of the year is lived through darkness (see Damm this volume). Long periods of darkness must have elicited a direct physiological response. A common form of depression known as Seasonal Affective Disorder is experienced by many people, especially in winter. Social gatherings may have helped people psychologically at the darkest of time of year. In a recent interview, eminent psychologist Maureen Gaffney (2014) has spoken about the importance of the seasonal celebrations at Christmas as harkening back to ancient gatherings at the darkest point of the year, the winter solstice, the point from when the days started to get longer. These gatherings, she suggests, might have served as 'an unconscious audit' of one's friends and alliances, as one was facing into tough (and cold) times to come. Gatherings at the darkest time of the year may have been fundamentally about assuaging fears and insecurities by surrounding oneself and one's family with the people that could be counted on, a show of social strength. Following Gaffney, it may be that gatherings that took place at sites like Durrington Walls and Newgrange at mid-winter in prehistory may also have centred on a similar 'audit', on forging and maintaining tribal alliances, and perhaps on questions of leadership and tribal stability too.

It goes without saying that, in the northern hemisphere, winter is synonymous with darkness. The end of October is associated with Halloween or *Oíche Shamana* in Ireland. Traditions and customs of this festival revolve around the belief that it was on this night that spirits, including departed loved ones, return. Candles were placed in the windows of houses to guide spirits home. Seán Ó Duinn (2011) has discussed the Halloween tradition of children dressing up as ghosts or monsters – now Americanized as 'trick or treating' – as, in fact, a symbolic representation of the Tuatha Dé Danann, the ancient gods, returning to farmsteads to exact a tribute for providing good harvests during the year. The 'trick' in this case would be a bad harvest in the year following if an appropriate tribute was not given. Magico-religious beliefs around the harvest must equally have been very strong in the consciousness of people as they began to practise agriculture for the first time in northern Europe; their lives depended on what happened to the seeds they planted in the dark earth. Connections between darkness, birth and regeneration may have taken on additional resonances in the religious rituals of the Neolithic.

Conclusion

Darkness is a pre-eminent characteristic of human experience and, though largely unacknowledged in archaeological and historical literature, a fundamental aspect of the human story. It is intimately connected to people in the past: throughout human evolution in our experience of the seasons and dark landscapes; through the countless ritual depositions of various kinds made in dark places; and more exclusively through transformative religious rites which often took place in dark locations away from the wider community. If we are to better understand our past and the more hidden aspects of the human journey, darkness is an essential subject.

References

Berry, W. 1970. 'To Know the Dark'. *Farming: a hand book*. New York, Harcourt, Brace, Jovanovich.
Bogard, P. 2013. *The end of night: searching for natural darkness in an age of artificial light*. London, Fourth Estate.
Bowers, B. 1998. *Lengthening the day: a history of lighting technology*. Oxford, Oxford University Press.
Chryssavgis, J. 2009. *In the heart of the desert: the spirituality of the desert fathers and mothers*. Bloomington IN., World Wisdom Books.
Danaher, K. 1972. *The year in Ireland*. Dublin, Mercier Press.
Danaher, K. 1988. *Folk tales of the Irish countryside*. Dublin, Mercier Press.
Davies, P. and Robb, J. 2004. Scratches in the earth: the underworld as a theme in British prehistory, with particular reference to the Neolithic and earlier Bronze Age. *Landscape Research* 29 (2), 141–51.
Dewdney, C. 2004. *Acquaintance with the night: excursions through the world after dark*. New York, Bloomsbury USA.
Dowd, M. 2015. *The archaeology of caves in Ireland*. Oxford, Oxbow Books.
Ekirch, R. 2006. *At day's close: a history of nighttime*. London, Weidenfeld & Nicolson.
Gaffney, M. 2014. Interview on RTÉ Radio 1, Marian Finucane Show, 20th December 2014.
Gunning, T. 2000. *The films of Fritz Lang: allegories of vision and modernity*. London, British Film Institute.
Hensey, R. 2015. *The origins of Newgrange*. Oxford, Oxbow Books.
John of the Cross. 2003. *Dark night of the soul* (translated by E. Allison Peers). Mineola, NY, Dover Thrift Editions.
Jones, A. and MacGregor, G. (eds.) 2002. *Colouring the past: the significance of colour in archaeological research*. Oxford, Berg.
Jonnes, J. 2003. *Empires of light: Edison, Tesla, Westinghouse, and the race to electrify the world*. New York, Random House.
Kasof. J. 2009. Cultural variation in seasonal depression: cross-national differences in winter versus summer patterns of seasonal affective disorder. *Journal of Affective Disorders* 115, 79–86.
Keenan, B. 1991. *An evil cradling*. London, Vintage.
Koslofsky, C. 2011. *Evening's empire: a history of the night in early modern Europe*. New York, Cambridge University Press.
Langdon, H. 1999. *Caravaggio: a life*. London, Pimlico Press.
Mercer, R. 1981. *Grimes Graves, Norfolk, Volume I: Excavations 1971–72*. English Heritage Publishing.
Miwa, Y. and Hanyu, K. 2006. The effects of interior design on communication and impressions of a counselor in a counselling room. *Environment and Behavior* 38, 484–502.
Moriarty, J. 1998. *A walkabout in dreamtime Ireland*. Unpublished lectures, All Hallows College, Dublin, February–March 1998.
Nakamura, H. and Masato, O. 1999. Effect of illuminance and color temperature on preference of atmosphere in lighting environment with daylight and artificial light. *Research Reports of Ashikaga Institute of Technology* 28, 177–82.

Nicoll, A. (ed.) 1966. *The development of the theatre*. New York, Harcourt, Brace & World.
Norbu, N. 1986. *The crystal and the way of light: sutra, tantra and dzogchen*. New York, Routledge and Kegan Paul.
Ó Duinn, S. 2011. *In search of the awesome mystery*. Dublin, Columba Press.
Pinkerton, W. 1856. Saint Patrick's Purgatory. *Ulster Journal of Archaeology* 4, 40–52, 101–17, 222–38.
Ricard, M. and Shabkar, T. R. 1994. *The life of Shabkar: the autobiography of a Tibetan yogin*. Albany, State University of New York Press.
Russell, M. 2000. *Flint mines in Neolithic Britain*. Stroud, Tempus.
Seymour, J. D. 1918. *St Patricks Purgatory: a mediaeval pilgrimage in Ireland*. Dundalk, Dundalgan Press.
Tanizaki. J. 1977. *In praise of shadows*. Translated from the Japanese by T. J. Harper and E. G. Seidensticker. London, Vintage Classics.
Tarlow, S. 2000. Emotion in archaeology. *Current Anthropology* 41 (5), 713–46.
Thomas, J. 2009. On the ocularcentrism of archaeology. In J. Thomas and V. O. Jorge (eds.) *Archaeology and the politics of vision in a post-modern context*, 1–12. Cambridge, Cambridge Scholars Press.
Tsultrim, A. 1984. *Women of wisdom*. London, Routledge & Kegan Paul.

Chapter 2

Darkness visible. Shadows, art and the ritual experience of caves in Upper Palaeolithic Europe

Paul Pettitt

Afraid of the dark

Yet from those flames, no light; but rather darkness visible
(John Milton *Paradise Lost 1*, 63)

Figurative and non-figurative art in the deep caves of western Europe appeared sometime around or before 40,000 years ago, and persisted in fits and starts until the last few thousand years of the Pleistocene. Although cave art cannot be said to have been ubiquitous to Upper Palaeolithic life, it was embedded in wider and more continuous artistic production from the ornamentation of the body through portable engraved, sculpted and painted objects (*art mobilier*) to engravings, sculpture and painting on rockshelter walls and the cave art of concern here. 'Cave art', whether figurative or non-figurative, was practised at least in certain phases over much of the Early, Mid and Late Upper Palaeolithic in southern France and northern Spain, and perhaps more rarely in regional pockets elsewhere from southern Spain and England in the west, Germany and Italy in Central Europe, to the Urals in the east.

Recent uranium-series dating projects are revealing a general picture of technical and stylistic development over the 25,000 years or more of the Upper Palaeolithic over which cave art was being produced (e.g. Delluc and Delluc 1991, 2001; Ripoll López *et al.* 1999, 73; Pettitt and Pike 2007; Gárate 2008; Pike *et al.* 2012). The earliest examples seem to consist of finger dots, hand stencils and simple animal outlines, and are as yet more common in rockshelters containing evidence of Early Upper Palaeolithic (Aurignacian) occupation than in deep caves. By the Mid Upper Palaeolithic (Gravettian), numerous examples exist in deep caves among which regional clusters can be identified (such as the caves of the Quercy, including Pech-Merle and Cougnac: Lorblanchet 2010). True compositional scenes and a high degree of naturalism are common, and animal figures have risen to prominence. With the Late Upper Palaeolithic (Solutrean, Badegoulian and Early, Middle and Late Magdalenian) – to which the majority of cave art dates – considerable complexity of production, compositional scenes displaying perspective and movement, and the great polychrome paintings of Lascaux, Altamira and elsewhere are evident. Surprisingly, this development follows closely the chronological schemes of Breuil (1952) and Leroi-Gourhan (1968) who were reliant upon style and a limited amount of relative data (e.g. superimpositioning), and who worked without absolute chronology.

The themes of European Upper Palaeolithic cave art do not correspond to what one might expect based on modern cross-cultural surveys of humans' 'ideal' concepts of figurative art. A preference for irregular (broken) landscapes with water and hills, and a predominance of the colour blue, rank highest which may reflect the cognitive memory of our evolution on the landscapes of the African savanna (Orians and Heerwagen 1992; Dutton 2009). European cave art could hardly be more different. Apart from a very few questionable claims that curvilinear lines represent rivers, or that a few clusters of dots represent constellations (or, more believably, that one engraved stone object represents a map: Utrilla *et al.* 2009), landscape features appear to be entirely absent from Palaeolithic art. Herbivorous prey animals – particularly horse, red deer and bison or aurochsen – overwhelmingly dominate the figurative subjects. Even where groups of these animals can be confidently associated with each other as constituent elements of 'scenes', which presumably recall events observed in real life, the animals float, isolated in space, with no ground beneath their feet or landscape details in the background. They are therefore 'unanchored' in normal space, and thus cave art does not consist of 'landscapes' in the sense that art historians generally mean by the term.

It goes without saying that as we have no informants to interview about the use of cave art, or contemporary texts to refer to about its meaning; we are restricted to formal technical, thematic and stylistic analyses of the art itself, in addition to a cautious use of the anthropology of art of small-scale societies, in order to make generalisations about how it may have functioned among Pleistocene hunter-gatherer societies. Today, few specialists are naïve enough to forward over-reaching 'umbrella' theories that purport to explain in a monolithic way the 'meaning' of a diverse canon of Palaeolithic art that was produced over some 25,000 years; such 'explanations' inevitably reveal more about our own concerns than they do about Palaeolithic society (see Bahn and Vertut 1988 for an excellent critique). Umbrella theories may sell popular books but are intellectually lazy, and almost as pointless as asking a random sample of people across the world today to define the 'function of art' on the back of a postcard. Umbrella theories may here and there reflect elements of a diverse set of functions – some cave art may have had aesthetic appeal, some may have functioned as 'hunting magic', some may have acted as a repository of information, for example – but no one theory will ever encapsulate the complexity of cave art over some 75% of the period that humans have been producing art.

To an extent, however, prehistorians have recently arrived at the opposite extreme to the generalising umbrella theories of the twentieth century. Dutton (2009, 64–84) noted how the anthropology of the 1960s to 1980s over-exaggerated the regional uniqueness of the art of small-scale societies, as part of a wider 'postmodern' trend that emphasized the regionally unique and culturally contingent nature of human behaviour. At the same time, the notion that however culturally contingent art was it should still comply with universal functions over large geographical areas, became as unfashionable as Darwinian explanations for culture and cultural change. It has therefore become fashionable to believe that Palaeolithic art is so distant chronologically, and was produced by societies so alien to us, that we can never recapture *any* of its meaning. Its chronological and contextual distance cannot be denied, and although we will never (or rarely) be able to recapture *specific* meanings about the images and their associations, prehistorians are skilled enough to recognize patterning in theme, technique and context and to make *some* generalisations from this. To suggest that we cannot understand any of it is therefore unfair. Unlike the art itself we are not completely in the dark.

Palaeolithic people were not postmodernists, moreover, and in terms of cave art at least, many similarities can be observed across space and over the duration of the Upper Palaeolithic which show that cave art *does* reflect geographically dispersed and chronologically persistent themes. In figurative art even thematic choices and associations between different animals remained relatively stable at least over the Mid and Late Upper Palaeolithic (Sauvet and Wlodarczyk 2008). The marked emphasis on the depiction of large herbivores presumably reflects the centrality of these crucial resources to the Upper Palaeolithic mind. The use of light and shadow and the topography of cave walls and ceilings as a central dimension in the depiction of such animals – discussed below – indicates that the 'artists' were 'reading' cave walls and interacting with them in meaningful ways. As we shall see, the interaction of darkness and topography often predetermined the location and nature of the graphic space onto which art was created. Thus while the sample of cave art we have to deal with is presumably a small subsample of a far wider and broader art phenomenon, and while our distance from its producers will inevitably simplify considerably the questions we can ask of it, there are things we can understand. We can shine our analytical light on a good number of its aspects, and in our explanations we should, therefore, not be afraid of the dark. In this spirit, I hope to show here how darkness itself can be understood as an integral part of much cave art, and to speculate about its meaning.

Transitions: from the light to the dark

Let us descend into the sightless world
(Dante Alighieri *The Divine Comedy* Part 1. *The Inferno,* Canto IV, 15)

Darkness is the most obvious factor that separates the underground environment from the 'open air' environment. Unlike the grasslands that were critical to the procurement of resources necessary to survive in the Upper Palaeolithic (food, clothing and shelter, fuel, water, mates), from the point of view of survival *it was never necessary to venture into deep caves* in the Upper Palaeolithic. In terms of human settlement, in caves, where light stops, life stops, and although evidence of 'prosaic' activities in the dark zones of caves is relatively well known, in almost all cases intense evidence of domestic activity is restricted to cave exteriors and large cave mouths. This is the case, for example, at large Late Upper Palaeolithic 'supersites' such as Lascaux and Altamira, the mouths and exterior slopes of which seem to have acted as the focus for seasonal aggregation (Leroi-Gourhan 1979; Conkey 1980). While the artistic activity found in their dark zones presumably occurred while the exterior of these sites was being occupied, however, this activity seems to have been distinct from the activities that were obviously practised in the light and around the campfire.

When we think of cave art we usually think of art on the walls and ceilings of deep caves – essentially the dark zone – but in most caves plenty of available wall space existed in areas that received daylight; enough to facilitate ritual and artistic activity where an artificial light was unnecessary. As most art was created away from such areas, however, one can only assume that darkness *per se* was an integral element to this activity. In a wider sense, darkness – and other characteristics of deep caves that are often perceived as *disadvantages* such as humidity, spatial constriction, inexplicable noises and danger (Arias and Ontañon 2012) – formed integral elements of the experience, and thus in a sense the 'function' of deep caves. We may assume that venturing into the dark zones was therefore voluntary (as it was not necessary to enter deep caves in order to survive), but this may be anachronistic; perhaps deep-seated cosmological views and their centrality to how Upper Palaeolithic groups perceived their world and their survival within it from time to time compelled individuals to venture into the dark, liminal arena and interact with the dangers it contained. Cross-cultural research has shown very clearly that caves often became part of cultural systems because of a repeated association with, 'worrysome beings ... or simply terrifying creatures ... [rendering it] likely that this is connected with a characteristic trait of caves: the darkness' (*ibid.*, 101).

For most of us in the modern world the profundity of impenetrable and inexplicable darkness is difficult to conceive, and certainly rarely experienced (Bogard 2013). Such an all-pervasive darkness may be associated with rest – a good night's sleep – yet to many societies across the world the night-time – when a natural darkness obscures the perceptible world – is a liminal place of disorientation and danger (Galinier *et al.* 2010). The darkness of caves – where no natural light shines – similarly marks their liminality, and to many societies they are places that are twixt this world and another (Moyes 2012 and papers therein). Anyone who has taken a guided tour through a show cave will no doubt have experienced the few seconds when the guide extinguishes their light source to leave visitors in darkness and an almost stifling silence. Dante and Milton captured this in words, writing in a world in which darkness was closer, more profound, more inexplicable and generally more palpable than in much of the modern world, and it is therefore no surprise that they were able to convey a more intimate sense of the lightless world than people today, most of whom live in worlds that are rarely, if ever, completely dark.

In caves, the contrast between light and dark, particularly gradations from daylight to twilight to darkness, is the most profound of a number of sensory restrictions or heightenings which were exploited during the course of controlled ritual performances in caves from at least the Upper Palaeolithic onwards (Arias and Ontañon 2012; Bergsvik and Skeates 2012; Bjerck 2012). In a number of cases it seems that artistic effort was focused in transitional areas of caves, those outer chambers where daylight penetrated, at least in muted form. This may explain the richness of the art in Altamira's Polychrome Chamber, where the artist drew bison, horses and deer with his/her back to the natural light (Ramos 1999), and the Great Hall of the Bulls at Lascaux, which Geneste *et al.* (2004) suggest would have been bathed in a reddish crepuscular light at dawn and dusk. I shall return to these liminal zones (within liminal worlds) below. Beyond these, however, one is quickly in a realm that can only be explored with the use of artificial light. The mobile light sources available to cave explorers in the Palaeolithic were either simple torches – bundles of branches for which indirect evidence occurs in the form of torch wipes (*mouchage du torche* – charcoal stubbings on cave walls) from the early Mid Upper Palaeolithic – and simple stone lamps for which there is some evidence from the Early Upper Palaeolithic, although most examples derive from Mid and Late Upper Palaeolithic contexts. In each case these light sources give off about 10 watts/1850 kelvin of light, the equivalent of a small candle or sunset/sunrise, or even lower (de Beaune 1987; Delluc and Delluc 2009). Hearths lit on cave floors would further provide similar light, although were not movable.

Two important characteristics of these light sources are that they (and thus everything they illuminate) are constantly moving; and that they reduce visual acuity and colour contrasts, emphasising only the warmer colours of the spectrum, i.e. yellow and particularly red (de Beaune 1987; Delluc and Delluc 2009). In this sense one might say that in terms of visual perception cave art is 'redshifted' (Shepard 1992) which, apart from its natural occurrence in or near many caves, may explain the ubiquity of the use of 'red ochre' (haematite) in cave art. While all these light sources were used – and perhaps produced in high numbers on open air sites (de Beaune 2004) – it is possible that these effects formed a meaningful link between the darkness of the night and the darkness of the cave. Already it should be apparent that the visual experience of Palaeolithic cave explorers would have been nothing like our own: unlike with electric lighting *nothing* would ever be still to their experience, and even with the use of numerous lamps at the same time (as may have occurred, for example, in the Well/Shaft of the Dead Man in Lascaux, with at least twenty-one unmodified or rudimentary forms in limestone, and two extremely well made forms in red sandstone: Delluc and Delluc 1979) hardly any of a cave system could be seen at any one time.

The remarkably low light levels available to Palaeolithic cave explorers would inevitably have constrained the means and extent to which they were able to navigate, scrutinize and give meaning to the subterranean world. Only a small part of this would be visible at any one time, and as the explorers progressed along their path the darkness would open up before them and close in again behind them (Groenen 2000, 107). Sight could not be relied upon for many things one would otherwise take for granted: long-distance viewing, the perception of large chambers or long passages in their entirety, the planning of safe or desirable routes without experiencing them first, or the scrutiny of any detail over a metre or so beyond the viewer. Because of this, senses other than sight inevitably become crucial. The physicality of cave exploration would therefore prioritize touch as a means of steadying, raising and lowering the body in the tiring process of navigating the cave, as well as feeling for danger.

Hand stencils – one of the icons of cave art, but actually a category of Palaeolithic 'art' that is poorly understood – reflect the importance of physical touch in the prosaic and ritual exploration of dark caves. Restricted, it would seem, to the Early and Mid Upper Palaeolithic (Garcia Diez *et al.* 2015), hand stencils represent some of the earliest examples of artistic activity. Most research has focused on their morphometrics (e.g. Janssens 1957; Sahly 1966; Wildgoose *et al.* 1982; Faurie and Raymond 2004; Guthrie 2005; Gunn 2006; Snow 2006) – whether they represent male or female hands – and why in some caves fingers appear to be missing or bent, although recent research into their contextual associations has shown that the majority were placed in relation to specific features on the cave walls (Pettitt *et al.* 2014; see Fig. 2.1). The most common associations in La Garma and El Castillo caves are with a 'gripping' position on convex bosses, and with the placing of the palms over slight concavities. In the first case this 'gripping' position reflects the placement of the hand to steady the body when ducking down beneath low roofs, and in the second case this 'ergonomic' position reflects a close-up search for small details that would not have been visible without very detailed scrutiny of the cave wall in the darkness. In addition to these, stencils were often placed in close proximity to natural cracks, which themselves appear formed of shadow in low light (Pl. 1). These observations reveal that a close physical scrutiny of the cave walls – which has been termed *palpation* (*ibid.*) – was a major factor in the placement of stencils.

It is therefore clear that the profound darkness of deep caves would significantly constrain the nature of movement around them, prioritising palpation as an important sensory guide as well as close-up – almost myopic – scrutiny of cave surfaces. Those light sources that were available would render nothing still; instead presenting a constantly changing microcosm of the moving visible within a macrocosm of darkness. It is therefore no surprise that darkness formed a constituent part of the recognition and deliberate creation of artistic space within deep caves.

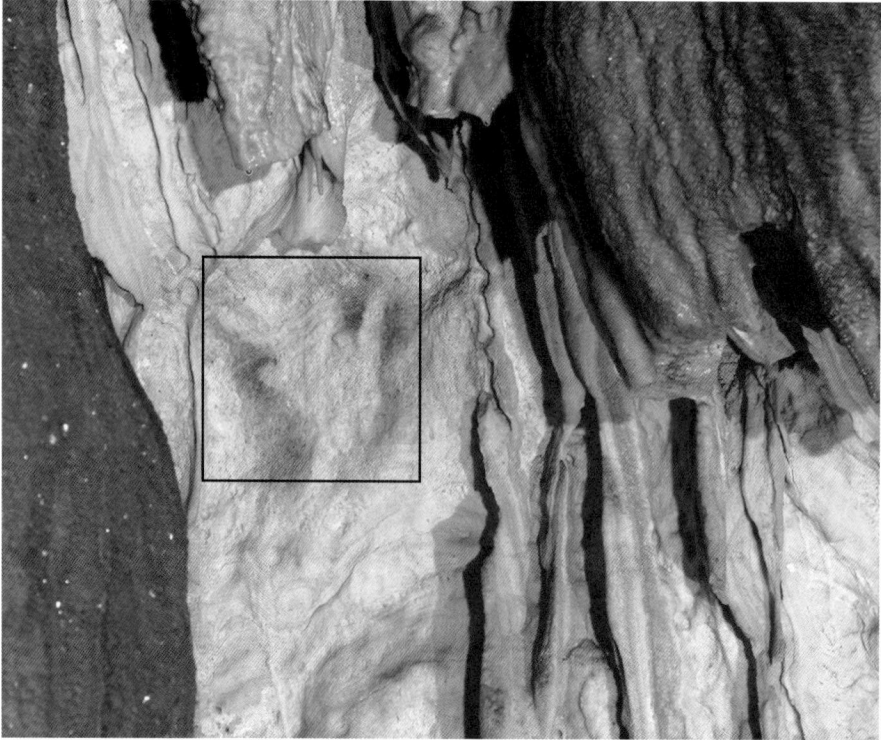

Figure 2.1: Hand stencil placed on stalactite, Ardales Cave, near Malaga, Spain (courtesy of Pedro Cantalejo Duarte).

Darkness and cave art

> *I came to a place where no light shone at all*
> (Dante Alighieri *The Divine Comedy* Part 1. *The Inferno*, Canto ~V, 30)

The context and nature of much cave art indicates that darkness was an important factor in the articulation of art with the subterranean space. It functioned to structure where art was placed, and in many cases to finish what to our modern eyes are incomplete images. Compositional scenes in Upper Palaeolithic art are comprised of associated depictions of animals that are 'framed' as graphic spaces within natural features of cave walls and ceilings – typically erosional niches – and shadows play the critical role in how these distinct 'canvasses' were identified (Vialou 2001). This can be seen, for example, in the Late Magdalenian panels of horse and bison placed within individual niches in Niaux Cave (Clottes 2010). Thus the active role of darkness in the definition of natural 'panels' formed a critical starting point for the often complex *chaînes opératoires* of art production (Lejeune 2001). Such 'dialogues' between the artist and cave were certainly in place by the Mid Upper Palaeolithic (Gravettian: e.g. Pigeaud 2001) and probably earlier (Pike *et al*. 2012; Pettitt *et al*. 2014). It has been noted above that no landscape context accompanies the animal figures. Viewed in the cold light of the present day they are truly without context, floating, as is often said, in the air. But this is not to view them in their *correct* context within the dark caves, where darkness itself forms the main context for the figures; it is a landscape in its own right.

Darkness itself forms the 'landscape context' of cave art, and is thus an integral part of it. The clearest demonstration of this is the numerous examples where it has been used to 'finish' otherwise incomplete images. Darkness therefore often forms a *component* of parietal images: it cannot be seen to have been peripheral to art, but an integral part of its composition. In the world of the deep cave nothing is complete; nothing is fixed; and things are rarely *definite*. Shapes emerge out of the darkness or are formed by it, and meaning was read into this. A major by-product of the modern human brain is its propensity to read meaning into natural shapes – hence the face of Jesus in a slice of toast or faces in the clouds (e.g. Atran 2002, 2006). Our ability to *interpret* and *give meaning* to natural shapes seems to have formed a major component of the creation of cave art from its inception in Europe. Hodgson (2003) has noted how the topography of cave walls and shadow can be suggestive of incomplete animal outlines, which triggers an 'implicit perception' – a hidden substructure of mental processing – which enables the human mind to read these suggestive outlines as complete images. Much cave art, therefore, functioned as synecdoche (Lorblanchet 1989, 115). By such a process of mental 'closure', cracks and fissures and rock bosses could be subtly and subconsciously identified with the salient features of prey – dorsal lines, heads, shoulders, antlers and the like – and thus the interplay of light and movement with the cave surface quite literally created animals out of the darkness. In view of this we should not be surprised at the amount of images in cave art that to our modern eyes appear to be either incomplete or 'indeterminate', that is, of unclear attribution (Lorblanchet 1989). It is a modern preoccupation to prioritize complete images and to seek to identify and pigeonhole these. By contrast, metamorphosis fundamentally underpins Palaeolithic art, and identifiable themes such as, 'horses, bison, ibex, and other animals, humans and signs are only the visible stitches in a continuous graphic fabric whose unity must be respected' (*ibid.*, 113). Thus, a continuum of images link the more obviously identifiable extremes of art. Painted and engraved forms will therefore blend together, and darkness will further extend this metamorphosis into the natural and endlessly moving realm.

As Groenen (2000, 107) has noted, in Palaeolithic cave art a fundamental distinction can be observed between a *visible sphere* which is defined by the depiction of aspects of the natural world as they are perceived; and the *invisible sphere*, which although this cannot be perceived directly, should not be underestimated as a major structuring principle in Palaeolithic art. Figures of the visible sphere can be associated with the invisible sphere – darkness – in two ways: they can be orientated *towards* it, or appear to be emerging *from* it (*ibid.*, 105). Consider the 'falling horse' from the Axial Gallery in Lascaux (Fig. 2.2). This

Figure 2.2: The 'falling horse' of Lascaux (Jean Vertut, courtesy of Paul Bahn).

skilled and technically sophisticated painting is nevertheless 'incomplete', positioned so that it appears to be falling out of or into a large crack – a pool of darkness. Smaller horses above it appear to be running towards this space; the whole scene suggesting animals entering or leaving this world via the darkness. Such transitions into and out of the darkness can be found in many caves: Groenen (*ibid.*, 106), for example, notes two cervids in the lower gallery of La Pasiega Cave (Cantabria, Spain) which are oriented towards a 'mouth of shadow' created by an aperture in the cave's wall.

A remarkable example of the interaction of cave surface, art and shadow is the so-called 'bison-man' of El Castillo Cave (Cantabria). Here, a natural column resembles an upright bison, the shape of which has been embellished with paint. The uppermost tip of the natural column was artificially modified in antiquity so that when its shadow falls on the nearby cave wall it resembles an upright bison-man similar to the bison painted on the column itself (Pl. 2). This cannot be coincidence given the obvious modification of the column, and there can be no clearer example of the interaction between cave topography, shadow and art in the Palaeolithic use of deep caves.

Darkness and liminality

During the European Upper Palaeolithic, caves formed an important arena for the exercise of the human imagination. In caves, darkness plays a significant role in desensitising or removing the explorer from the 'world above' and as such, places of separation are well suited to the liminal or transitional phases of *rites de passage* and other activities (Bjerck 2012, 59). Under such circumstances the imagination was free to roam, perhaps loosened from the constraints it normally operated under in the daylit world. Perhaps it should be no surprise, then, that the particular imagination at work with cave art was not that which reflects the landscapes in which human hunter-gatherers evolved, but rather the resources that the then current resource landscape provided and which were critical for survival in Pleistocene climates. In the darkness of caves these resources met a deeper, less conscious world, where ambiguity reigns. The notion that supernatural powers inhabit rock is widespread among small-scale societies; although perhaps somewhat uncritically invoked by proponents of 'shamanistic' interpretations of cave art (e.g. Lewis-Williams 2002), caves are commonly seen as 'osmotic membranes' separating this world from others (Bjerck 2012, 60). In mythologies across the world, caves are associated with animals that frequent their nooks and crannies – snakes, lizards and bears – who are seen as capable of travelling between worlds.

One should not underestimate the significance of the darkness in this perspective; Groenen (2000, 107) has spoken of the 'fearsome presence' of the invisible sphere in caves. In the constantly shifting light, tangible things quickly lose their form, appear and disappear as the viewer traverses the mysterious space. It is no surprise that much of the art can be understood in terms of liminality, therefore; it appears, blurs, constantly changes in form, and disappears, as if continually in flux. This changeable appearance of the art is central to the perceptive functioning of the human brain. Caves are themselves liminal in several ways, not least as they tend to lack an obvious termination – their innermost extremes often tapering away into the darkness (Bjerck 2012, 61). Liminality begins with the entrances to caves, which experience natural light and dark. As the sun rises, light will spread, illuminate the cave mouth and gradually penetrate into the cave as far as the maximal daylight zone allows. As the sun sets, the darkness of the cave spreads outwards to encompass everything. In a way this is similar to the process of carrying an artificial light through the cave; it brings light into the darkness in front of it at the same time that it loses light to the darkness behind it. Perhaps this significance of extending 'natural' transitory light artificially into the darkness was not lost on Palaeolithic cave explorers. As noted above, if crepuscular light may have penetrated the original entrance of Lascaux into the Great Hall of the Bulls, it may well have had significance itself.

It is not just darkness that conveys this sense of liminality. As Lorblanchet (1989, 114) has noted of the often complex entanglements of partial images and marks, 'figurative components extricate themselves from a formless "magma", from such a web of lines is born a hoof, such curving lines give birth to a nameless muzzle, a wavering line of a backbone, an eye conceals itself, and *the space is vibrant with awakening life*' (my emphasis). It should be clear that the engraving of masses of partial images and the attendant synecdoche it invites, functioned similarly to darkness, constantly evoking ever-changing appearances, transformations and disappearances.

Conclusions

While much of what we say about cave art must inevitably remain speculative, enough data exist to reveal at least that darkness was itself an important constituent of the medium. It is probably safe to conclude that darkness was one of the profound aspects of deep caves that affected Palaeolithic explorers and that it was given meaning in whatever belief systems were being played out in the dark and shifting arenas of this mysterious world. While we will presumably never capture the specific beliefs that came and went and from time to time presumably underpinned the production of (the biased and lucky sample of) art that remains today, we may make a few simple observations that shine a little light into the deep darkness of prehistory.

- In deep caves, visibility is a problem. Beyond the zones lit by natural light, only the introduction of artificial light can penetrate the profound darkness that pertains in these areas. Such light sources as were available to Palaeolithic 'artists' – simple stone bowl lamps of animal fat and grasses, simple torches, and small hearths lit on the cave floor – gave off a diffuse and shifting light.
- Artists were obviously aware that the *natural* state of deep caves was one of profound darkness. The provision of artificial light was therefore as necessary to the artistic enterprise as the provision of materials with which to create the art.
- The specific position of art in deep caves indicates that the *exploration* of these profoundly dark areas was one of the contexts in which art was created. In many cases art was created in positions that would have been relatively uncomfortable,

whereas opportunities where art could be created in relative comfort were avoided; decision making cannot therefore be said to pertain to comfort or practical considerations.
- The exploration of deep caves by the diffuse light available rendered only a small area – typically one or two metres radius from the light source – visible. By contrast, the greater majority of deep caves were at any time in perpetual darkness.
- Travelling through caves with a portable light source would constantly remodel what was visible and what was not. Areas of the cave's floor, walls and ceiling were continually coming into and going out of the light.
- The interaction of the light source with topographic features within the cave created a constantly moving 'dialogue' between the explorer, his/her light source, and the cave's features, mediated through the interplay between light and dark. The use of such interplay indicates that this was recognized, exploited and given meaning by individuals who came to leave 'art' in these places.
- In view of the importance of liminality and transition in the thinking of small-scale societies, it is tempting to see in the shifting and ambiguous sensory world of cave art similar concerns. These are occasionally reflected in the form of figurative art itself.

Acknowledgements

I am grateful to Marion Dowd and Robert Hensey for their invitation to participate in the 'Into the earth: the archaeology of darkness' conference and to contribute to this volume. Their patience awaiting my manuscript was heroic. It has been a pleasure to add some simple observations about the Palaeolithic to what was a stimulating enterprise. I am grateful to Elizabeth Archibald, Principal of St. Cuthbert's Society, Durham, for taking an interest in my work, and for the Milton quote. Marc Groenen and Paul Bahn generously provided photos for the illustrations. My research into the context of hand stencils was funded by The Leverhulme Trust.

References

Arias, P. and Ontañon, R. 2012. La Garma (Spain): long-term human activity in a karst system. In K. A. Bergsvik and R. Skeates (eds.) *Caves in context. The cultural significance of caves and rockshelters in Europe*, 101–17. Oxford, Oxbow Books.
Atran, S. 2002. *In gods we trust: the evolutionary landscape of religion*. Oxford, Oxford University Press.
Atran, S. 2006. The scientific landscape of religion: evolution, culture, and cognition. In P. Clayton (ed.) *The Oxford handbook of religion and science*, 407–29. Oxford, Oxford University Press.
Bahn, P. and Vertut, J. 1988. *Images of the Ice Age*. London, Windward.
Bergsvik, K. A. and Skeates, R. (eds.) 2012. *Caves in context. The cultural significance of caves and rockshelters in Europe*. Oxford, Oxbow Books.
Bjerck, H. B. 2012. On the outer fringe of the human world: phenomenological perspectives on anthropomorphic cave paintings in Norway. In K. A. Bergsvik and R. Skeates (eds.) *Caves in context. The cultural significance of caves and rockshelters in Europe*, 48–64. Oxford, Oxbow Books.

Bogard, P. 2013. *The end of night. Searching for natural darkness in an age of artificial light*. London, Fourth Estate.

Breuil, H. 1952. *Four hundred centuries of cave art*. Paris, Sappho.

Clottes, J. 2010. *Les cavernes des Niaux. Art préhistoriques en Ariège-Pyrénées*. Paris, Errance.

Conkey, M. 1980. The identification of prehistoric hunter-gatherer aggregation sites: the case of Altamira. *Current Anthropology* 21, 609–30.

de Beaune, S. 1987. Palaeolithic lamps and their specialization: a hypothesis. *Current Anthropology* 28 (4), 569–77.

de Beaune, S. 2004. Un atelier magdalénien de sculpture de la steatite au Rocher de la Caille (Loire)? In A.-C. Welté and E. Ladier (eds.) *Art mobilier paléolithique supérieur en Europe Occidental*, 177–86. Liège, ERAUL 107.

Delluc, B. and Delluc, G. 1979. L'éclairage. In A. Leroi-Gourhan and J. Allain (eds.) *Lascaux inconnu*, 121–42. Paris, Éditions du CNRS.

Delluc, B. and Delluc, G. 1991. *L'Art pariétal archaïque en Aquitaine*. Paris, Gallia Préhistoire Supplement 28.

Delluc, B. and Delluc, G. 2001. L'art á l'Abri Pataud (Les Eyzies, Dordogne). In M. Lejeune (ed.) *L'Art du paléolithique supérieur: L'art pariétal dans son contexte naturel*, 87–94. Liège, ERAUL 107.

Delluc, B. and Delluc, G. 2009. Eye and vision in Palaeolithic art. In P. Bahn (ed.) *An enquiring mind: studies in honor of Alexander Marshack*, 77–97. American School of Prehistoric Research Monograph Series. Oxford, Oxbow Books.

Dutton, D. 2009. *The art instinct*. Oxford, Oxford University Press.

Faurie, C. and Raymond, M. 2004. Handedness frequency over more than ten thousand years. *Proceedings of the Royal Society of London Series B* 271, S43-5.

Galinier, J., Becquelin, A. M., Bordin, G., Fontaine, L., Fourmaux, F., Roullet Ponce, J., Salzarulo, P., Simonnot, P., Therrien, M. and Zilli, I. 2010. Anthropology of the night. Cross-disciplinary investigations. *Current Anthropology* 51 (6), 819–45.

Gárate, D. 2008. The continuation of graphic traditions in Cantabrian pre-Magdalenian parietal art. *International Newsletter on Rock Art* 50, 18–25.

García-Diez, M., Garrido, D., Hoffmann, D. L., Pettitt, P. B., Pike, A. W. G. and Zilhão, J. 2015. The chronology of hand stencils in European Palaeolithic rock art: implications of new U-series results from El Castillo Cave (Cantabria, Spain). *Journal of Anthropological Sciences* 93, 1–18.

Geneste, J.-M., Horde, T. and Tanet, C. 2004. *Lascaux: a work of memory*. Perigueux, Fanlac.

Groenen, M. 2000. *Sombra y luz en el arte paleolítico*. Barcelona, Ariel.

Gunn, R. G. 2006. Hand sizes in rock art: interpreting the measurements of hand stencils and prints. *Rock Art Research* 23, 97–112.

Guthrie, R. D. 2005. *The nature of Paleolithic art*. Chicago, University of Chicago Press.

Hodgson, D. 2003. Seeing the 'unseen'. Fragmented cues and the implicit in Palaeolithic art. *Cambridge Archaeological Journal* 13 (1), 97–106.

Janssens, P. A. 1957. Medical views on prehistoric representations of human hands. *Medical History* 1, 318–22.

Lejeune, M. 2001. Quelques réflexions sur le role de la paroi rocheuse dans l'art du paléolithique supérieur. In M. Lejeune (ed.) *L'Art du paléolithique supérieur: L'art pariétal dans son contexte naturel*, 15–9. Liège, ERAUL 107.

Leroi-Gourhan, A. 1968. *The art of prehistoric man in Western Europe*. London, Thames and Hudson.

Leroi-Gourhan, A. 1979. La stratigraphie et les fouilles de la Grotte de Lascaux. In A. Leroi-Gourhan and J. Allain (eds.) *Lascaux inconnu*, 45–74. Paris, Éditions du CNRS.

Lewis-Williams, D. 2002. *The mind in the cave. Consciousness and the origins of art*. London, Thames and Hudson.

Lorblanchet, M. 1989. From man to animal to sign in Palaeolithic art. In H. Morphy (ed.) *Animals into art*, 109–43. London, Hyman.

Lorblanchet, M. 2010. *Art pariétal. Grottes ornées du Quercy*. Parc-Saint-Joseph, Éditions du Rouergue.

Moyes, H. (ed.) 2012. *Sacred darkness. A global perspective on the ritual use of caves*. Boulder, University Press of Colorado.

Orians, G. H. and Heerwagen, J. H. 1992. Evolved responses to landscapes. In J. H. Barcow, L. Cosmides and J. Tooby (eds.) *The adapted mind: evolutionary psychology and the generation of culture*, 555–79. New York, Oxford University Press.

Pettitt, P., Maximiano Castillejo, A., Arias, P., Ontañon Peredo, R. and Harrison, R. 2014. New views on old hands: the context of stencils in El Castillo and La Garma caves (Cantabria, Spain). *Antiquity* 88, 47–63.

Pettitt, P. B. and Pike, A. W. G. 2007. Dating European Palaeolithic cave art: progress, prospects, problems. *Journal of Archaeological Method and Theory* 14 (1), 27–47.

Pigeaud, R. 2001. Dialogue avec la paroi: cas des representations paléolithiques de la Grotte ornée Mayenne-Sciences (Thorigné-en-Charnie, Mayenne). In M. Lejeune (ed.) *L'Art du paléolithique supérieur: L'art pariétal dans son contexte naturel*, 21–43. Liège, ERAUL 107.

Pike, A. W. G., Hoffman, D. L., García-Diez, M., Pettitt, P. B., Alcolea, J., González-Sainz, C., de las Heras, C., Lasheras, J. A., Montez, R. and Zilhão, J. 2012. Uranium-series dating of Upper Palaeolithic art in Spanish caves. *Science* 336, 1409–13.

Ramos, P. 1999. *The cave of Altamira*. New York, Harry Abrams.

Ripoll López, S., Ripoll Perelló, E., Collado Giraldo, H., Mas Cornellá, M. and Jordá Pardo, J. F. 1999. Maltravieso. El santuario extremeño de las manos. *Trabajos de Prehistoria* 56, 59–84.

Sahly, A. 1966. *Les mains mutilées dans l'art préhistorique*. Toulous, Privat.

Sauvet, G. and Wlodarczyk, A. 2008. Towards a formal grammar of the European Palaeolithic cave art. *Rock Art Research* 25 (2), 165–72.

Shepard, R. G. 1992. The perceptual organization of colors: an adaptation to regularities of the terrestrial world? In J. H. Barcow, L. Cosmides and J. Tooby (eds.) *The adapted mind: evolutionary psychology and the generation of culture*, 495–532. New York, Oxford University Press.

Snow, D. R. 2006. Sexual dimorphism in Upper Palaeolithic hand stencils. *Antiquity* 80, 390–404.

Utrilla, P., Mazo, C., Supena, M. C., Martínez-Bea, M. C. and Domingo, R. 2009. A Palaeolithic map from 13660 cal BP: engraved stone block from the Late Magdalenian in Abauntz Cave (Navarra, Spain). *Journal of Human Evolution* 57, 99–111.

Vialou, D. 2001. Architecture de l'art parietal paléolithique. In M. Lejeune (ed.) *L'Art du paléolithique supérieur: L'art pariétal dans son contexte naturel*, 7–14. Liège, ERAUL 107.

Wildgoose, M., Hadingham, E. and Hooper, A. 1982. The prehistoric hand pictures at Gargas: attempts at simulation. *Medical History* 26, 205–7.

Chapter 3

Between symbol and senses: the role of darkness in ritual in prehistoric Italy

Ruth D. Whitehouse

Introduction

Italy is characterized by 'underground' sites that were used for ritual purposes in prehistory, especially in the Neolithic, Copper and Bronze Ages. I have discussed these sites for some twenty years (Whitehouse 1990, 1991a, 1991b, 1991c, 1992, 1995, 1996, 2001, 2007) and so in this short paper I shall just summarize the salient points of my earlier analyses. My 1992 book (Chapters 3 and 4) described a number of 'underground' sites which included rockshelters, crevices and artificial rock-cut structures, as well as natural caves. The present discussion concentrates on the large natural caves: not caves used for occupation, which of course do occur in Italy, but caves that are unsuitable for occupation because of their location and/or their form, and which have produced evidence of ritual use in the form of such features as wall paintings, attention to water features, deposition of unusual objects and burials. The sites in question were used during the Neolithic, the sixth to fifth millennia BC in Italy, and the floruit of the cult use seems to have been in the later sixth and early fifth millennia. I shall briefly describe three sites to illustrate the discussion of darkness in cult practice. The descriptions are intended to introduce some specificity into what is otherwise a generalising discussion. The term 'the caves', used throughout this paper, refers to a broader number of sites, of which the three described here are particularly good examples.

Grotta di Porto Badisco (Grotta dei Cervi)

This cave (Fig. 3.1), situated in the south of the Salento peninsula in southern Puglia (the 'heel' of Italy), consists of three long narrow corridors, subdivided into a number of zones, with some relatively roomy areas where it is possible to stand upright and to move around fairly freely, and other much more restricted passages where one has to crouch or manoeuvre on all fours, sometimes with floor, ceiling and both walls pressing against the body. There is some evidence that the cave may have been used for burial and also for rituals related to stalagmites, but the outstanding evidence for cult in this cave consists of the paintings that cover much of the wall area. These include figurative designs ('matchstick men'), depicted individually or forming scenes of hunting and

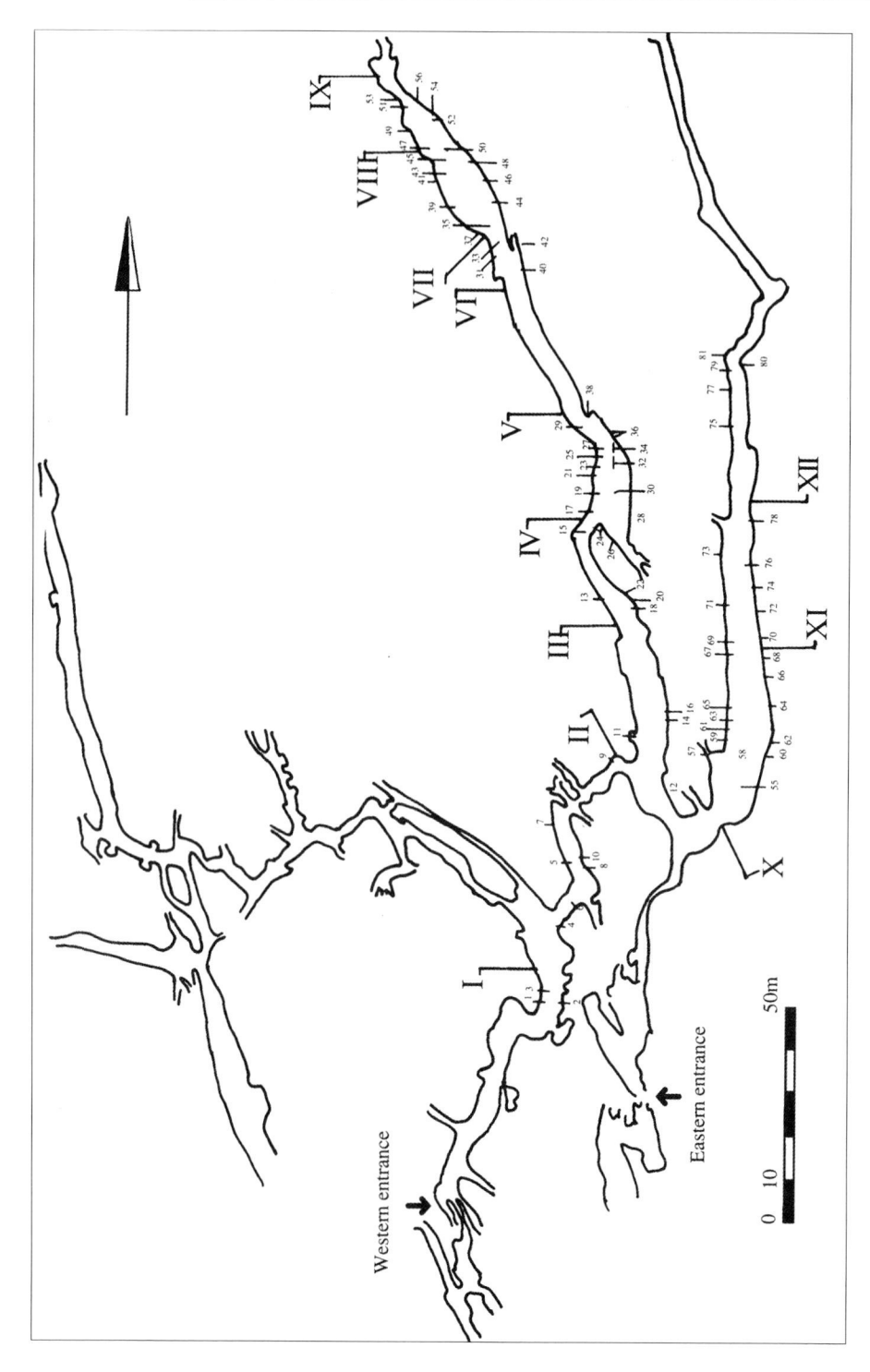

Figure 3.1: Plan of Grotta di Porto Badisco, showing the different zones and groups of wall paintings (after Graziosi 1980).

other subjects, abstract motifs and, in one zone deep in the cave, nearly one hundred small handprints pressed onto the cave ceiling and walls (main reference: Graziosi 1980; also Whitehouse 1992 with additional references).

Grotta Scaloria

This cave (Fig. 3.2) is situated further north in Puglia, on the lower foothills of the Gargano promontory, just north of the Tavoliere plain, which is the location of the main area of Neolithic settlement in the sixth millennium BC, characterized by hundreds of ditched enclosures (*villaggi trincerati*) identified through aerial photography. The cave, entered originally via a swallowhole in the limestone, consists of two chambers, but was linked in the past by a passage to the neighbouring cave of Grotta di Occhiopinto, which has its own separate entrance via another swallowhole. The upper chamber of Grotta Scaloria was relatively accessible and may have had multiple uses, including domestic ones. In its later phases, still Neolithic, it was filled with a dense anthropogenic rubbish deposit containing a mixture of domestic waste and human bones; there were also a few more or less intact burials. The lower cave, reached by a steep descending passage, was devoted to a cult of stillicide water: several stalagmites had been truncated, and painted pottery vessels placed on the flattened surfaces to collect the water dripping from the stalactites above (in some cases forming new stalagmites in the pots). An artificial pool in the floor of the chamber also collected water running down the walls and from the ceiling (main reference: Elster *et al.* in press; Tiné and Isetti 1982; also Whitehouse 1992 with additional references).

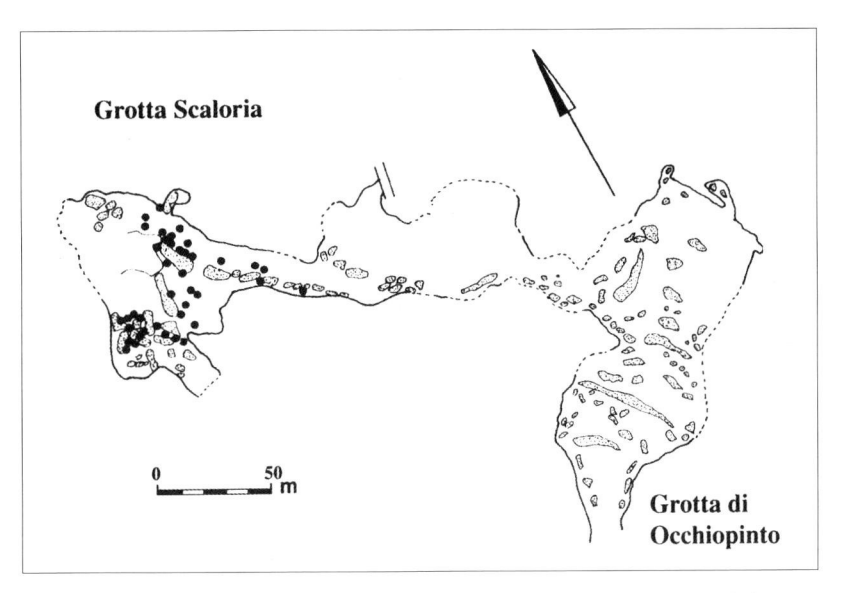

Figure 3.2: Plan of Grotta Scaloria/Grotta di Occhiopinto cave complex. Stippled areas represent stalagmites; solid dots represent pottery vessels (after Tinè and Isetti 1982).

Pozzi della Piana

Further north and across the Apennine mountains in Umbria, Pozzi della Piana (Fig. 3.3) consists of a large underground complex of galleries and chambers, entered via a number of almost vertical shafts. Although well known to cavers, it has been much less explored by archaeologists than the other two sites described above, but has nonetheless produced evidence of cult use in the Neolithic and perhaps also the Bronze Age. Here again, ritual activity centred on stillicide water: in the deepest part of the complex, furthest from natural daylight, was a pool surrounded by stalagmites and stalactites. Evidence of human exploitation of the water came in the form of a number of small pottery drinking vessels placed inverted in niches in the cave walls around the pool (Passeri 1970).

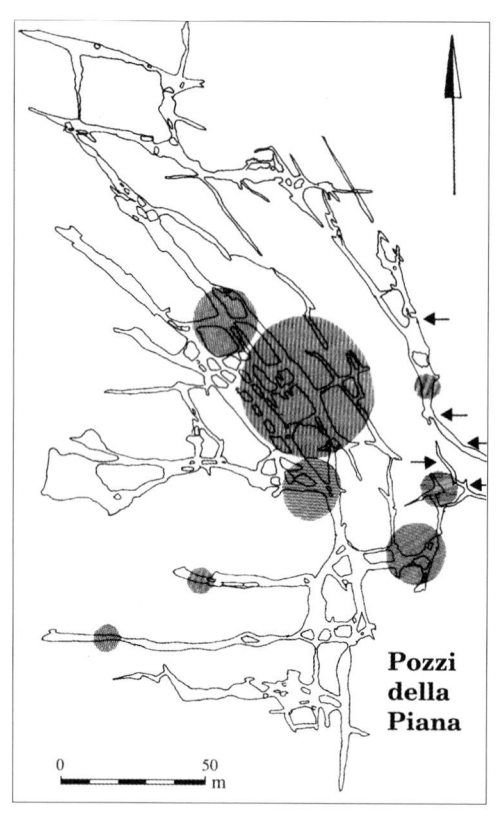

Figure 3.3: Plan of the underground complex of Pozzi della Piana. Shaded areas represent greatest concentrations of archaeological finds; small arrows indicate positions of entrances (after Passeri 1970).

How the caves were used and understood

My original interpretation of the sites involved, *inter alia*, the identification of recurring ritual themes present in various caves and also the recognition of a social function for the cult. The three main ritual themes identified were: a) secrecy, b) a hunting cult, and c) a cult of 'abnormal' water. The secrecy theme was constituted by the hidden nature of the caves themselves and the fact that the areas of greatest cult activity seem always to have been in the deepest, least accessible parts of the caves, furthest from natural daylight. Evidence for the hunting cult is provided by the hunting scenes painted on the walls of Grotta di Porto Badisco and a few other caves and rockshelters, and by the occurrence of unusually high levels of bones of wild animals (especially red and roe deer) in some cave deposits. Evidence for a cult of 'abnormal' water takes the form of attention to stalagmites, stalactites and stillicide water, as in Grotta Scaloria and Pozzi della Piana, but also to water in other unusual forms, such as steaming or bubbling water.

In terms of social function, I have made the case that the sites were used for rites of passage, including initiation rites. The arguments for this interpretation concentrate on the marginality of the caves to the main areas of settlement and their hidden nature, as well as the evidence for the types of ritual practised in them. The interpretation also draws heavily on ethnographic analogy. Here I shall simply take both the ritual themes and the social function as starting points for the current discussion. Readers who are interested can find the fullest account in *Underground Religion* (Whitehouse 1992).

Darkness

What role did darkness play in the cults centred on these caves? Darkness is a salient feature of the sites. In all cases, as one moves into the caves, one rapidly loses any illumination from natural daylight and the darkness soon becomes complete (though of course it could be alleviated by the use of artificial light, which is discussed below). Darkness is certainly integral to the role of the three caves outlined above, and of course caves in general. I suggest that it would have worked both in terms of symbolism and in terms of sensory experience. The following discussion addresses both these aspects, initially separately and then together.

Darkness as symbol

Darkness might have worked symbolically in two ways: as part of a system of symbols, as understood in structuralist anthropology, and as metaphor.

Systems of symbols

My original interpretation in 1992 concentrated on a structuralist approach, drawing especially on the work of Edmund Leach (e.g. 1971, 1976), who based his own work on that of French anthropologist and founder of structural anthropology, Claude Lévi-Strauss (e.g. 1958, 1962). Structuralism is founded on the idea that human thought is based fundamentally on patterns of binary contrasts, where words and concepts hold meaning not in themselves but as parts of systems that contain also their opposites. Thus, to take very simple examples, in a colour system, the meaning of black would be constructed in its opposition to white, while in relation to the present discussion, darkness would take its meaning from its contrast to light. In the case of the Italian caves, a number of binary contrasts distinguish the sacred sphere, represented by the cult sites, from the secular sphere, represented by settlement sites (Table 3.1). The settlement sites represent the everyday world of work, domestic life and human relations, while the cult sites stand for the 'other world' of the supernatural, relations with the ancestors, and the divine. Nowadays I am less enamoured with structuralism than I was twenty years ago and it is certainly unfashionable today. However, although I now believe that binary thinking of the kind regarded as fundamental by structuralism is not the only way people think, I still think it is *one* of the ways people think – which explains the pervasive occurrence of binary classifications in both the ethnographic and archaeological records.

In the context of Neolithic Italy, darkness figures as one of a series of contrasts which serve to identify the secrecy theme: where settlements are above ground, cult caves are

Table 3.1: Structural contrasts in Neolithic Italy. Row 3, referring to illumination, has particular relevance for the current discussion.

Characteristic	Secular sphere (settlements)	Sacred sphere (cult sites)
Location	above ground, open	underground, hidden
Accessibility	easy	difficult
Illumination	light	dark
Space	abundant	restricted
Animals	domesticated	wild
Plants	domesticated	wild?
Mode of exploitation	farming	hunting (and gathering?)
Water	'normal': cold, liquid, moving	'abnormal': hot, gaseous, solid, still
Artefacts	everyday materials, utilitarian	special materials, non-utilitarian
Context of artefact discard	domestic rubbish	deliberate deposition
Condition of artefacts	worn, broken	unused, complete

underground; where settlements are open and easy to access and move around, cult sites are difficult to find and to get into; and where settlements are light, cult caves are dark. So darkness is one of the defining characteristics of the secrecy theme, taking its meaning from its contrast with light, and also from its association with the other components of the secrecy theme, as seen in Table 3.1.

Metaphor
The other main way that symbols work is as metaphor (for discussions of metaphor from different perspectives see, for example, Aristotle [1984]; Richards 1936; Shibles 1971; Ricoeur 1978; Ortony 1993). Chris Tilley (1999) has shown us (us archaeologists, that is – those in many other disciplines knew it long ago) that metaphor is essential to human communication and interpretative understandings of the world – a truly fundamental way of thinking, arguably more fundamental than the binary classifications of structuralist anthropology. Metaphor works by comparison – the unknown is compared to the known, the abstract compared to the concrete, the complex compared to the simple – as a primary way of extending understanding of the world. Metaphors may be simple, but more often they are complex and multi-layered and this is especially true in the case of items that play major roles in human sensory and emotional experience. These include bodily functions and products (e.g. bodily fluids such as blood, breast milk and semen figure strongly in symbol systems based on metaphor), but also external states experienced by the senses, such as heat and cold, dry and wet and, relevant to the present topic, darkness and light.

Darkness is understood metaphorically in many cultures to represent, for instance, death or evil (think of phrases like 'forces of darkness'). In the case of something as widespread and generic as darkness, metaphorical uses are likely to have been multiple and various, but here I explore two possible meanings in relation to the Italian cult caves. First, I suggest that in this context darkness is a metaphor for *invisibility*.

Why invisibility? This relates to the interpretation of the caves as used for rites of passage. In classic anthropological theory, going back to Van Gennep (1960 [1909]) who first described rites of passage, these rites mark major changes in the social roles and standing of the participants. They include classic life crisis rites, marking major stages or events in life (or the social interpretations of these), such as birth, attainment of adulthood (menarche, puberty), marriage, parenthood and death. They also include rites of initiation into secret societies, religious sects etc. – which may have been how some of the caves were used, especially Grotta di Porto Badisco.

Rites of passage have been much debated since Van Gennep first described them and the category has been both challenged and refined in the anthropological literature (Bowie 2000 for an overview). In archaeology the concept has appeared in interpretation only relatively recently and still seems under-exploited (see Garwood 2012). Rites of passage, as classically understood (Table 3.2), involve three stages: *segregation*, in which the participants are symbolically detached from their previous state (pre-liminal rites); *margin* (or limes), characterized above all by ambiguity (liminal rites); and *aggregation*, in which the participants are symbolically accepted into their new state (post-liminal rites). The most critical stage is the central, liminal one, described by Victor Turner as the 'betwixt and between' state (1967, 93–111). Among the defining characteristics of the liminal stage is invisibility: the subject of the ritual is structurally invisible – taken out of functioning society, no longer in one social role and not yet in another. And this is how darkness works as a metaphor – it stands for invisibility quite simply because in the dark people cannot be seen. Combined with the secret locations and underground nature of the sites, darkness makes the participants almost literally invisible.

A second metaphorical meaning of darkness, again in association with the confined spaces in the caves, is as the *womb*. Rites of passage are often considered in terms of death and rebirth: as the participant moves from one social persona to another, s/he metaphorically dies and is reborn as another person. Victor Turner (1967) writes of, 'how, by the principle of the economy (or parsimony) of symbolism, logically antithetical processes of death and growth may be represented by the same tokens, for example, by huts and tunnels that are at once tombs and wombs'. This description fits the Italian cult caves perfectly: the participant in the rite of passage enters a tomb and re-emerges from a womb. Darkness, of course, is a primary characteristic of both tombs and wombs (or perhaps, more accurately, of *most* tombs and *all* wombs).

Experiencing darkness

The other aspect that I wish to discuss is the sensory experience of darkness, in the context of the Neolithic caves. I start with describing my own experience – generalized from visits to several different caves, including Grotta di Porto Badisco and Grotta

Table 3.2: The structure of rites of passage. Row 4 demonstrates how the movement into and out of darkness fits into the structure of the rites.

Rites of Passage		
segregation/separation	liminality/transition	aggregation/reincorporation
detachment from previous state	'betwixt and between' state	acceptance into new state
pre-liminal rites	liminal rites	post-liminal rites
	ambiguity invisibility	
movement from light into darkness	darkness	movement from darkness into light

Scaloria described above – and then consider what the experience of the original participants might have been like. This section is difficult to illustrate because, by definition, one cannot photograph darkness. Here I offer a miscellany of images of Mediterranean caves of my acquaintance to give some idea (Fig. 3.4). In most cases entering the caves involves stooping and then climbing or even crawling in. Once inside I can turn and still see daylight – an experience both reassuring and disturbing. It is reassuring because I am still orientated and know the way out; disturbing because as long as I am looking at the bright light filling the entrance, I am virtually blinded and cannot see anything within the cave. As I turn away from the light I can let my eyes gradually adapt to the semi-darkness; I can then make out the form of the chamber and the blackness of the openings leading to side chambers or deeper into the cave. As I move into the cave, away from the entrance, and particularly if I turn a corner, I lose all trace of natural daylight and am plunged into complete darkness. Obviously I can take a torch with me (and of course on my actual visits I always did), but even modern torches only illuminate small areas at a time; moreover, I tend to switch it off for periods, partly to experience deliberately the complete darkness, partly to save the battery.

The darkness, whether complete or partial, has a number of effects on the senses. One is disorientation: without visual guides I rapidly lose any sense of direction or distance. I do not know which direction I am facing or how far I am from the entrance. I also lose all sense of time, how much time has passed or what time of day or night it is. Equally I have no idea what is happening in the outside world (a colleague once told me how disturbed he felt when he emerged from a cave to find that he had missed a huge storm, which had caused a lot of damage, but of which he had been completely unaware). Another effect of the darkness and the inability to see is the sharpening of the other senses: hearing, smell and touch. I become very aware of strange sounds, smells and sensations on the skin, all of which are very different in the caves from those I encounter in the outside world. For instance, sound behaves strangely in caves, sometimes bouncing off the walls, creating echoes whose original source cannot be

3. *Between symbol and senses: the role of darkness in ritual in prehistoric Italy* 33

Figure 3.4: Miscellany of images of Mediterranean caves (Ruth Whitehouse).

located; at other times apparently absorbed and travelling only very short distances, so I cannot hear another person only a few metres away in a different chamber. My sense of smell responds to the dampness, the lack of fresh air, and the sour scents of the fauna, often bats or rodents, that normally frequent the cave. In terms of touch, I am critically aware of the general humidity of the environment, and the proximity of the cave walls, floor and ceiling, often pressing on parts of my body normally free to air. Changes from dry to damp, from smooth to rough, from hard to powdery, as well as the movement from confined to more open spaces, take on a significance they would not hold in the world outside. And in terms of vision itself, if I can see anything at all, the restricted beam of my torch casts little pools of light but creates additional shadows in the surrounding areas. All this is disorienting and rather frightening. That, at least, has been my experience.

So how might my experience compare with that of participants in the Neolithic cave rituals? I am a twenty-first-century individual with twenty-first-century sensibilities. I am not claustrophobic or afraid of the dark as such, but I am not particularly brave. I have never gone into a cave without a good prior knowledge of what to expect and, in more complex caves, I have always been accompanied by a guide, at least for the first visit. What would have been the experience of Neolithic visitors? We may assume that their physiological responses would have been similar to mine, though their past experiences and cultural training would probably have led them to interpret these responses quite differently. On the one hand, they would have been more used to at least semi-darkness than a modern urban-dwelling person; they might also have been more used to caves in general; they would certainly have been more agile than me. They are likely to have taken lights with them too, presumably lamps using animal fat or vegetable oil, which would have cast a variable and flickering light, impacting the darkness less consistently than my electric torch.

Would they have had guides too? This raises an important issue that was brought into sharp focus at the 'Into the earth: the archaeology of darkness' conference by Brian Keenan's enthralling and moving contribution – that is, the crucial difference between a voluntary and an enforced sojourn in a cave or other underground location. Several of the speakers at the conference discussing archaeological or historical examples seem to have assumed that occupation of the sites was by choice, the occupants propelled by hermit-like motivation, in search of peace, seclusion and sensory deprivation, with the aim of achieving a spiritually better state, perhaps communication with the divine. However, though this might have been the case, equally it might not. While it is unlikely that any of our prehistoric or historic cave users would have experienced kidnapping or captivity of the brutality suffered by Brian, their presence in the caves may still not have been voluntary. In the case of the Italian Neolithic caves, if I am right in my interpretation that they were used for rites of passage, the initiands would have had no choice in the matter. They would have been taken, possibly even by force, into the cave by ritual specialists, whose job it was to lead the participants through the rites, ensuring their correct performance, imparting secret knowledge, and making sure that the social transformation was successfully accomplished. At one level the presence of these ritual leaders might have been reassuring: they would have been members of the community known to and trusted by the participants/initiands. On the other hand, the ritual leaders would have been in complete control and, if we follow certain ethnographic examples (good examples are found in the ethnographic literature on initiation rites in Papua New Guinea, e.g. Allen 1967; Barth 1975; Langness 1977; Herdt 1982), we might imagine that they would have manipulated both the people themselves and the environment of the cave to enhance the sensations of disorientation and fear that are part of the physiological response to the situation. In particular, if the sites *were* used for initiation rites, the ethnographic parallels suggest that the experience might have been frightening, painful and humiliating. Darkness, of course, is not the only contributor to these experiences, but it would have been an important one.

Symbol and senses together

What was the role of embodied experience in the rites? Could the symbolism have worked in a more abstract way, or did it require the corporeal sensations? This question takes us back to the nature of rites of passage. In his original description of these rites, Van Gennep recognized that they involve a change both in social identity and individual consciousness. Anthropologists since Van Gennep's day have tended to concentrate on the social side, but the individual aspect is equally important. For the rite to be effective, it is necessary for the participant to feel a fundamentally changed person at the end of the ritual process and this can only happen if the emotions are engaged. Without this, the manipulation of symbols by ritual leaders, however creative and elaborate, would remain an arid intellectual exercise without the power to change people's lives.

So, how does the sensory experience of these caves relate to the cave as metaphor? To understand this, we need to turn to another anthropologist, Pierre Bourdieu. He has taught us that through the dialectical relationship between the human body and space that is structured by myth and ritual, both structures and values are incorporated into bodily understanding; in other words, bodies take metaphors seriously (Bourdieu 1977, 89–94). Bourdieu was writing about built space, but his ideas apply equally to natural spaces used by humans and work perfectly in the case of the cult caves. I have suggested elsewhere (Whitehouse 2001, 166) that the physical context of the caves – their tunnels, passages and corridors to be negotiated and thresholds to be crossed – provided a metaphor for the journey of the rite of passage. The sensory experiences of the individual moving through the caves during such a rite would have served to instil a feeling of irrevocably changed personhood, matching the change of status being socially marked by the rite. And, in this context, darkness – *standing for* invisibility, death and rebirth and *experienced* as disorienting, confusing and frightening – would have contributed to this feeling of transformation. Brian Keenan's account of his own personal transformation through captivity, confinement and darkness, provides us with a privileged glimpse into what, *mutatis mutandis*, the experiences of the Neolithic initiands might have been like (Keenan 1992).

References

Allen, M. 1967. *Male cults and secret initiation in Melanesia*. Melbourne, Melbourne University Press.

Aristotle (trans. W. Ross) [1984]. *Poetics*. In W. Ross (ed.) *The works of Aristotle*, 1457b 6–9. Oxford, Oxford University Press.

Barth, F. 1975. *Ritual and knowledge among the Baktaman of New Guinea*. New Haven, Yale University Press.

Bourdieu, P. 1977. *Outline of a theory of practice*. Cambridge, Cambridge University Press.

Bowie, F. 2000. *The anthropology of religion*. Oxford, Blackwell.

Elster, E., Isetti, E., Robb, J. and Traverso, A. in press. *Grotta Scaloria*. Los Angeles, UCLA Cotsen Institute of Archaeology.

Garwood, P. 2012. Rites of passage. In T. Insoll (ed.) *The Oxford handbook of the archaeology of ritual and religion*, 261–84. Oxford, Oxford University Press.

Graziosi, P. 1980. *Le pitture preistoriche della Grotta di Porto Badisco*. Florence, Istituto Italiano di Preistoria e Protostoria.

Herdt, G. H. (ed.) 1982. *Rituals of manhood. Male initiation in Papua New Guinea*. Berkeley, University of California Press.

Keenan, B. 1992. *An evil cradling*. London, Hutchinson.

Langness, L. L. 1977. Ritual, power and male dominance in the New Guinea Highlands. In R. D. Fogelson and R. N. Adams (eds.) *The anthropology of power*, 3–22. London and New York, Academic Press.

Leach, E. 1971. *Rethinking anthropology*. London, Athlone Press.

Leach, E. 1976. *Culture and communication: the logic by which symbols are connected. An introduction to the use of structuralist analysis in social anthropology*. Cambridge, Cambridge University Press.

Lévi-Strauss, C. 1958. *Anthropologie structurale*. Paris, Plon.

Lévi-Strauss, C. 1962. *La pense sauvage*. Paris, Plon.

Ortony, A. (ed.) 1993. *Metaphor and thought*. Cambridge, Cambridge University Press.

Passeri, L. 1970. Ritrovamenti preistorici nei Pozzi della Piana (Umbria). *Rivista di Scienze Preistoriche* 25, 225–51.

Richards, I. 1936. *The philosophy of rhetoric*. Oxford, Oxford University Press.

Ricoeur, P. 1978. *The rule of metaphor*. London, Routledge.

Shibles, W. 1971. *Metaphor: an annotated bibliography and history*. Whitewater, Language Press.

Tilley, C. 1999. *Metaphor and material culture*. Oxford, Blackwell.

Tiné, S. and Isetti, E. 1982. Culto neolitico delle acque e recenti scavi nella Grotta Scaloria. *Bullettino di Paletnologia Italiana* 82, 31–70.

Turner, V. 1967. *The forest of symbols: aspects of Ndembu ritual*. Ithaca, New York and London, Cornell University Press.

Van Gennep, A. 1960 [1909]. *The rites of passage*. London, Routledge and Kegan Paul.

Whitehouse, R. D. 1990. Caves and cult in Neolithic southern Italy. *Accordia Research Papers* 1, 19–37.

Whitehouse, R. D. 1991a. Cult and culture in Neolithic southern Italy. *Journal of Mediterranean Studies* 1 (2), 242–51.

Whitehouse, R. D. 1991b. The social function of religious ritual: the case of Neolithic southern Italy. *Origini* 14, 387–98.

Whitehouse, R. D. 1991c. Ritual knowledge, secrecy and power in a small-scale society. In E. Herring, R. Whitehouse and J. Wilkins (eds.) *Papers of the fourth conference of Italian archaeology. 1. The archaeology of power. Part 1*, 195–206. London, Accordia Research Centre.

Whitehouse, R. D. 1992. *Underground religion: cult and culture in prehistoric Italy*. London, Accordia Research Centre, University of London.

Whitehouse, R. D. 1995. Thick description and contextual archaeology in the interpretation of prehistoric ritual: a case study from southern Italy. In W. H. Waldren, J. A. Ensenyat and R. C. Kennard (eds.) *The IIIrd Deya conference of prehistory: ritual, rites and religion in prehistory*, 1–31. British Archaeological Reports. International Series 611. Oxford, Tempus Reparatum.

Whitehouse, R. D. 1996. Continuity in ritual practice from Upper Paleolithic to Neolithic and Copper Age in southern Italy and Sicily. In V. Tinè (ed.) *Forme e tempi della neolitizzazione in Italia Meridionale e in Sicilia*, 385–410. Rossano, IRACEB/IIAS.

Whitehouse, R. D. 2001. A tale of two caves. The archaeology of religious experience in Mediterranean Europe. In P. Biehl and F. Bertèmes (eds.) *The archaeologies of cult and religion*, 161–7. Budapest, Archaeolingua Foundation.

Whitehouse, R. D. 2007. Underground religion revisited. In D. Barraclough and C. Malone (eds.) *Cult in context. Reconsidering ritual in archaeology*, 97–106. Oxford, Oxbow Books.

Chapter 4

Experiencing darkness and light in caves: later prehistoric examples from Seulo in central Sardinia

Robin Skeates

Introduction

Caves are often represented simply as dark underground places. Indeed, total, constant darkness is sometimes held to be a characteristic feature of true caves. Biologists and ecologists have long been fascinated by the fact that life can flourish in this absolute darkness, including cave animals with distinctive troglomorphic features (such as being eyeless and depigmented). Yet, for humans, caves are physically and mentally challenging places without light. Cave guides often play upon this dimension by briefly turning off artificial lights underground to enable visitors to sense the darkness – an experience that can be both emotive and memorable. It is hardly surprising, then, that lighting technologies have been used to facilitate and enhance visits to these dark places throughout human history. For example, the nature and impact of flaming torches has been extensively considered with regard to the production and viewing of paintings in French Palaeolithic caves (e.g. Bahn and Vertut 1997; Le Quellec 2011; Azéma and Rivère 2012). The symbolic and structural potential of dark and light contrasts has also been emphasized by Whitehouse (1992) in relation to dark and secluded Neolithic cult caves in Italy. In this chapter, I want to present another view: how the particular effects of light and darkness might have been actively used and experienced by later prehistoric people, and how these effects mediated between people's bodies, cave architecture and cultural objects.

My examples derive from the Seulo Caves Project (Skeates 2011; Skeates *et al.* 2013). This project seeks to develop detailed and contextual understandings of a group of over ten caves and rockshelters located within the present-day territory of Seulo in central Sardinia, which were occupied between the Middle Neolithic and Final Bronze Age (*c.* 4250–850 cal BC). So far we have undertaken archaeological excavations in five of these sites, but for the purposes of this chapter I will focus on the two caves which seem best-suited to a discussion of light and darkness: Grutta 1 de Longu Fresu (a small Middle Neolithic cult cave), and Grutta de is Janas (a large cave complex with evidence of both Late Neolithic and Bronze Age activities) (Fig. 4.1).

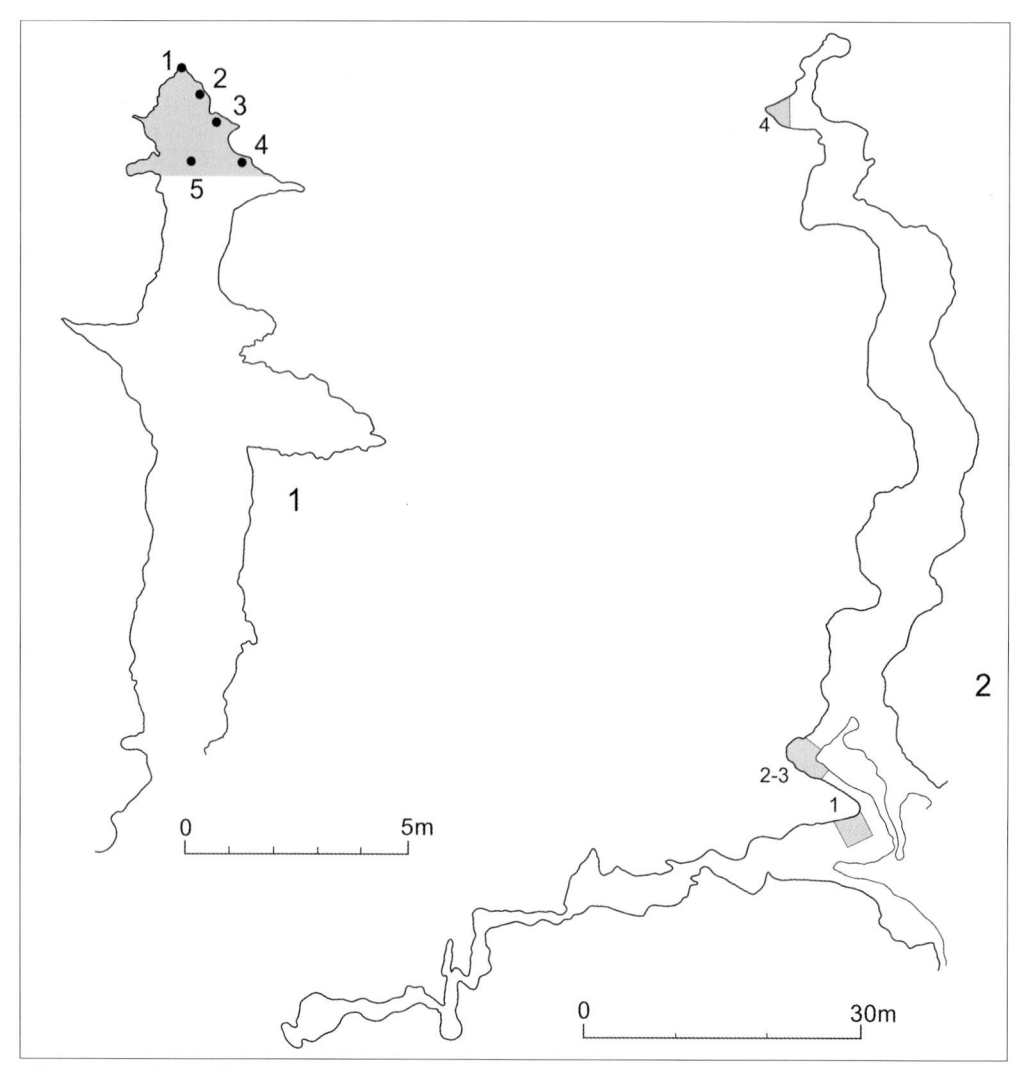

Figure 4.1: Plans of (1) Grutta 1 de Longu Fresu (1. niche with human long bone, 2. human skull, 3. greenstone axe-head, 4. painting, 5. stone structure) and (2) Grutta de is Janas (chambers: 1. upper, 2. large lower, 3. small lower, 4. inner) (Yvonne Beadnell).

My approach here is to combine scientific data with more subjective observations. Using a light meter, I attempted to measure light levels in different parts of these caves, but the equipment was only effective in the best-lit areas. By contrast, we gathered a much richer dataset based on oral testimonies and discussions of our team members' experiences and perceptions of the caves, gained over many hours of moving through and working in these spaces. United with the excavation data, I have used these 'phenomenological' insights (cf. Tilley 2004; Hamilton *et al.* 2006) to offer below some interpretations of how light and darkness might have been used and experienced by the prehistoric groups whose remains we encountered. My assumption is that (with the possible exception of some of the chambers in Grutta de is Janas), the general configuration of these caves, and of natural lighting in relation to them, has not changed significantly between prehistory and the present day. Perhaps more problematic is my use of flash photography to illustrate this chapter, since it exposes details of the caves that are hard to see with other forms of lighting. But even these artificially bright images fail to penetrate completely the darkness of the caves.

Ritual enlightenment: Longu Fresu Cave

Grutta 1 de Longu Fresu is located at the bottom of the minor Longu Fresu valley. It has a small and somewhat hidden entrance (1.15m wide and 0.55m high). This leads to a tunnel-shaped corridor (15m long, 1.5–7.5m wide and 0.5–3.5m high), along the sides of which eight niches have been formed by small springs (Fig. 4.1). This natural cave was modified into, and used as, a place for the performance of small-scale, and potentially secret, rituals during the Middle Neolithic (*c.* 4250–4000 cal BC). This interpretation is based on the results of our excavations in the final two metres of the cave, which have revealed a contemporaneous set of special features (Fig. 4.2). A small group of paintings was added to one of the innermost niches, extending over an area of at least 30cm by 30cm, but is today partly obscured by a coating of flowstone. Nevertheless, it is possible to discern at least two schematic, linear representations of anthropomorphic (or combined human-animal) figures, with legs, arms and either an elongated head or horns. The style of these paintings is comparable to that of other Neolithic cave art in the Central Mediterranean region (cf. Graziosi 1973). About a metre and a half beyond these paintings, the skull of an adult human is cemented to the cave wall by flowstone, and in the disturbed cave deposits between the skull and the paintings an additional 104 disarticulated human bones were recovered. Together, these represent the original deposition of at least one complete adult body on the floor at the back of

Figure 4.2: Interior of Grutta 1 de Longu Fresu (1. niche, 2. skull, 3. stone structure, 4. paintings) (Jeff Veitch).

the cave, its later disturbance and disarticulation, and the secondary caching of large bones (including long bones and at least three skulls) along the side walls and niches of the cave. A greenstone axe-head also lay in the same deposits (Pl. 3). This was the only artefact found during our excavations, which points to its intentional, votive deposition – a practice that was widespread in the Central Mediterranean Neolithic (cf. O'Hare 1990). These innermost cave deposits appear to have been delimited by a small, semi-circular stone structure (0.9m long and wide), formed by a truncated group of stalactites upon which one or more large stone blocks seem to have been placed.

Natural and artificial light and darkness mediated between people's bodies, architectural space and material symbols during ritual performances at Longu Fresu Cave. This is best understood when one physically experiences the cave: moving into, along, and out of it. The restricted cave entrance is dark. This instils a sense of fear and hesitancy amongst some modern visitors about entering the invisible underground space beyond. Once inside, one's eyes gradually adapt to the dark environment. The level of light falls off with distance from the entrance, becoming particularly dark after 6.5m. It is surely no coincidence that the Neolithic cultural material that we identified in this cave was all found in the dark zone, concentrated especially in the darkest and innermost two metres of the passage. Furthermore, the ritual nature of this material – human remains, cave paintings, a votive axe-head and a possible stone structure – leads one to think in terms of the intentional use of this dark place for ritual secrecy or retreat. However, the entrance of the cave is south-facing and, with direct sunlight shining on it, natural light penetrates right to the back of the cave. This provides one with just enough light to orient oneself, particularly in relation to the sunlit entrance – of course, only during daylight hours. But this light is insufficient to illuminate the side niches of the cave, including the niche within which the small group of cave paintings were installed, adjacent to a small spring. It is an interesting paradox that this visually stimulating artwork appears to have been intentionally positioned in one of the darkest parts of the cave. We must, then, imagine the original makers and audiences of this art as having used torches, however dim, to illumine the art and its meanings. Forms and colours are also indistinct in this dimly-lit environment, and require artificial light to be brought to life. The potentially symbolically important vulva-like appearance of the cave niches, and the deposits of iron oxides that have stained them red, are only visible with torches and flash-photography. Likewise, the dark grey pigment of the paintings and the visually attractive bright green colour of the axe-head could only have been seen with the aid of artificial lighting (Fig. 4.2, Pl. 3). From this, it is easy to think in terms of the intentional concealment and revelation of the Neolithic symbols (the freshwater spring, the anthropomorphic paintings, the greenstone axe-head and the human skulls) during ritual performances, leading ritual participants into special knowledge – perhaps relating to humans and their relations with the supernatural. The light of the entrance then serves as a symbolic and spatial reference-point, generally for the outside world, and more specifically in helping people negotiate their way back to the exit.

But light and the sense of sight do not operate alone in Grutta 1 de Longu Fresu. Bodily movement and positioning in relation to the space of the cave is particularly important. In fact, squeezing in and out of the entrance, and carefully making one's way along the cool, musty, humid and silent corridor, is a full-bodied experience. And, alongside other people, it is also an intimate experience. For the Middle Neolithic we might imagine small-scale rites of passage (including both mortuary rites and rites of initiation) being enacted here, involving multi-sensory experiences of symbolic revelation and religious enlightenment.

Firelight: Grutta de is Janas

Grutta de is Janas is the largest cave system in the Seulo area (Fig. 4.1). The main entrance today leads directly to the large northern branch. This is up to 12m wide and 7m high, it extends inwards for 114m, and contains some spectacular speleothems – noted in print by travellers and scientists since the early nineteenth century (e.g. Angius 2006 [1833/56]). A smaller entrance leads, via a 13m long corridor, to the shorter western branch. The two branches are connected, at least 10m in from the two entrances, by three inter-connected chambers. The Upper Chamber, which is best reached today via the small entrance corridor, extends over an area of 11m by 6.5m, and has a low ceiling, 0.5–1.5m in height (Fig. 4.3). This space is connected to the two lower chambers by a small vertical shaft. The larger of the lower chambers is similar in size to the Upper Chamber, while the smaller one, which is surrounded by a wall of stalagmites, is around 3m in diameter. It is within these three chambers that some shallow but rich Late Neolithic deposits were formed.

Figure 4.3: Upper Chamber, Grutta de is Janas (Robin Skeates).

No human remains or convincing examples of art have been found in this cave, but these dark deposits are extensively burnt and contain patches of ashes as well as fragments of charcoal. Large quantities of animal bones (especially sheep/goat, but also cattle) and pottery fragments (assignable to Ozieri style bowls and jars) were found here, as well as a range of special artefacts (some imported from other parts of Sardinia), including long flint blades, freshly-flaked obsidian arrowheads, a polished bone point, seashell pendants, a polished red stone bead, and a rare stone figurine head (Fig. 4.4). Radiocarbon dates on the animal bones provide a timespan of c. 3800–3550 cal BC. It is just conceivable that these deposits might have been formed as a consequence of repeated short-term occupations of those chambers of the cave closest to the entrances by small groups of mobile herders and their animals, who might have 'cleansed' the living space by burning the accumulated organic deposits at the end of their seasonal occupations (cf. Boschian and Montagnari-Kokelj 2000). But, given the deposition of special artefacts and of large quantities of animal bones and pottery vessels in these three low-ceilinged chambers, a more ceremonial interpretation is equally possible, involving the ritual consumption and sacrificial destruction of valued meat and artefacts in the threshold of a spiritually-charged underworld. We cannot be certain if one or either of these scenarios is valid, and it should be noted that they are not mutually exclusive.

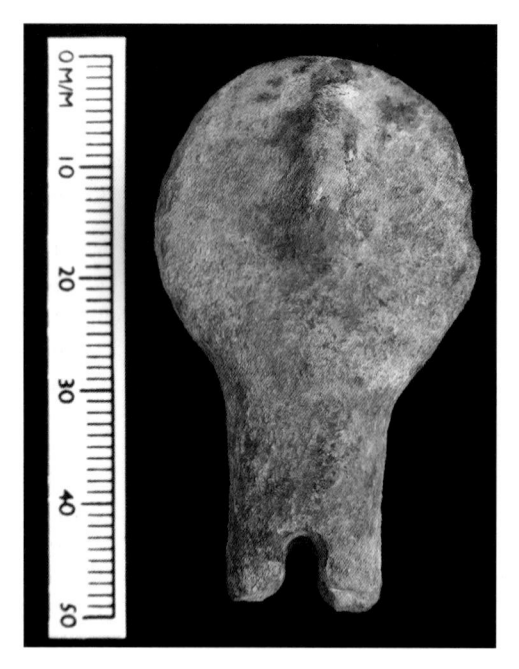

Figure 4.4: Head of stone figurine from large Lower Chamber, Grutta de is Janas (Jeff Veitch).

Light and darkness would again have mediated between people's bodies, architectural space and material culture in this series of three cave chambers. Today, despite the cave's two south-facing entrances, these spaces are completely dark and need to be lit artificially. In the past one can imagine the use of torches, to light people's way down and along the entrance corridors, and to illuminate their depositions of some visually attractive cultural material. However, it is currently difficult to gauge the precise balance that existed in the Late Neolithic between natural light, artificial light and darkness in this part of the cave system closest to the current entrances, because a large rock-fall – which overlies (and therefore post-dates) the Neolithic deposits in all three of the excavated chambers – may have blocked additional cave entrances that could potentially have allowed in some natural light. Leaving this issue to one side, what is particularly striking about these chambers is the large quantity of ashes and charcoal found in the floor deposits. The majority of the identifiable charcoal is represented by small branch-wood of shrubby taxa. This evidence points towards multiple fires set in each of the chambers, fuelled by easily combustible material, and implies not only dancing flames and dynamic firelight but also concentrated heat and smoke within these confined spaces. Indeed, the heat was so intense that an obsidian arrowhead was partly melted, pottery fragments were re-fired, and patches of the cave bedrock were burnt. It is consequently difficult to envisage people remaining in these chambers with such a fire burning. Nevertheless, the light generated by these events would have been sufficient to illuminate the chambers and their burning cultural materials, and also to cast some light and shadows into the first few metres of the two adjacent branches of the cave system – enough to give people some indication of their enormity and a sense of liminality. At night, firelight glowing, then fading, in the cave could also have been seen from just outside the cave entrances. Dynamic light effects and darkness would, then, have actively contributed to human experiences and knowledge of Grutta de is Janas in the Late Neolithic, whatever the precise activities performed there.

Passage into the darkness: Grutta de is Janas (interior)

The northern branch of the Grutta de Janas cave system extends inwards, more or less horizontally, from the modern entrance for a distance of more than 100m (Fig. 4.1). In the central section the cave roof is particularly high, and there are some spectacular speleothems to be seen which create a cathedral-like atmosphere and comprise the centre-piece of modern touristic visits to the cave (Fig. 4.5). Numerous low chambers and cavities also lead off to the sides. Towards the end of the northern branch, just before the point at which it descends steeply into the abyss of a final series of chambers, and some 95m inside the modern cave entrance, we investigated another chamber (we identified no archaeological remains beyond this point in the cave system). It is a small circular space, tightly bounded by a curving wall of stalagmites (Pl. 4). The floor area measures 2m by 1.7m, which only affords room for a maximum of two or three people. Overlying the bedrock, our excavations revealed a largely intact deposit, just 12cm deep. This contained a few cultural remains: some tiny charcoal fragments; two fragments of copper; twenty plain pottery sherds, all probably derived from a single bowl; and two animal bones identified as a fragment of a sheep/goat radius and a juvenile pig tibia. The pig bone was radiocarbon dated to *c.* 2250–2100 cal BC which, together with the style of the bowl, places the associated deposit in the Early Bronze Age. This period is particularly significant because it saw not only an extension of use boundaries within Grutta de Janas (compared to the Late Neolithic, when deposits were concentrated in the chambers closest to the cave entrances), but also the more extensive exploration and occupation of caves in the wider landscape of Seulo, and indeed throughout Sardinia (cf. Skeates 2012). Below, I consider what part darkness might have played in this process.

Darkness and exclusively artificial light mediated between people's bodies, cave space and cultural objects during special journeys along the northern branch of the Janas system. Having moved about 10m in from the naturally-lit modern-day cave entrance, the darkness in this part of the cave system is absolute. This environment provides an ideal home for a colony of bats, which has a roost high-up on the cave ceiling. But, for humans, this blinding darkness calls for caution. Indeed, the floor of the northern branch is strewn with dangerous obstacles, including large stalagmites and angular boulders, all made wet and slippery by the humidity of the cave. Within living memory, adventurous young people from the local town of Seulo would come here, with a kerosene lamp, to explore the inner reaches of the cave. They repeatedly wrote their names on the stalagmites as a record of their achievements, to be lit upon by later visitors. But today, this route is completely transformed by the installation of a health-and-safety conscious touristic walkway, complete with handrails as well as artificial lighting: making the whole experience much more accessible – both physically and visually (Fig. 4.5). In fact, the journey along the northern branch can now be achieved rapidly, within a few minutes, but would originally have taken visitors much longer. Whatever the conditions underfoot, artificial lighting would always have been essential for people to negotiate this route. Our experience of using torches here (without the overhead cave lighting) was a tantalising and often frustrating one. Despite keeping

Figure 4.5: Speleothems, modern walkway and lighting along the middle section of the northern branch of Grutta de is Janas (Jeff Veitch).

our eyes wide open, we strained to see details of the spectacular and evocative natural architecture that our torches picked out on the roof and walls of the cavern. These shadowy features were brought alive by the play of our torches, but also constantly framed by areas of impenetrable darkness (Fig. 4.6). And when our batteries ran out, we groped our way back to the safety of the cave entrance, as quickly as possible. Considering the flaming torches or simple clay lamps of the Early Bronze Age, we can be justified in imagining that similar experiences were shared by prehistoric visitors.

During the Early Bronze Age, such a journey into darkness involved the (arguably) votive deposition of a restricted assemblage of objects on the floor of the small inner chamber described above. The tiny charcoal fragments found here in the otherwise brown sediment are too few to be interpreted as remains of a brightly burning fire set in the chamber, but did perhaps derive from flaming torches. Aided by such artificial light, a human journey to this place intentionally penetrated one of the deepest and darkest parts of the cave – going well beyond those chambers near the entrance that had been utilized during the Late Neolithic. The configuration of the inner chamber, with its curtain of stalactites, would have concentrated artificial light in this small space, and on the restricted group of people and objects situated within it. The shine of the copper artefact might have been picked up by torchlight. But the plain dark grey bowl would have offered only limited visual stimulus. And, looking outwards, the scene would have been framed by utter darkness. In this dim and distant environment, far from the outside world and its familiar people and places, it is possible to imagine the restricted sight but heightened other senses of the people who placed the objects in the chamber:

Figure 4.6: Darkness along the middle section of the northern branch of Grutta de is Janas (Robin Skeates).

isolation, disorientation, fear, wonder, a sense of achievement, and – perhaps especially – spiritual alertness. If ever there was a place to communicate with the supernatural, and to offer gifts, this dark liminal place was it. And perhaps a trace of this early significance continues to this day, carried by the place name 'Grutta de is Janas', which means 'Cave of the Fairies', with reference to the enduring folklore of Sardinia which tells of these small, winged, supernatural beings guarding great treasures underground and their occasional good and bad interventions in the human world.

Conclusion

In this chapter I have tried to challenge the widespread perception of caves simply as dark places, by considering how particular effects of light and darkness might have been used and experienced by people in two caves in central Sardinia during the Neolithic and Bronze Age, and how these effects mediated between people's bodies, cave architecture and cultural objects. I am well aware of the limitations of my approach to recording, interpreting and illustrating this difficult area of archaeological enquiry. However, I still regard its consideration as necessary, particularly within cave archaeology where darkness is often as fundamental as water is to maritime archaeology.

Darkness in caves can seem absolute and impenetrable. It can therefore instil feelings of blindness, fear, hesitancy and disorientation in visitors. It is surely because of this potency of darkness that the dark zones of caves were sometimes intentionally used by groups of prehistoric people, particularly as liminal places situated between the worlds of the living and the supernatural. Here, they concealed and revealed key material symbols during the course of controlled, small-scale, ritual performances which might in part be understood as rites of passage – physically and conceptually – into darkness and enlightenment.

At the same time, people adapt their eyes and other senses to the darkness of caves, particularly with the aid of penetrating sunlight and artificial lighting. In contrast to the bright electric lights used to illuminate caves today, dim and shadowy prehistoric firelight, torches and lamps would have struggled to contend with the darkness of deep caves. However, they would have been sufficient to enable people to orient themselves in relation to entrances, to bring alive some of the visually striking dimensions of the cave architecture and introduced cultural artefacts, and to unlock their symbolic potential, while still framed by the darkness.

References

Angius, V. 2006 [1833/56]. *Città e villaggi della Sardegna dell'Ottocento* (ed. L. Carta). Nuoro, Ilisso.
Azéma, M. and Rivère, F. 2012. Animation in Palaeolithic art: a pre-echo of cinema. *Antiquity* 86, 316–24.
Bahn, P. and Vertut, P. 1997. *Journey through the Ice Age*. London, Weidenfeld & Nicolson.
Boschian, G. and Montagnari-Kokelj, E. 2000. Prehistoric shepherds and caves in the Trieste Karst (Northeastern Italy). *Geoarchaeology* 15, 331–71.

Graziosi, P. 1973. *L'arte preistorica in Italia*. Firenze, Sansoni.

Hamilton, S., Whitehouse, R., Brown, K., Combes, P., Herring, E. and Seager Thomas, M. 2006. Phenomenology in practice: towards a methodology for a 'subjective' approach. *European Journal of Archaeology* 9, 31–71.

Le Quellec, J.-L. 2011. Palaeolithic art in motion. *Antiquity* 85, 1082–3.

O'Hare, G. B. 1990. A preliminary study of polished stone artefacts in prehistoric southern Italy. *Proceedings of the Prehistoric Society* 56, 123–52.

Skeates, R. 2011. The Seulo Caves Project, Sardinia: a report on archaeological work undertaken in 2009 and 2010. *Cave and Karst Science* 38, 131–6.

Skeates, R. 2012. Caves in need of context: prehistoric Sardinia. In K. A. Bergsvik and R. Skeates (eds.) *Caves in context: the cultural significance of caves and rockshelters in Europe*, 166–87. Oxford, Oxbow Books.

Skeates, R., Gradoli, G. M. and Beckett, J. 2013. The cultural life of caves in Seulo, central Sardinia. *Journal of Mediterranean Archaeology* 26, 97–126.

Tilley, C. 2004. *The materiality of stone: explorations in landscape phenomenology: 1*. Oxford and New York, Berg.

Whitehouse, R. 1992. *Underground religion: cult and culture in prehistoric Italy*. London, Accordia Research Centre, University of London.

Chapter 5

The dark side of the sky: the orientations of earlier prehistoric monuments in Ireland and Britain

Richard Bradley

Newgrange and Balnuaran of Clava

I started work on this chapter towards the end of 2013. It was then that I visited Balnuaran of Clava near Inverness, where I had excavated almost twenty years before (Bradley 2000). One reason I was there was to observe the midwinter solstice from the tombs in the prehistoric cemetery. I might have visited similar structures that day, for the distinctive architecture of other passage tombs achieves a comparable effect: an intense beam of sunlight extends along an entrance passage and illuminates the centre of the monument. I would have seen that happening at Newgrange, too (O'Kelly 1982). At first sight the correspondence is not surprising as those monuments share the same ground plan, but there is a problem. Newgrange is a Neolithic tomb dating from the end of the fourth millennium BC. The Clava Cairns were built over a thousand years later. There is another important difference. Newgrange faces the midwinter *sunrise* but, a millennium afterwards, the Clava passage tombs were aligned on the *setting sun* at the same time of year. Two questions come to mind. Why were so many Neolithic monuments directed towards the rising sun when those built during the Bronze Age normally faced the sunset? And did the dwellings of the living share the same alignments as the houses of the dead?

There have been two phases of research into relationships of this kind. The first was during the early twentieth century when the subject engaged the interest of Norman Lockyer (1906) and Boyle Somerville (1923). They undertook accurate surveys of many ancient structures, and Lockyer, in particular, drew on his expertise as an astronomer. But their work was soon forgotten and it was not until much later that their interpretations of the chambered tombs at Balnuaran Clava and Bryn Celli Ddu were confirmed by new fieldwork (Bradley 2000, 122–6; Burrow 2010). One reason for the neglect is that these pioneers were not archaeologists.

Much the same happened in the 1960s with the work of Alexander Thom who suggested that past societies could calculate the movements of the sun and moon. He inferred the existence of specialized methods of surveying in the past. Thom made new plans of many monuments and interpreted them according to his knowledge of astronomy (Thom 1967, 1971, 1978). It was a long time before his interpretations were checked in detail (Ruggles 1999). There was an important difference between the complex statistical procedures required to test Thom's hypotheses and the simple orientations that could be observed on the ground. Earlier researchers, like Thom, had made excessive claims. Ruggles suggested that future investigations should pay more attention to ancient cosmologies. This chapter builds on his approach.

Orientations

It is important to distinguish between different kinds of alignment. There are a number of options to consider, as some are much more specific than others. This analysis focuses on the predictable movements of the sun; the significance of the moon is debateable and will be considered later.

Certain points are particularly significant (Table 5.1). There is a difference between the effects of solar illumination inside closed structures like passage tombs, and those observed at open monuments like stone circles. In a tomb such as Newgrange the passage acts like a lens, intensifying the light and focusing it on the chamber walls. In other contexts this effect is lost, although the outsides of buildings may be lit. Figures 5.1–5.3 and Plates 5–6 illustrate what happens during the midwinter solstice at Balnuaran of Clava.

At stone circles, solar orientations take a different form and may have been relatively uncommon. In some cases they can only be identified because a pair of stones point towards significant points in the solar year, and this is even more apparent where the axis of the monument is emphasized by other features. They include the earthwork avenue at Stonehenge (Parker Pearson 2012, 238–48), and an outlying monolith at Long Meg and her Daughters (Burl 1994). Otherwise, there is a problem of deciding where observers should stand. Should they view celestial events by looking across the diameter of the enclosure, or ought they to congregate in its centre? Henge monuments are different again, for here the horizon may be hidden behind the earthwork bank, so that the only long distance view is through an entrance. At the central henge in the Thornborough complex the entrance picks out the midwinter sunrise (Harding 2013, fig. 6.12).

Table 5.1: Sources of variation among the alignments of prehistoric monuments.

Increasing light:	**Decreasing light:**
Morning; rising sun	*Evening; setting sun*
Specific times of year:	**Specific times of year:**
Midwinter; midsummer; the equinoxes (?)	*Midwinter; midsummer; the equinoxes (?)*
Specific events:	**Specific events:**
Sunrise; sunset	*Sunrise; sunset*
Impermeable structures:	**Permeable structures:**
Chambered tombs; houses	*Stone circles; henges*

5. *The dark side of the sky*

Figure 5.1: View of the midwinter sunset looking along the passage of the south-west cairn at Balnuaran of Clava (Ronnie Scott).

Figure 5.2: The entrance to the north-east passage tomb at Balnuaran of Clava at the time of the midwinter sunset (Ronnie Scott).

Figure 5.3: View of the midwinter sunset looking along the passage of the north-east cairn at Balnuaran of Clava (Ronnie Scott).

In many cases such precision was not important. At best the structure of a particular monument indicates a general direction, and this can be achieved in several different ways. Most chambered tombs lack the lengthy passages found at Clava and Newgrange. Instead, they open directly into a chamber or a series of chambers. Their orientation may be emphasized by an elongated mound. Similarly, the monoliths used in stone circles can be graded by height so that the tallest are on one side of the circuit and the lowest ones are opposite. The clearest example is at Stonehenge (Parker Pearson 2012, chapter 8). Particular parts of the ring can also be emphasized by cup marks, and in certain cases these features are found together. The 'stone circle' at Beltany, Co. Donegal provides a well-documented instance (Lacey 1983, 72–3).

At Balnuaran of Clava these relationships are even more explicit (Bradley 2000, chapters 2 and 5). Here two passage graves and a ring cairn are enclosed by rings of upright stones. The higher monoliths are on the south-west side and the lowest are towards the north-east. The contrast between them extends to the use of quarried slabs for the tallest uprights and erratics for some of the others. The colours of the rocks were important, too. Thus pillars of red sandstone face the setting sun, but their counterparts on the far side of the monument contain inclusions of quartz. These conventions apply to all three well-preserved cairns in the cemetery and extend to the interior of both passage graves.

The cemetery at Balnuaran of Clava is relevant for another reason. If the passage tombs were aligned on the setting sun at midwinter, the backs of their cairns faced the midsummer sunrise. There is nothing to indicate an exact alignment, but there still seems to be a concern with this direction. It may explain why pieces of quartz are commoner along the eastern edges of these monuments. Another example is provided by the Scottish stone circle of Croftmoraig (Piggott and Simpson 1971; Bradley and Sheridan 2005; Bradley 2012). It is located on a natural mound and the monoliths were arranged around a glacial erratic embedded in its surface. From here there is a dramatic view of the midsummer sunset to the north-west behind Schiehallion, one of the most prominent mountains in the southern Highlands. This effect is best observed from the middle of the ring, but it does not depend on any alignment between the individual stones. In a later phase, however, an oval setting was constructed inside the existing circle. In this case its long axis (which is defined by a pair of matching uprights) is directed towards the path of the sun as it travels down a hillside to the south-west. In this case the significant feature is that it appears to settle on the horizon at the time of the midwinter solstice. On other occasions it would have been too high for this to happen.

Changes over time

Croftmoraig and Balnuaran of Clava share a feature which distinguishes them from Newgrange. Not only are they directed towards the setting sun, but both were built during the Bronze Age. These attributes may be related.

There are four phases in the evolution of earlier prehistoric architecture, each of them epitomized by the orientations of important monuments. To a certain extent the same applies to domestic buildings. The sequence is summarized in Table 5.2.

The main points are readily apparent. In the first phase, which corresponds to the Early and Middle Neolithic, few monuments had precise alignments, but many long barrows and long cairns were directed towards the morning sun. It is striking that the two structures that were most obviously orientated on the sunset were among the latest of their kind. One was the Dorset Cursus, the largest earthwork of its type in Britain (Barrett *et al.* 1991, 36–58), and the other was the great tomb of Maeshowe (Richards 2005, chapter 9). Less than 20% of the passage tombs in Ireland had solar alignments. They were directed towards the solstices more often than the equinoxes and were directed towards the sunrise and sunset in roughly equal proportions (Prendergast 2011).

The second phase is the Late Neolithic period. Again, individual monuments, including henges, timber circles and stone circles, were aligned on either the sunrise or the sunset, and there are even cases in which both these orientations were combined, for instance, the pairing of Durrington Walls with its neighbour Woodhenge, or the opposing axes of the sarsen setting at Stonehenge (Parker Pearson 2012, 48–9, 79–81, 161). The evidence is similar to that from passage graves, and it may be no accident that the structures built during this phase share their circular outline. A new development is the recognition of domestic dwellings associated with Grooved Ware in Ireland and Orkney. As Jessica Smyth has observed, their entrances were often directed towards the

Table 5.2: *The principal orientations of prehistoric structures between 3700 and 800 BC, illustrated by typical examples. There is most evidence for westerly alignments after 2400 BC. References to the 'sunrise' and 'sunset' are to the first and last appearance of the sun from the monument in question. References to the 'morning' and 'evening' sun describe the longer process that can be observed as it climbs or descends the sky.*

Date range BC	North-east to south	South to north-west
3700–3000	**Structures facing the morning sun:** *Long barrows; long cairns; court cairns; passage tombs*	**Structures facing the evening sun:** *Passage tombs*
	Structures aligned on the sunrise: *Dorchester on Thames cursus; passage tombs (e.g. Newgrange)*	**Structures aligned on the sunset:** *Dorset cursus; passage tombs (e.g. Maeshowe)*
3000–2400	**Structures facing the morning sun:** *Henges; timber circles; stone circles; roundhouses*	**Structures facing the evening sun:** *Henges; stone circles*
	Structures aligned on the sunrise: *Henges (e.g. Thornborough); timber circles (e.g. Woodhenge); stone circles (e.g. Stonehenge)*	**Structures aligned on the sunset:** *Henges (e.g. Durrington Walls); stone circles (e.g. Long Meg and her Daughters; Stonehenge)*
2400–1500	**Structures facing the morning sun:** *Roundhouses*	**Structures facing the evening sun:** *Wedge tombs; Clava Cairns; Scottish recumbent stone circles*
	Structures aligned on the sunrise: *Rare or absent*	**Structures aligned on the sunset:** *Clava passage tombs (e.g. Balnuaran of Clava); timber circles (e.g. Seahenge)*
1500–800	**Structures facing the morning sun:** *Roundhouses; domestic enclosures*	**Structures facing the evening sun:** *Late stone circles*
	Structures aligned on the sunrise: – – –	**Structures aligned on the sunset:** *Late stone circles (e.g. Drombeg)*

rising sun (2013, 412, 2014, chapter 5). That is particularly important at the settlement of Barnhouse because the orientation of its houses contrasts with that of Maeshowe only one kilometre away. It is a contrast that assumes more importance with time.

The third phase extends from 2400–1500 BC and takes in both the Chalcolithic and Early Bronze Age. It was then that the developments prefigured by monuments like Maeshowe and Durrington Walls become still more important. By this stage few structures explicitly reference the sunrise, and many more are directed towards the south-west, west and sometimes the north-west. Examples include Irish wedge tombs and their Scottish counterparts, the Clava Cairns. It was during this period that the passage graves at Balnuaran were aligned on the midwinter sunset. More importantly, it was when other circular monuments shared that emphasis on the western half of the sky. Among them are the recumbent stone circles of Scotland whose monoliths were graded by height (Welfare 2011), but the distribution of this practice extends into most parts of Britain and even includes the timber circle known as Seahenge (Brennand and Taylor 2003). Here one group of taller posts was to the north-east and another was to the west. The entrance was located on the south-western side and it seems possible that the monument was aligned on both the midsummer sunrise and the midwinter sunset. Similar conventions were followed on both sides of the Irish Sea. The same emphasis on the south-west is evident at the excavated cairn of Kintraw in Argyll (Simpson 1967) and at Beltany (Lacey 1983, 72–3). Such evidence is particularly striking because the few excavated dwellings of this period normally faced south-east.

That contrast is even more evident in a final phase from 1500–800 BC. Roundhouses become much more common, and a few are associated with enclosures. Both have orientations between the east and south. Until recently, less was known about the ceremonial monuments of this period, but new research in Scotland and Ireland has shown that stone circles remained important (Bradley 2011, chapter 6). In Munster, they were associated with other kinds of monument and share a south-western alignment. That certainly applies to the stone circle at Drombeg which is orientated on the midwinter sunset (O'Brien 2002). The oval stone setting at Croftmoraig is aligned on the same event and was used from 1400–1200 BC (fieldwork by the writer in 2012).

Thus there were two phases during which public monuments shared a common orientation. Until the late fourth millennium BC some monuments may have acknowledged the position of the rising sun, although few were provided with exact alignments. The situation did not change until the adoption of passage graves, but only limited proportions of these tombs were directed towards celestial events. The second phase in which specialized structures shared the same axis was between the introduction of metalwork and the end of the Bronze Age. The evidence is strongest between about 2400 BC and 1500 BC, but recent work shows that even after this time older traditions of monumental architecture continued or were revived (Bradley 2011, chapter 6). In this case there was still an emphasis on the west. In between these two periods and, in particular, between about 3000 BC and the middle of the third millennium BC, individual constructions were directed towards both the sunrise and the sunset.

The dark side of the sky

How are archaeologists to explain the striking contrast between the passage tombs at Newgrange and Clava? Both are related to the darkest days of the year but the Neolithic monument is orientated on the midwinter sunrise and its Bronze Age counterpart on the setting sun. Then there is another question to ask. The Clava cemetery was built on the site of an older settlement (Bradley 2000, 121–2). How were the alignments of tombs related to those of domestic dwellings? This question is considered in a later section of this paper.

This paper has emphasized the orientation of Neolithic and Bronze Age monuments in relation to the sunrise and sunset. This is important in two ways. The solstices mark the turning points of the year, and people would have been aware of the distance that it travelled and its height above the horizon. Every day can be divided between the period when the amount of light increases and a time when the sky becomes darker with the coming of night. Sunrise and sunset marked the two extremes, and their positions were acknowledged by a series of monuments.

Other studies have placed more emphasis on the moon, but in most cases this approach envisages a longer period of observation. Aubrey Burl suggests that recumbent stone circles in Scotland shared a lunar alignment because their dominant axis extended outside the solar arc, but included the position of the moon over an eighteen and a half year period (2000, chapter 12). The problem with this idea is that it assumes that these monuments *must have had* an astronomical orientation of some kind. As Adam Welfare (2011) has argued, the direction in which they faced may have been more significant than their exact configuration. The Clava Cairns illustrate this point. Again they face south-west and the directions of their passages are consistent with the position of the moon at one stage in its monthly cycle, yet the only precise alignments – those at Balnuaran – are on the midwinter *sunset*. Of course, any monument that faces the sunset must also be directed towards the moon since the lunar arc is wider than the arc described by the sun. On the other hand, what they do share is an emphasis on the dark side of the sky.

That is consistent with the character of prehistoric monuments in these islands. There is an important difference between those built and used during the Late Neolithic period and structures employed after that time. Henges, stone circles, timber circles and passage tombs can all be directed towards the rising or setting sun, and occasionally they do have exact astronomical alignments. These places played various roles in prehistoric society. Whilst some monuments were associated with the dead, they also provide evidence for large gatherings and feasts. Sites like Newgrange or Durrington Walls are associated with substantial collections of artefacts and faunal remains. The same is true during the Chalcolithic, but the structures which date from the Bronze Age have an entirely different character. There are fewer finds and food remains are rare. Their main association is with human bones. There is little evidence for activities directed towards the living.

Perhaps the changing character of these monuments is illustrated by the change from structures directed towards the rising sun to those associated with the onset of darkness. One explanation has been suggested by William O'Brien (2002, 2012, 259–61) who observes that in Munster the dead were thought to travel south-west to enter the underworld at an island off the Beara Peninsula. There is medieval literary evidence to this effect. His model has a wider application. It applies not only to Irish monuments like wedge tombs but also to Scottish stone circles and to Stonehenge where the remains of the dead are found at a site whose most obvious alignment was on the midwinter sunset. The same ideas could even have played a part in southern Europe. Michael Hoskin (2001) shows that virtually all the chambered tombs in the Mediterranean are orientated towards the east or south-east. In only three regions (the Balearic Islands, Provence and eastern Languedoc) do the monuments face west. As was the case in Britain and Ireland, these structures were among the last to be built.

There is no suggestion of direct contacts between these regions, but again they may be places where the dead were associated with darkness and the setting sun.

One problem is the role of the earliest monuments in Ireland and Britain, which were usually directed towards the east or south-east. They were found with the remains of the dead, but they also appear to have been directed towards the rising sun. Perhaps this pattern is found because such monuments were closely related to the rectilinear houses occupied at the time. There are a few cases in which mounds or cairns were superimposed on the remains of timber buildings, but in other respects the alignments of these houses are more diverse. It is not always easy to distinguish between the front and back of such dwellings, but about a third of those in Ireland faced east and another 25% were directed towards the south-east (Smyth 2006, fig. 7, 2014, fig. 3.1). Unlike chambered tombs, wooden houses had to withstand strong winds and this may be one reason why they did not share a common orientation.

By 3000 BC the structures found in settlements had changed their character and a tradition of circular houses replaced these rectangular buildings. This development ran in parallel with the adoption of circular mounds. At a time when western alignments were becoming more common among public monuments, domestic dwellings were directed towards the rising sun. Comparatively few houses are known between 3000 BC and 1500 BC, but after that time they are frequent discoveries. It would be easy to suppose that the rising sun helped to light the interior, but that does not provide a satisfactory explanation, for domestic enclosures with the same orientation have been identified during recent years. In this case it would have served no practical purpose. In fact the orientations of prehistoric structures became increasingly polarized. The process started with the use of passage tombs and was more pronounced after the introduction of metalwork. The basic pattern is summarized in Table 5.3.

To summarize the argument, these observations suggest an increasingly powerful association between the sunrise and the domestic world. It was the exact opposite of the connection between human remains and the night. Just as the entrances of houses brought light into the world of the living, it was the stone structures – circles and chambered tombs – of the Neolithic and the Bronze Age that provided a 'door into the dark' (Heaney 1969). That is a good way to characterize these monuments

Table 5.3: The dominant orientations of monuments and domestic buildings, and the relationships between them.

	Alignment(s) of monuments	**Alignment(s) of houses**	**Relationship**
Phase 1	Morning: rising sun	Varied	*Partial overlap*
Phase 2	Morning: rising sun Evening: setting sun	Morning: rising sun	*Similarity and contrast*
Phase 3	Evening: setting sun	Morning: rising sun	*Contrast*
Phase 4	Evening: setting sun	Morning: rising sun	*Contrast*

Acknowledgements

I would like to thank Marion and Robert for organising such a stimulating conference, and Ronnie Scott for allowing me to use his photographs of Balnuaran of Clava. It will be evident that this paper is influenced by the ideas of William O'Brien and Adam Welfare.

References

Barrett, J., Bradley, R. and Green, M. 1991. *Landscape, monuments and society. The prehistory of Cranborne Chase*. Cambridge, Cambridge University Press.

Bradley, R. 2000. *The good stones. A new investigation of the Clava Cairns*. Edinburgh, Society of Antiquaries of Scotland.

Bradley, R. 2011. *Stages and screens. An investigation of four henge monuments in northern and north-eastern Scotland*. Edinburgh, Society of Antiquaries of Scotland.

Bradley, R. 2012. Croftmoraig. *Discovery and excavation in Scotland* 13, 146.

Bradley, R. and Sheridan, A. 2005. Croft Moraig and the chronology of stone circles. *Proceedings of the Prehistoric Society* 71, 269–81.

Brennand, M. and Taylor, M. 2003. The survey and excavation of a timber circle at Holme-next-the-Sea, Norfolk, 1998–9. *Proceedings of the Prehistoric Society* 69, 1–84.

Burl, A. 1994. Long Meg and her Daughters. *Transactions of the Cumberland and Westmorland Archaeological Society* 94, 1–11.

Burl, A. 2000. *The stone circles of Britain, Ireland and Brittany*. New Haven, Yale University Press.

Burrow, S. 2010. Bryn Celli Ddu passage tomb, Anglesey: alignments, construction, dates and ritual. *Proceedings of the Prehistoric Society* 76, 249–70.

Harding, J. 2013. *Cult, religion and pilgrimage*. York, Council for British Archaeology.

Heaney, S. 1969. *Door into the dark*. London, Faber.

Hoskin, M. 2001. *Tombs, temples and their orientations. A new perspective on Mediterranean prehistory*. Bognor Regis, Ocinara Books.

Lacey, B. 1983. *Archaeological survey of Co. Donegal*. Lifford, Donegal County Council.

Lockyer, N. 1906. *Stonehenge and other British stone monuments astronomically considered*. London, Macmillan.

O'Brien, W. 2002. Megaliths in a mythologised landscape: south-west Ireland in the Iron Age. In C. Scarre (ed.) *Monuments and landscape in Atlantic Europe*, 152–76. London, Routledge.

O'Brien, W. 2012. *Iverni. A prehistory of Cork*. Cork, The Collins Press.

O'Kelly, M. 1982. *Newgrange. Archaeology, art and legend*. London, Thames and Hudson.

Parker Pearson, M. 2012. *Stonehenge*. London, Simon and Schuster.

Piggott, S. and Simpson, D. 1971. The excavation of a stone circle at Croft Moraig, Perthshire. *Proceedings of the Prehistoric Society* 37 (1), 1–15.

Prendergast, F. 2011. *Linked landscapes: spatial, archaeoastronomical and social network analysis of the Irish passage tomb tradition*. Unpublished PhD thesis, University College Dublin.

Richards, C. 2005. *Dwelling among the monuments*. Cambridge, McDonald Institute for Archaeological Research.

Ruggles, C. 1999. *Astronomy in prehistoric Britain and Ireland*. New Haven, Yale University Press.

Simpson, D. 1967. Excavations at Kintraw, Argyll. *Proceedings of the Society of Antiquaries of Scotland* 99, 54–9.

Smyth, J. 2006. The role of the house in Early Neolithic Ireland. *European Journal of Archaeology* 9, 229–57.

Smyth, J. 2013. Tara in pieces – change and continuity at the turn of the third millennium BC. In M. O'Sullivan, C. Scarre and M. Doyle (eds.) *Tara from the past to the future*, 408–16. Dublin, Wordwell.

Smyth, J. 2014. *Settlement in the Irish Neolithic: new discoveries at the edge of Europe*. Oxford, The Prehistoric Society.

Somerville, H. B. 1923. Orientations of prehistoric monuments of the British Isles. *Archaeologia* 73, 193–224.

Thom, A. 1967. *Megalithic sites in Britain*. Oxford, Oxford University Press.

Thom, A. 1971. *Megalithic lunar observatories*. Oxford, Oxford University Press.

Thom, A. 1978. *Megalithic remains in Britain and Brittany*. Oxford, Clarendon Press.

Welfare, A. 2011. *Great crowns of stone. The recumbent stone circles of Scotland*. Edinburgh, Royal Commission on the Ancient and Historical Monuments of Scotland.

Chapter 6

In search of darkness: cave use in Late Bronze Age Ireland

Marion Dowd

On a caving expedition to the Burren in 1989, members of the Cork Speleological Group decided to explore Robber's Den, Co. Clare. They climbed the vertical cliff face to the cave entrance – a rope is typically used to make this short ascent. The entrance leads into a small chamber which is naturally lit by daylight and commands panoramic views over a broad karst plateau. An opening in the floor of this chamber drops down into a dim and dark lower chamber. Rectangular in shape, this space has been used at various times in the past as indicated by intermittent finds of animal bones and artefacts. A narrow gap in the floor of this second chamber provides access into an extremely tight narrow passage shrouded in complete darkness. The journey through the passage is torturous; twisting and contorting the body, all the time feeling trapped between massive solid walls of limestone. It is not a trip for the faint-hearted or claustrophobic and is unquestionably off-putting to all but experienced cavers (Fig. 6.1). When the explorers squeezed through this constrictive passage in 1989 they emerged into a third chamber, again enveloped in complete darkness. An underground river runs through a deeper section of the cave interrupting the silence with the sound of flowing water. Probably thinking they were the first to venture so far into Robber's Den, the cavers must have been surprised to discover the skeletal remains of an adult female lying on the cave floor (Anderson and McCarthy 1991; Cremin

Figure 6.1: Caver Terry Casserly squeezing through the narrow passage into the third chamber of Robber's Den (Colin Bunce).

1991). The woman was over thirty-five years old at the time of death. Her dental health was poor with evidence for dental abscesses, calculus on the majority of the teeth, and indications of periodontal disease. She had suffered osteoarthritis and degenerative changes to the spine (Fibiger forthcoming). Beside the skull, on the cave floor, were two decorated lignite rings neatly resting one on top of the other. Radiocarbon dates revealed that this woman had died towards the end of the Late Bronze Age (Dowd 2015, 143).

Late Bronze Age material in caves

A core issue raised by the Late Bronze Age skeleton from Robber's Den is how it got there and what it represents. Even though caves in Ireland have been used for a wide variety of purposes from the Early Mesolithic through to post-medieval and modern times, the occurrence of archaeological material deep inside caves is not common (Dowd 2015). Broadly speaking, prehistoric activities revolve around burial, excarnation and votive deposition in the outer parts of caves, frequently within the daylight zone and usually less than 20m inside cave entrances (often less than 10m). However, over a period of approximately 400 years, during the Late Bronze Age (1000–600 BC), individuals or small groups of people began undertaking long and sometimes arduous journeys into the absolute deepest and darkest parts of caves. Human bodies and disarticulated bones, animal remains and artefacts, mark these excursions underground. Occasionally, people modified the underground landscape. This paper explores the evidence for these Late Bronze Age journeys into darkness, and examines possible reasons for this specific phenomenon, which is so strikingly different to how people in Ireland interacted with caves in all previous and subsequent archaeological periods.

Currently eleven caves have been identified that contain material of Late Bronze Age date (Fig. 6.2) (Dowd 2015, Chapter 6). The evidence ranges from intact cadavers (Robber's Den); to disarticulated human bones (Glencurran Cave, the Catacombs); metalwork hoards (Kilgreany Cave, Brothers' Cave); and deposits of animal remains and non-metal artefacts – particularly pottery (Glencurran Cave, Moneen Cave, Kilgreany Cave, Ballynamintra Cave, Carrigmurrish Cave, Brothers' Cave, Killuragh Cave). Only three of these sites have been excavated to modern archaeological standards (Robber's Den, Glencurran Cave and Moneen Cave). Almost all the others were investigated in the late nineteenth and early twentieth centuries and, as a consequence, contextual information is quite limited. While these eleven caves vary in shape and size, there is a consistent use of the deepest and darkest chambers. Here, in areas furthest from cave entrances and from daylight, is where Late Bronze Age material is found.

Negotiating darkness

The location of Late Bronze Age material within many caves displays a deliberate intention to take a physically arduous route *through* and *into* darkness. Such difficult and potentially hazardous trips must have been symbolically redolent. These were,

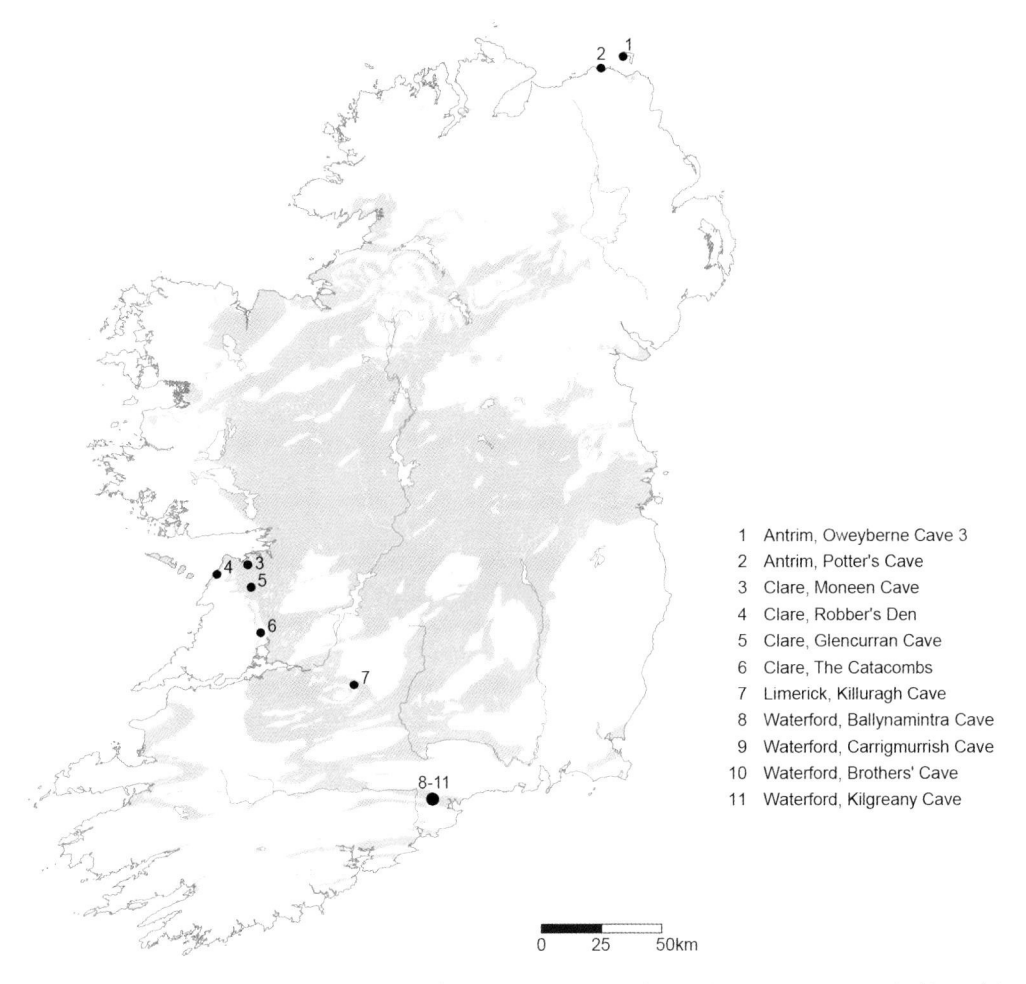

6. *In search of darkness: cave use in Late Bronze Age Ireland* 65

Figure 6.2: Irish caves with material of Late Bronze Age date. Limestone regions indicated in grey (Thorsten Kahlert).

1 Antrim, Oweyberne Cave 3
2 Antrim, Potter's Cave
3 Clare, Moneen Cave
4 Clare, Robber's Den
5 Clare, Glencurran Cave
6 Clare, The Catacombs
7 Limerick, Killuragh Cave
8 Waterford, Ballynamintra Cave
9 Waterford, Carrigmurrish Cave
10 Waterford, Brothers' Cave
11 Waterford, Kilgreany Cave

plausibly, journeys into a liminal realm where the spirit world could be accessed, and where emotional, mental or psychic revelation awaited. In the south-east of Ireland, in the Dungarvan valley, there was an increased use of caves during the Late Bronze Age. Each of the caves in question had been foci for ritual or funerary activities in the Neolithic and/or Early Bronze Age, strongly suggesting that by the Late Bronze Age they were regarded as established sacred places in the landscape that had inherited ritual status (Dowd 2015). One of these sites, Brothers' Cave, was entered via a large circular opening on the ground surface measuring 7m in diameter. Ropes or ladders may have been employed to descend the 8m vertical drop onto the cave floor beneath. Though not particularly large, this cave system is quite complex. Close to the entrance, but within the darkness of the cave, is an area that becomes waterlogged after periods of prolonged rain. It was aptly named the 'Bog' by Colonel Richard W. Forsayeth who excavated the site between 1906 and 1913 (Forsayeth 1931; Dowd and Corlett 2002). The colonel recovered more than thirty-seven amber beads from this location, almost certainly representing a necklace. In Ireland, prehistoric amber beads and necklaces are typically found in bogs and overwhelmingly represent votive deposits of Late Bronze Age date (Eogan 1999). Brothers' Cave could have been similarly viewed: a liminal and transitory place in the landscape, an underground location that alternated between being wet and dry.

In addition to the amber deposit in the Bog, a Late Bronze Age metalwork hoard (a bronze axe, sickle and chisel, and a bone point – Fig. 6.3) was deposited on the floor of a cramped low narrow passage that Forsayeth named the 'Gut', some 30m from the Bog. Two bone points, five amber beads and a fragment of leather (a pouch or bag?) were recovered nearby (Forsayeth 1931). The Gut is the furthest part of Brothers' Cave

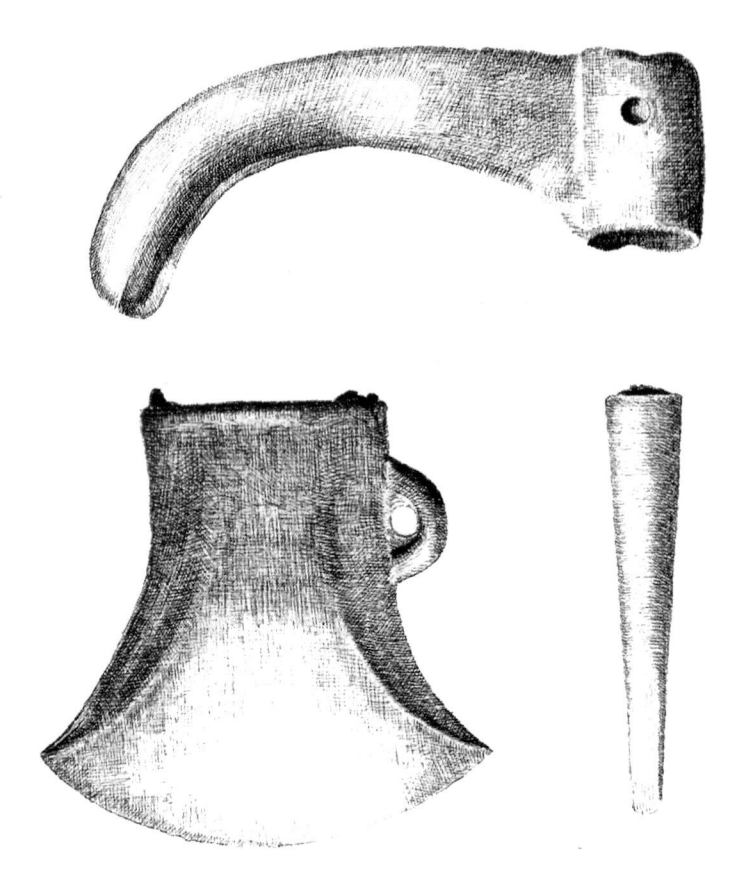

Figure 6.3: Metalwork hoard from the Gut in Brother's Cave, illustrated by Colonel Richard W. Forsayeth in 1906 (Dowd and Corlett 2002).

Plate 1: Paul Pettitt with hands positioned over a pair of hand stencils on the Panel of Hands in El Castillo Cave, Cantabria, Spain. Note the association with natural cracks in the cave ceiling, and the extension of arms in the form of shadows (Becky Harrison, courtesy of Gobierno de Cantabria).

Plate 2: The 'bison-man' column, painting and shadow, El Castillo Cave, Cantabria, Spain (Marc Groenen).

Plate 3: Greenstone axe-head from Grutta 1 de Longu Fresu, Sardinia (Jeff Veitch).

Plate 4: Inner Chamber, Grutta de is Janas, Sardinia (Robin Skeates).

Plate 5: The entrance to the south-west passage tomb at Balnuaran of Clava, Scotland at the time of the midwinter sunset (Ronnie Scott).

Plate 6: The entrance to the north-east passage tomb at Balnuaran of Clava, Scotland at the time of the midwinter sunset (Ronnie Scott).

Plate 7: Moneen Mountain with location of Moneen Cave indicated, Co. Clare, Ireland (Ken Williams).

Plate 8: Area of Glencurran Cave, Co. Clare, Ireland, where ritual offerings were deposited during the Late Bronze Age (Ken Williams).

Plate 9: The Great Orme mines, Wales, and visitor entrances in 2013 (Sian James).

Plate 10: The ahu *platform at Nau Nau, Anekena, Rapa Nui (Easter Island) (Colin Richards).*

Plate 11: Several massive hare nui *overlook the* ahu *complex at Te Peu on the west coast of Rapa Nui (Easter Island) (Adam Stanford).*

Plate 12: Chief's house on Rapa Nui (Easter Island) in 1872, by Pierre Loti (alias Julien Viaud 1850–1923) (after Heyerdahl and Ferdon 1961, fig. 11).

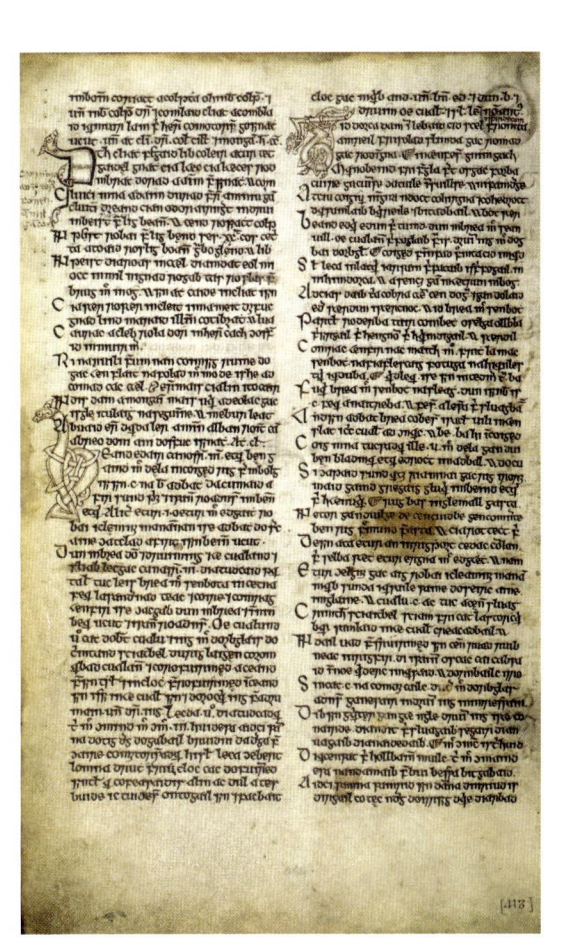

Plate 13: Extract on the theme of darkness from the fourteenth-century Book of Ballymote, RIA MS 23 P 12, folio 196v (© Royal Irish Academy). Courtesy of Irish Script on Screen.

Plate 14: Inuit woman playing a string game. The figures can be boats or sledges, but animals and humans are also popular. In some areas the game is restricted to the long dark season (Malaurie 2002, 373).

Plate 15: Descending Peter Bryant's Bullock Hole, Co. Fermanagh, Northern Ireland (Axel Hack).

from the prehistoric entrance (the present main opening is the result of nineteenth-century quarrying). This was effectively the 'end' of the cave, the deepest area that could be reached by humans. To identify this location and its significance, Bronze Age people must have spent considerable periods of time exploring underground, becoming familiar with the various and complex chambers and passages, getting lost and finding their way, and creating a mental or physical map of the cave. Following this, the Gut was selected as the appropriate area at which to leave a votive deposit. Was this a place that was as far from the world of the living and as deep into the spirit world as was possible to travel? The Late Bronze Age material from Brothers' Cave indicates repeat journeys underground. The cave may have been visited on a recurring monthly, seasonal or annual basis, or perhaps more sporadically, dictated by irregular events such as social, economic or environmental upheavals.

Darkness for a select few

When Colonel Richard Forsayeth discovered the axe, chisel and sickle in Brothers' Cave in 1906 they were, 'lying with merely a slight wash of earth above them, on a space that could almost be covered with the hand … They appeared to have been laid down, not accidentally dropped … they were not secreted, but open to the view of any passer-by' (Forsayeth 1931, 180). That there was no effort to conceal or bury the hoard reveals two things. Firstly, there was no expectation on the part of the individual who brought the hoard into the cave that it would be subsequently removed or disturbed: the hoard was 'safe' there. Secondly, and related to this, is that caves were arguably the domain of a select few, such as ritual practitioners or shamans, during the Late Bronze Age. There may have been a direct correlation between a certain cave and a particular ritual practitioner (for instance, the woman from Robber's Den). A cave may have served as the reserved or designated spiritual 'working' space of a particular ritual specialist for the duration of her or his lifetime. The implication is that rituals conducted inside caves were to some extent personal and private, even if they were undertaken on behalf of the wider community above ground. In Tzinacapan, Mexico, for instance, every *curandero* (curer) has his own special cave in which he analyses problems and restores social, spiritual and environmental harmony. The *curandero* will receive particular signs or dreams telling him when to visit his cave (Heyden 2005, 26–7).

While potent places in the landscape such as caves were physically accessible, taboos or cultural restrictions may have meant they were off-limits for the majority of the population. Nevertheless, the wider community potentially played an important role in cave rituals while all the time remaining outside in the daylight and world of everyday life. For instance, some cave rituals possibly commenced with a community procession to, and gathering at, a cave entrance. This would have been particularly effective in cases where the entrance consisted of a large hole on the ground surface that led via a vertical descent into a deeper cave system (e.g. Brothers' Cave and Carrigmurrish Cave), or caves where the entrance was higher than the surrounding ground level thus requiring people to strain and look upwards (e.g. Robber's Den). By leaving the group, entering the cave world, and disappearing from view, the ritual practitioner/s made a powerful social, symbolic and ritual departure from the community.

The Bronze Age people who visited Moneen Cave on a sporadic basis from approximately 2100–800 BC had to climb the gentle slopes of Moneen Mountain – a journey that can take up to an hour depending on the departure point (Dowd 2013). At present, the bare karstic landscape in which the site is set means that anyone walking up the mountain is quite exposed and can be seen from great distances (Pl. 7). Palaeobotanical research, however, suggests that the karst uplands of the Burren supported pine woodland up until about 600 BC (Feeser and O'Connell 2010). Those who visited Moneen Cave possibly travelled through trees with the wider community gathered towards the base of the mountain watching, waiting, wondering. Moneen Cave, unlike the other sites discussed here, is an extremely small chamber (max. 3.4m × 3m and 2m high) with no dark zone. It is entered via a narrow opening in the cave roof. For Bronze Age communities, the potency of Moneen may have revolved around the journey *to* the site rather than *within* the cave itself. A community could have observed the progress of significant individuals uphill carrying offerings such as an antler hammerhead (Early Bronze Age), or shellfish, meat and pottery sherds (Late Bronze Age), then disappearing underground through a hidden opening in the rock. On rare occasions, during very cold weather, a plume of steam issues from the cave entrance and is visible from the surrounding lowlands (Denise Casserly pers. comm.). This may have been perceived as a message or a sign from the spirit world, a call for another visitation to Moneen Cave. A similar phenomenon has been noted at the Cave of the Winds, in the Great Plains of North America: this cave appears to 'breathe' with changes in the weather – 'inhaling' when a high-pressure system approaches and 'exhaling' with the advent of a low-pressure system in the form of vaporous clouds (Blakeslee 2012, 354). This striking phenomenon may have led communities in the past to perceive both caves as living entities.

What exactly happened within the darkness of caves was veiled in secrecy. Specialized knowledge of cave rituals, spiritual knowledge gained therein, and encounters underground were probably concealed from the wider community. In the Fiji Islands, for example, when a chief died he was first interred in his house. A period of time later, his bones were brought by night to a distant inaccessible cave in the mountains, the location of which was known only to a few trusted people (Fison 1881 in Weiss-Krejci 2012, 124). In Bronze Age Ireland the person/s who entered the dark cave world might have been seen as going into an otherworld, while those outside remained vigilant of the duration of the absence – whether hours, days or weeks. Changes that occurred in the external world during this time – changes in the weather, the health of people or livestock, crop growth, political or social affairs etc. – were possibly directly linked to what was taking place deep underground in the dark. Emotional responses of those outside may have included anxiety, fear, terror, awe, suspense, relief or joy. Ritual specialists could deliberately capitalize on anticipated emotional responses by extending the duration of time spent inside a cave to exact stronger reactions from those outside. The experience of the emerging ritual participant would also have been visibly intense: disorientation and confusion as s/he was blinded by light and colour, and overwhelmed by smells, movement and life in readjusting to the everyday world. Physical manifestations of the sojourn underground likely included muddied bodies and clothing, dishevelled hair, and even bruises, bloodied wounds or more serious injuries sustained – evidence of the physical and spiritual perils of navigating the underground.

Being in the dark

The surviving archaeological assemblages make it difficult to establish the precise nature of Late Bronze Age rituals in caves and the frequency with which they were visited. For instance, Glencurran Cave was visited on numerous occasions throughout the Middle and Late Bronze Age, but there is no way of knowing how regular or irregular such trips were. The site was used for at least one interment – that of a two to four year old child, seemingly laid on a bed of rushes (*Juncus spp.*), and accompanied by clothing or jewellery fixed with over forty perforated cowrie and flat periwinkle shells (Dowd 2009, 94). The burial was just one event in a history of funerary and ritual activities that spanned up to seven hundred years. Over that time an array of objects and materials were placed on the floor at the 'end' of the cave as it would have appeared in prehistory (Pl. 8). Deposits included disarticulated human bones (with a preference for clavicles); newborn calves, lambs and piglets; joints of meat; sherds of Late Bronze Age pottery; lithics; and items of personal ornamentation composed of amber beads, perforated animal teeth, perforated shells and bone beads (Dowd 2007, 2009). As with any instance of votive deposition at sacred places, the reasons propelling such acts are numerous and include expressions of gratitude, supplication, repentance, devotion, veneration, as well as bolstering political and social status (Bradley 1998). The objective may have been achieved regardless of whether the offering was a prestigious metalwork hoard (e.g. Kilgreany Cave) or a single sherd of pottery (e.g. Ballynamintra Cave). In fact, the most salient factor may have been the act of entering the cave and spending time in the dark.

An intriguing additional use of caves suggested by finds from Glencurran is that certain individuals sought out the subterranean for ritual retreat in the Late Bronze Age, spending lengthy periods of time alone in the dark. In the world above ground many of the identifiable places of religious activity – stone circles and alignments, certain bogs, rivers and lakes – suggest public affairs in relatively exposed settings where rituals could have been witnessed by many. There may have emerged at this time a need amongst ritual specialists to retreat from public view and public spaces. Caves offered one of few locations in the landscape where solitude was guaranteed, particularly if they were out of bounds for the majority of the population. At Glencurran Cave there was evidence from the dark zone of chert knapping and the manufacture of shell beads and bone objects. The items in question were found scattered amongst disarticulated human bones, animal remains and artefacts (Dowd 2009). Carrying out craft or manufacturing activities at this location makes no practicable sense unless the objects were created as a result of spiritual experiences within the cave, or to absorb the special nature of the place itself. That this 'work' took place on ritual floors was no doubt significant. The unusual predominance of clavicles in the human bone assemblage from Glencurran may point towards rituals such as osteomancy (divination using bones).

Many scholars have associated prehistoric ritual retreat in caves with rites of passage and initiation where, for instance, a group of initiates entered a cave as adolescents and, a period of time later, emerged from this liminal space and time as adults (e.g. Eliade 1964; Whitehouse 1992; Stone 1995; Heyden 2005; Bjerck 2012; Skeates 2012, this volume; Whitehouse this volume). Much more frequently documented in historic and ethnographic sources, however, is the use of caves for spiritual retreat by a solitary ritual specialist, monk or hermit. Solitary seclusion in caves is sometimes the preferred form of monasticism for Buddhist monks and nuns (Mackenzie 1999; Aldenderfer 2012; Hobbs 2012), as was similarly the case for many early Christian ascetics (Ryan 1931; Hughes 1948; Taylor 1993; Manning 2005; Dowd 2015). In these particular cases the theme is no doubt linked to respective traditions that Buddhist saints meditated in caves in search of enlightenment, and that Jesus Christ sought out caves for closer communion with God (Taylor 1993). In modern Zimbabwe there are also many examples of mediums, priests and witches who live in isolation in caves from where they dispense messages or advice from the spirit world (Ranger 2012).

The Irish Late Bronze Age evidence similarly points towards ritual specialists retiring to caves for periods of time to engage in contemplation, spiritual growth or to enter altered states of consciousness – which are highly likely to arise naturally in the darkness and silence of the cave environment (for discussion, see Clottes and Lewis-Williams 1998; Lewis-Williams 2002; Clottes 2003; Ustinova 2009; Mlekuž 2012; Dowd 2015). The butchered bones of cattle, sheep and pig from Glencurran Cave and Moneen Cave might reflect food consumed by a retreatant pursuing spiritual enlightenment rather than representing food offerings to a sacred place or spiritual being. Two sea caves in Antrim – Potter's Cave on the coast at Ballintoy and Oweyberne Cave 3 on the coast of Rathlin Island – have also produced evidence of temporary occupation during the Bronze Age in the form of charcoal fragments, stakeholes, animal bones and pottery sherds (Forsythe and McConkey 2012; Dowd 2015). In both caves activities were focused in the outer areas within the daylight zone. Here we may have the localized use of caves for short-term shelter while on trips to the coast to source flint nodules and marine resources. However, we should not assume that occupancy was necessarily secular in nature. These caves, located as they are at distinctly isolated and liminal parts of the landscape, may have been adapted for ritual retreat where complete darkness was not an essential requirement.

Manipulating darkness

While some individuals in Late Bronze Age society were making incursions deep underground they were also, on occasion, deliberately altering and manipulating the physical environment: interactions with these wild places involved humanising them. This is most apparent at Glencurran Cave. The area that was the focus of votive deposition occurred some 40–50m inside the entrance (Pl. 8). Two low passages extend from this area and, until the twentieth century, both were almost completely choked with geological sediments. These low passages were noticed by Bronze Age people because the openings were blocked by drystone walling, thus defining and 'containing' the sacred area (Dowd 2009). One of the passages would have been large enough for human entry and may have been used as a space for extreme isolation – with a ritual specialist walling themselves in or being walled in. If this sounds unlikely, we need only consider the medieval *reclusorium* or anchorhold located within the Christian monastery, normally abutting the church, which permitted the anchorite to remain in spiritually significant isolation while remaining within the religious community (Ó Clabaigh 2010). These were often small, cramped cells with no doors or windows, only a little opening in the wall through which the recluse could communicate or obtain food.

Further intriguing evidence of human interactions with the dark landscape of Glencurran Cave is a semi-circular drystone structure built against the cave wall (Fig. 6.4). It was constructed at the point where the sloping entrance passage ends and the level cave floor begins; this area also marks the transition between the outer daylight zone and the inner dark zone of the cave. The stone structure was filled with multiple layers of creamy white calcite that had been dug up from the floor deeper inside the cave in the dark zone (extraction pits are still visible). Some of the layers contained chunks of hard calcite that had been cleaved off the cave ceiling (chisel marks and scars

Figure 6.4: Drystone structure in Glencurran Cave, marking the beginning of the dark zone (Peter Rees).

have been recorded). Great effort was made not to contaminate the pristine colour of this strikingly creamy bright clay. The only intrusive or deliberate placements within the layers were occasional animal bones and a small bronze ring (similar to Late Bronze Age examples from Dún Aonghasa – Cotter 2012, 48–9). A human mandible and a whetstone had been wedged into gaps in the drystone wall of the structure. The construction of this edifice involved detailed knowledge of the resources available in the cave – stones, white clays and calcite – knowledge that can only have been acquired through spending lengthy periods of time underground investigating and exploring. Its location strongly suggests that the structure marked both a physical and spiritual boundary, and radiocarbon dates place its construction towards the end of the Late Bronze Age. It may even have been built as part of a closing ceremony associated with the final phase of religious activities at Glencurran.

Concluding remarks

The skeleton of the Late Bronze Age woman found in Robber's Den, described in the opening paragraph of this chapter, demonstrates a concerted effort on the part of those who deposited the remains to seek out a location in darkness that involved not a difficult journey, but a torturous one. It is likely that two people were involved in bringing the body into the deepest chamber: one person in front pulling, and one behind pushing. The corpse could have been moved with relative ease through the first and second chambers, albeit within cramped and confined conditions but with some available natural light. However, the final trip through the extremely narrow passage must have occurred in complete darkness. It is difficult to imagine carrying a torch or lamp when navigating this passage as both hands are needed to push, squeeze and crawl through (and that is without the added encumbrance of hauling a corpse). Trying to negotiate a cadaver through this constricted space must have been extremely difficult, particularly if rigor mortis had set in. We cannot exclude the possibility that people of small stature, such as older children or adolescents, transported the corpse as they could have entered the deepest chamber with greater ease.

Robber's Den was not simply a convenient final resting place for a deceased member of the community. This was an extreme journey, for the purpose of meeting an extreme objective. It may be that in life this woman was considered so potent, or such a threat, that her remains were confined to the deepest, darkest and most inaccessible part of Robber's Den as a form of punishment, or perhaps to ensure that the route back to the world of the living would be too difficult for this revenant to traverse. Alternatively, she may have been directly associated with caves in her lifetime. Perhaps she was one of the select few who entered these special places for spiritual and religious reasons and this location was therefore considered appropriate to house her remains for posterity. The journey also alludes to the difficulties of labour and childbirth and the precarious journey an infant makes with great effort through the birth canal. The woman placed at the end of the constrictive passage in Robber's Den may allude to cyclical concepts of birth, death and rebirth.

Robber's Den and other caves with Late Bronze Age material reveal an ideological or cultural shift at the onset of the Irish Late Bronze Age, one that led to a specific interaction with caves and the need to seek out places of absolute darkness, isolation and silence for religious purposes. Why this phenomenon lasted for no more than 400 years or so remains unknown (albeit sometimes there is a suggestion of Middle Bronze Age origins). There may have been a perceived juxtaposition between underground and over ground; inside and outside; private and public; darkness and light; secrecy and knowledge. Caves were plausibly equated with the womb and associated with femininity and fertility, nurture and growth. Whatever the motivation, journeys underground culminated in the deposition of human bodies and bones, animal remains and artefacts. Within these dark landscapes signs of the past were open to view – animal bones, human bones, and objects that had been deposited decades or centuries earlier. Late Bronze Age materials were placed on cave floors amongst these older remnants of previous lives and past beliefs. That items were left exposed on cave floors and were not subsequently removed tell us that journeys into darkness were the exception rather than the rule in late prehistoric Ireland.

References

Anderson, L. and McCarthy, M. 1991. Report on an excavation at Robbers Den cave, Ballynahowan, Co. Clare June 3–4th 1989. *Irish Speleology* 14, 11–3.

Bjerck, H. B. 2012. On the outer fringe of the human world: phenomenological perspectives on anthropomorphic cave paintings in Norway. In K. A. Bergsvik and R. Skeates (eds.) *Caves in context. The cultural significance of caves and rockshelters in Europe*, 48–63. Oxford, Oxbow Books.

Blakeslee, D. J. 2012. Caves and related sites in the Great Plains of North America. In H. Moyes (ed.) *Sacred darkness. A global perspective on the ritual use of caves*, 353–62. Boulder, University Press of Colorado.

Bradley, R. 1998. *The passage of arms*. Oxford, Oxbow Books.

Clottes, J. 2003. Caves as landscapes. In K. Sognnes (ed.) *Rock art in landscapes – landscapes in rock art*, 11–30. Skrifter 4. Trondheim, Tapir Akademisk Forlag.

Clottes, J. and Lewis-Williams, D. 1998. *The shamans of prehistory*. New York, Harry N. Abrams.

Cotter, C. 2012. *The Western Stone Forts Project: excavations at Dún Aonghasa and Dún Eoghanachta. Volume 2*. Dublin, Wordwell Ltd.

Cremin, B. 1991. Extension of Robbers Den Cave, Co. Clare. *Irish Speleology* 14, 8–9.

Dowd, M. 2007. Living and dying in Glencurran Cave, Co. Clare. *Archaeology Ireland* 21 (1), 36–9.

Dowd, M. A. 2009. Middle and Late Bronze Age funerary and ritual activity at Glencurran Cave, Co. Clare. In N. Finlay, S. McCartan and C. Wickham Jones (eds.) *Bann flakes to Bushmills: papers in honour of Peter C. Woodman*, 86–96. Oxford, Oxbow Books.

Dowd, M. 2013. About a boy: excavations at Moneen Cave in the Burren. *Archaeology Ireland* 27 (1), 9–12.

Dowd, M. 2015. *The archaeology of caves in Ireland*. Oxford, Oxbow Books.

Dowd, M. and Corlett, C. 2002. Brothers in caves – lost archives of subterranean Waterford rediscovered. *Archaeology Ireland* 16 (1), 8–10.

Eliade, M. 1964. *Shamanism: archaic techniques of ecstasy*. New Jersey, Princeton University Press.

Eogan, G. 1999. From Skåne to Scotstown: some notes on amber in Bronze Age Ireland. In A. F. Harding (ed.) *Experiment and design*, 75–86. Oxford, Oxbow Books.

Feeser, I. and O'Connell, M. 2010. Late Holocene land-use and vegetation dynamics in an upland karst region based on pollen and *Coprophilous* fungal spore analyses: an example from the Burren, western Ireland. *Vegetation History and Archaeobotany* 19 (5–6), 409–26.

Fibiger, L. forthcoming. Osteoarchaeological analysis of the human skeletal remains from Irish caves. In M. Dowd (ed.) *The Irish Cave Archaeology Project: studies on human remains and artefacts from Ireland's caves*. Oxford, Oxbow Books.

Fison, L. 1881. Notes on Fijian burial customs. *The Journal of the Anthropological Institute of Great Britain and Ireland* 10, 137–49.

Forsayeth, R. W. 1931. The Brothers' cave. *Journal of the Royal Society of Antiquaries of Ireland* 61, 179–201.

Forsythe, W. and McConkey, M. 2012. *Rathlin Island, an archaeological survey of a maritime landscape*. Belfast, The Stationery Office.

Heyden, D. 2005. Rites of passage and other ceremonies in caves. In J. E. Brady and K. M. Prufer (eds.) *In the maw of the earth monster: Mesoamerican ritual cave use*, 21–34. Austin, University of Texas Press.

Hobbs, J. J. 2012. Ritual uses of caves in West Malaysia. In H. Moyes (ed.) *Sacred darkness. A global perspective on the ritual use of caves*, 331–41. Boulder, University Press of Colorado.

Hughes, P. 1948. *A history of the church, Volume 2*. London, Sheed and Ward Ltd.

Lewis-Williams, D. 2002. *The mind in the cave*. London, Thames and Hudson.

Mackenzie, V. 1999. *Cave in the snow*. New York, Bloomsbury Publishing.

Manning, C. 2005. Rock shelters and caves associated with Irish saints. In T. Condit and C. Corlett (eds.) *Above and beyond: essays in memory of Leo Swan*, 109–20. Wordwell Ltd., Wicklow.

Mlekuž, D. 2012. Notes from the underground: caves and people in the Mesolithic and Neolithic karst. In K. A. Bergsvik and R. Skeates (eds.) *Caves in context. The cultural significance of caves and rockshelters in Europe*, 199–211. Oxford, Oxbow Books.

Ó Clabaigh, C. 2010. Anchorites in late medieval Ireland. In L. H. McAvoy (ed.) *Anchoritic traditions of medieval Europe*, 153–77. London, Boydell & Brewer Ltd.

Ranger, T. 2012. Caves in black and white: the case of Zimbabwe. In H. Moyes (ed.) *Sacred darkness. A global perspective on the ritual use of caves*, 309–16. Boulder, University Press of Colorado.

Ryan, J. 1931. *Irish monasticism, origins and development*. Dublin, The Talbot Press Ltd.

Skeates, R. 2012. Constructed caves: transformations of the underworld in prehistoric Southeast Italy. In H. Moyes (ed.) *Sacred darkness. A global perspective on the ritual use of caves*, 27–44. Boulder, University Press of Colorado.

Stone, A. J. 1995. *Images from the underworld: Naj Tunich and the tradition of Maya cave painting*. Austin, University of Texas Press.

Taylor, J. E. 1993. *Christians and the holy places*. Oxford, Clarendon Press.

Ustinova, Y. 2009. Caves and the ancient Greek oracles. *Time and Mind* 2 (3), 265–86.

Weiss-Krejci, E. 2012. Shedding light on dark places: deposition of the dead in caves and cave-like features in Neolithic and Copper Age Iberia. In K. A. Bergsvik and R. Skeates (eds.) *Caves in context. The cultural significance of caves and rockshelters in Europe*, 118–37. Oxford, Oxbow Books.

Whitehouse, R. D. 1992. *Underground religion: cult and culture in prehistoric Italy*. London, Accordia Research Centre, University of London.

Chapter 7

Digging into the darkness: the experience of copper mining in the Great Orme, North Wales

Sian James

Out of the dark we came, into the dark we go (Haggard 1885)

The darkness experienced in underground mines is all-encompassing; suffocating for some, strangely comforting for others. For millennia people have felt the need to excavate into the earth to search for its treasures, which leads them deep into the unknown and forces them to overcome, or come to terms with, the challenges that darkness poses. The Great Orme Mines, Llandudno, offer a unique opportunity for investigating two very different periods of copper mining: Bronze Age and post-medieval. This paper presents the archaeological evidence from each phase to offer tantalising glimpses into how miners used technology and ritual to deal with the experience of digging into the darkness.

The Great Orme mines

The name Great Orme has Scandinavian or Norse origins, *ormr* meaning snake, and *hofuth* meaning head or headland (Ayto and Crafton 2005, 488). It is a peninsula of carboniferous limestone standing 207m above the modern town of Llandudno on the north coast of Wales. The limestone formed around 320 million years ago. Cracks in the rock allowed copper-bearing minerals to seep through from deep within the earth's crust. Ever since the Bronze Age, miners have been able to excavate these soft copper ores by working the seams of ore visible on the surface and following them into the earth.

The Great Orme has had a long history of occupation and various activities have taken place there, as evidenced by the archaeological and historical records (Bannerman and Bannerman 2001). There is a wealth of local folklore relating to the numerous caves and mine tunnels on the Great Orme. A belief in subterranean spirits, *knockers* or *coblyn*, has been documented since Agricola (1556). Victorian guide books to Llandudno commented on the miners' belief in knockers: 'Some venture to affirm that the knockers are nothing more than the rushing or dropping of water; certain it is, that miners are by no means terrified at their vicinity, feeling that they are fellow-workmen and good friends' (Williams 1995, 41). The stress and danger of working in underground dark environments clearly made an impact on those who ventured inside.

Two main phases of mining are currently recognized at Great Orme: the first during the Bronze Age, and the second in post-medieval times. In the 1930s Oliver Davies reported Roman coins and pottery some distance from the mine, but suggestions of Roman mining are thus far unproven (Lewis 1996, 42). There are several copper bearing lodes and ores running along beds of strata, these were utilized both in prehistoric and historic times (Bick 1991).

The Bronze Age witnessed wide-scale mining for copper from around 1800 BC in the Pyllau Valley area of the Great Orme. With five miles of tunnels discovered so far, it makes this area the largest known prehistoric copper mine in the world. Excavations have led to the discovery of around 3,000 stone hammers and nearly 30,000 animal bone fragments. Two human bones have been found at the mine, both dated to the Middle Bronze Age. Radiocarbon dates show that the mine was worked around 1800–1200 BC – in the later part of the Early Bronze Age and earlier half of the Middle Bronze Age. On other areas of the Great Orme an ore processing site has been recorded (Denison 2001, 6), along with remains of a smelting site (Chapman 1997). Mining ceased when workers hit the water table at a depth of 67m; by this time iron was becoming the latest metal technology and demand for mined copper seems to have declined (Pare 2000, 1; Bradley 2007, 230).

After a long hiatus, developments in machinery and industrial pumps allowed copper to be mined once more on the Great Orme from the 1700s until the late 1800s. This activity ranged from random prospecting to the sinking of deep mine shafts (Gravett and Jowett 1997, 6). Finds from this phase of mining include various iron mining tools, such as chisels, picks and shovels, as well as powder horns, straw fuses, ladders and chains (Lewis 1996, Appendix C7). Miners lived in the settlements of Cwlach and Maes-y-Facrell, close to the mine workings. As copper became harder to extract (and competition from cheaper sources abroad took over the industry) and tourism in Llandudno boomed, the workers eventually changed trades or locations and mining declined completely (Senior 2001, 480). The old mine shafts were capped and the workings filled in with spoil from the surrounding area.

Although the copper mines at Great Orme have only recently been identified as Bronze Age in origin, previous miners and explorers had recognized earlier workings. For instance, in 1849 a large cavern was discovered by Victorian miners, containing stone hammers, bone tools and a few bronze objects (Anon 1849; O'Brien 1996, 47). These finds were considered to be possibly Roman in date, a view shared by Oliver Davies during his investigations on the Orme in 1938–9. It was not until modern excavation, beginning in 1976 with Duncan James' exploration into the ancient workings under Bryniau Poethion, that radiocarbon dates linked the mines to the Bronze Age (James 1990). The Great Orme Exploration Society (GOES), together with the Gwynedd Archaeological Trust (GAT) and others, carried out a series of excavations to understand the extent and nature of the prehistoric activity. In 1987 a scheme to landscape an area in the Pyllau Valley to facilitate a car park caused the local council to survey the underground workings. A team from Ashton Mining

Consultants abseiled down one of the deep mine shafts known in the area and broke through into the ancient workings (Lewis 1996, 43). The survey revealed Bronze Age mining activity represented by a labyrinth of underground tunnels and chambers. In 1989, Great Orme Mines Ltd. was formed with the goal of continuing exploration on the site and opening the mines to the public. Planning permission was granted and the mines were opened in 1991 (Pl. 9).

For over twenty years the site has been archaeologically explored and excavated leading to a wealth of discoveries. During this time researchers have used technology to overcome the difficulties of working in the dark and dangerous conditions underground. The disorientation caused by dripping water and other sounds, the numerous tunnels, the passage of time, the limited space and light, allow modern day excavators to empathize with the ancient and historical miners. Coping with the restricted dark conditions involves focusing on the task ahead, knowing the passages intimately, and having confidence in team members. When stripped of modern technology, such as when a headlamp fails, experience allows excavators to overcome any inner demons; in the dark the mine is a more sinister place than in the light.

Bronze Age mining at Great Orme

People in the Bronze Age would have been much more used to regular darkness than people today. Without competition from electric or gas illumination, the blackness of night would have been more absolute. However, without light pollution from artificial light sources, stars and the moon would have appeared brighter so night-time was not necessarily gloomy or dim. Many prehistoric monuments incorporate solar alignments, most famously Stonehenge; however, architecture from this period also references other celestial movements, such as the recumbent stone circles in Aberdeenshire tracking the rising of the moon (Cummings 2008, 153). As well as marking, celebrating or commemorating the movement of the heavens, these monuments might hint at mechanisms enlisted by prehistoric communities to deal with the darkness and welcome the forthcoming light. Coping strategies may have been felt necessary when venturing into the darkness of caves or mines too.

The monuments and material culture left behind suggests the people of Bronze Age Wales were a society concerned with industrial and religious activities and had a wide network of connections (Lynch 1995, 41). This can be seen in the Whitby jet disc from Pen y Bonc, Anglesey, or the possible Irish influence evident in the Mold Cape, Denbighshire (Lynch 2000, 110–2). It is possible that the Great Orme mines fuelled or funded a demand for metalwork in Britain and beyond, much of which appears to have been for ritualistic use. The brightly coloured copper ores at Great Orme would certainly have attracted early miners. Green malachite was the main ore at the site, together with blue azurite, golden cuprite and chalcopyrite, and probably native orange copper (Bick 1991). There is little settlement evidence for the miners as yet, but it is likely that the community included not just those involved in the actual ore extraction (Wager 2002, 91), but also workers involved in fuel collection, smelting and farming.

Artefacts from the Bronze Age phases of mining consist mainly of stones and animal bones. Around 3,000 beach stones have been recovered, ranging in size from 2–29kg (Great Orme Mines Ltd. 2004, 14). These are considered tools for ore extraction and processing, although about ninety-five percent display no modifications or wear from usage, such as pitting or breakages (Gale 1995; Lewis 1996). Most of the other five percent were not nearly as utilized as those from Copa Hill or other prehistoric mines (Timberlake 1994, 134, 2003, 96). It is probable that many of the unused stones were intended for future use in the mining process as they match the size and shape of known stone hammers. These stones are easily distinguishable from the limestone host rock on the Great Orme by their smooth, rounded appearance and texture. This would have made it easy for miners working underground to have used touch rather than sight to identify them in the limited light or darkness. Some of the stone deposits, especially those found in groups, appear to have been deliberately placed at particular locations as tools left behind by miners. Several caches of three or four stone mauls have been discovered, apparently *in situ* (Lewis 1996, 100, 118). These might be deliberate deposits left by miners as offerings to substitute for the copper taken from the ground. Leaving gifts of this nature might be seen as an exchange process with the earth (*ibid.*, 118; Beecroft 2005). If the miners believed in demons or spirits in the underground, as some later miners did (Owain 1988, 18), then the caches of stones could serve as offerings in return for safety or for the bounty of copper.

The most common animal bones found at the Great Orme mines are rib or long bones, usually of cattle (Hamilton-Dyer 1994; James 2011). Sheep/goat and pig are the next most common species, with a few deer, horse, dog and other species also represented. This pattern of primarily domesticates with some wild animals is common on most Bronze Age sites (Pryor 2006, 149) and implies the mine was reliant on a farming economy with limited interest in hunting. Recent research has identified that the bones left in the mine were selected based on species and skeletal element for use as tools in the ore extraction process (James 2011). Like the stone hammers, bones tools were also commonly left unutilized in the mine. This may have been for storage in preparation for use, or perhaps these were offerings (Lewis 1996, 129). Traditionally, hoards have been defined as functional if they can be easily returned to, but ritual if access is difficult or impossible (Parker Pearson 1993, 34) – as might be the case here. Some of the locations where bone was deposited are very awkward to access, certainly on a day-to-day basis. The sequence of retrieving tools might not only be the workings of a functional *chaine opératoire* but the result of an established ritual (Insoll 2004, 11) linked to success and the ability to work in the dark.

Some areas of the mine appear to have been blocked up with stone walls. This has been noted both on the surface and underground, and may have helped with ventilation through a process known as drafting (Lewis 1996, 101, 111). Additional air movement through convection could be achieved by blocking tunnels and cutting additional shafts in parallel, as was done at Rio Tinto (Davies 1935, 24). Fires could also be set to increase air movement, a practice mentioned by the Greek author Theophrastus, but these would have to be carefully positioned to avoid adding to ventilation problems (Humphrey *et al.* 1997). Walling up an area could be of practical use, perhaps signifying that all the ore had been extracted, or it could make parts of the mine more secure (Lewis 1996, 101). On the other hand, walls might serve as a warning that an area was unsafe, or routes might be blocked due to an accident or incident that had occurred in the area beyond. Perhaps miners would not enter an area where a death had taken place; a wall might be the only surviving evidence of a ritual closing ceremony (Beecroft 2005).

Apart from charcoal, there is little other evidence of lighting the underground during the Bronze Age. Evidence for the burning of marrow on bones is uncommon (James 2011). A 'Roman' oil lamp has been recovered from surface spoil tips (Lewis 1996, 137). In the *Kuttenberger Kanzionale*, depicting fifteenth-century mining, some of the workers have lamps similar to this 'Roman' lamp, but most seem to be working without light (Ford 1994, 81). Some miners at Great Orme may have worked without the benefit of light, perhaps especially children working in small tortuous tunnels. It may have been possible to feel the difference between the soft copper ore and the harder limestone without sight.

Some of the tunnels at Great Orme are so small they are only accessible today by expert cavers. The method of ore extraction – following the copper veins, extracting the malachite, and leaving the solid limestone behind – is the reason for this. Some tunnels are only 20cm wide (Great Orme Mines Ltd. 2003, 21). This, along with the small tools found in such areas, supports the theory that small adults or children, possibly as young as five or six years old, worked in certain parts of the mines (Williams 1995, 12; Lewis 1996, 105; Pryor 2003, 272). This not only makes archaeological excavation impossible for some areas, but suggests certain tunnels were untouched by post-medieval miners, though they too employed children.

After being trapped temporarily in Grimes Graves as a boy, Francis Pryor could well understand, 'why miners have always had a healthy respect for the forces they believed existed below the ground' (Pryor 2003, 155). Miners the world over are known to be highly superstitious, with many folk traditions and ritual observations peculiar to their work. This is due to the dangerous nature of underground mining and the unpredictable manner in which the prized ore is found (O'Brien 2014, 254). Similar settings may have been experienced by those venturing into Early Neolithic chambered tombs where there was little room to move in a damp, dark enclosed space (Cummings 2008, 152). A bone flute recovered from Penyrwyrlod, south-east Wales (Britnell and Savory 1984), suggests that music may have been played in such spaces, and acoustic studies have shown that the sound produced would have created remarkable effects (Watson 2001). Shouting, whistling or making loud noises was generally taboo in post-medieval mines (Beecroft 2005). However, this may not necessarily have been the case in prehistoric times, thus music and sound may have been a coping mechanism or signalling method in the darkness of Bronze Age mines.

Post-medieval mining at Great Orme

The first documentary evidence for mining at Great Orme dates from 1692 when Sir Thomas Mostyn got a lease for twenty-one years of mining rights (Williams 1995, 14).

By 1849 the Great Orme was known as *The Welsh California* and was scarred with the pock-marks of prospecting pits (*ibid.*, 26). By 1856 Captain Vivian, a Cornish miner who gave his name to Vivian's Shaft, commented that the 'spirit of adventure' had gone out of the miners as the ore appeared to be running out. Another remark concerning the loss of 'mining spirit' was made by Sarah Lloyd, wife of David Lloyd (the lease owner in the 1860s). Miners' working conditions were not much better in the post-medieval period than they were for their prehistoric counterparts. They had a short lifespan, faced dangers of accidents at work and the risk of respiratory and arthritic conditions, as well as many other health problems (Black 1999, 17).

The evidence for mining folklore and superstition is considerable (Williams 1995, 41). Wales has a long tradition of omens, superstitions and belief in luck (Davies 1971, 3); work in mines proved to heighten these beliefs. Although these ideas would have served the practical purpose of allowing miners to work in perilous surroundings, they are swathed in elaborate rituals that were carried out on a day-to-day basis in the belief that they would ensure safety (Ash *et al.* 1973, 403). Superstitions proliferate in occupations that have an element of danger (*ibid.*, 78), or when the worker is in a constant struggle with nature (Davies 1971, 2). Mining falls into this category, as does fishing; some workers at Great Orme did both (Williams 1995, 39).

Many different types of artefact were deposited during the post-medieval phase of mining at Great Orme, not all have any obvious practical use down a mine. These deposits include clay pipes, horse shoes, cat skeletons, a dog skeleton, clogs and other personal items. Cats have been the subject of various ritual activities for millennia; they were commonly associated with evil and were often used in ritual sacrifice (Fontana 1993, 85). Cats were long favoured familiars of witches and were sometimes killed with their owner if they were convicted of witchcraft (Palmer 2001, 69). Three cats have been recorded from post-medieval locations at Great Orme; all were found in areas not easily accessible so it appears they were deliberately placed rather than being natural occurrences (Lewis 1996, Appendix C3). It was commonplace up until Victorian times to kill and wall-up a cat in the foundations or structure of a building to bring strength and good luck (Pennick 1986, 11; Merrifield 1987; Hutton 1991, 292). Perhaps the emphasis was on committing the animal to the darkness by any means possible, rather than focusing on the location of the deposit. To see a cat on the way to a mine appears to have been very unlucky, especially if the cat was black or white. Even uttering the word *cat* was taboo down most mines (Ash *et al.* 1973, 403).

In an area known as Location 14, a pair of miner's clogs was discovered deliberately placed with a stone under each heel. It is relatively common for mines of post-medieval date across Britain to have shoe or clog deposits in some part of the workings (Williams 1995, 41). This is usually attributed to a belief in knockers; by making such an offering, miners would be kept safe while underground (Lewis 1996, Appendix C3). Parts of around twenty-five leather shoes (including one child's boot) were discovered in the Tudor period coal mines of Coleorton in Leicestershire (Hartley 1994, 93). The suggestion that these were ritual deposits was rejected due to lack of supporting evidence. At Great Orme the clog offerings were probably made as a closing deposit in that area in the hope that good luck would follow in the next area (Williams 1995, 41).

Clay pipes are a relatively common find. Smoking may have helped the miners to relax and given them a focus whilst working in harsh conditions. Miners may have taken solace in the glimmer of light produced by the pipe of a fellow worker down a tunnel, reassuring them that they were not alone in the gloom. Pipes were disposable items and are usually individual finds; personal discoveries such as these allow archaeologists come closer to the experience of mining in the past.

Evidence for general lighting in the mine is scarce. Candles are known to have been used in mines elsewhere. A clay base served not only to steady the candle, but could be fixed to hats or helmets when climbing ladders or moving about the tunnels (Williams 1995, 40). Candles were a measure of time in the underground; these were called 'watch candles' and may have been a feature at the Great Orme mines (*ibid.*, 40). The light emitted by a candle, together with the noise of dripping water and hammering, would have created environments ripe for the birth of superstitions (Davies 1971, 2).

In post-medieval Europe knockers or mine spirits appear in various guises, from dwarfs dressed in traditional miners' dress (Agricola 1556, 217), to invisible beings (Ash *et al.* 1973, 403; Owain 1988, 18). Isaac describes coblyn or knockers as having many tasks, the primary one being to guide miners towards metal deposits (*ibid.*, 18). The 'miners have a notion that the knockers are of their own tribe and profession and are a harmless people who mean well' (Davies 1971, 13). Not generally believed to be dangerous, knockers were known to retaliate by throwing stones at people who had ridiculed them, made loud or irritating noises underground, not shared food, or not left gifts (Ash *et al.* 1973, 141). Sceptics called belief in such beings 'childishness of intellect' (Davies 1971, 15), but the mining environment produces many acoustic anomalies that can confuse and deceive the senses, so it is easy to see how superstitions take hold. Offerings such as clogs and animal remains at the Great Orme may reflect beliefs in subterranean spirits, or offerings to appease these mine folk (Lewis 1996; Beecroft 2005).

The Gentleman's Magazine (Anon. 1849) described that:

> *In October 1849, the miners at Llandudno near Conway broke, in the course of their labours, into what appeared to be an extensive cavern, the roof of which, being one mass of stalactite, reflected back their lights with dazzling splendour. On examination, the cavern turned out to be an old work, probably Roman; the benches, stone hammers, etc., used by that ancient people having been found entire, together with many bones of mutton, which had been consumed by these primitive miners. These bones are, to all appearance, as fresh, though impregnated with copper, as they were when denuded of their fleshy covering. The cavern is about forty yards long.*

Post-medieval miners at Great Orme may have drawn solace from the findings of tools and workings from 'old Welsh' or 'Celtic' miners (Beecroft 2005) showing that even 'primitive miners' could overcome the harsh conditions. On the other hand, signs of previous miners might have caused post-medieval workers to imagine spirits and ghosts of earlier peoples remaining in the gloom of the mine. Even today, while excavating areas of the mine, especially deep underground, it is impossible not to think of the earlier workers and empathize with their plight.

Conclusions

The artefacts that miners at Great Orme left behind are not only testament to periods of high productivity, vast exchange networks, and organized communities, but are evidence of how technology and ritual were utilized when working underground. The remains reveal how people in the past negotiated small confined spaces devoid of light, without any sense of time, and under constant threat of danger. For post-medieval workers, stories concerning mine spirits or knockers were a way of explaining the mysterious sounds heard in the blackness. Standardized bone tools and easily identifiable stone hammers helped Bronze Age miners locate working implements in the dark. By leaving tools in tunnels and workings, miners may have felt that underground forces were suitably placated giving them confidence to return to the darkness time after time. Fire would have enabled both prehistoric and post-medieval people to overcome the gloom of the underground, but this appears to have been used practically, in fire setting and drafting, and sparingly since many areas show no signs of burning. Perhaps coming from a world where darkness was more commonplace than today, miners were more acclimatized to working in the subterranean environment of the Great Orme.

References

Agricola, G. (trans. H. Hoover and L. Hoover) 1556. *De re metallica*. New York, Dover Publications Inc.

Anon. 1849. *Gentleman's Magazine*. London, F. Jeffries.

Ash, R., Ashe, G., Briggs, K., Ellis Davidson, H. and Hole, C. 1973. *Folklore, myths and legends of Britain*. London, Reader's Digest Association Ltd.

Ayto, J. and Crafton, I. (eds.) 2005. *Brewer's Britain and Ireland: the history, culture, folklore and etymology of 7500 places in these islands*. London, Weidenfiled & Nicolson.

Bannerman, D. and Bannerman, N. 2001. *The Great Orme explained*. Llandudno, Campbell Bannerman Publications.

Beecroft, S. 2005. *Evidence of ritual activity at the Great Orme*. Unpublished MA thesis, University of Liverpool.

Bick, C. (ed.) 1991. *Early metallurgical sites in Great Britain BC 2000 to AD 1500*. London, The Institute of Metals.

Black, J. 1999. *Eighteenth-century Europe* (2nd edition). Hampshire, Macmillan Press Ltd.

Bradley, R. 2007. *The prehistory of Britain and Ireland*. Cambridge, Cambridge University Press.

Britnell, W. and Savoy, H. 1984. *Gwernvale and Penywyrlod: two Neolithic long cairns in the Black Mountains of Brecknock*. Bangor, Cambrian Archaeological Association.

Chapman, D. 1997. Great Orme smelting site, Llandudno. *Archaeology in Wales* 37, 56–7.

Cummings, V. 2008. The architecture of monuments. In J. Pollard (ed.) *Prehistoric Britain*, 135–59. Oxford, Blackwell Publishing.

Davies, L. 1971. *Aspects of mining folklore in Wales*. Folk Life 9. Wales, W. E. Jones.

Davies, O. 1935. *Roman mines in Europe*. Oxford, Clarendon Press.

Denison, S. 2001. In brief: Great Orme. *British Archaeology* 58, 6.

Fontana, D. 1993. *The secret language of symbols*. London, Pavilion Books Ltd.

Ford, T. 1994. Fifteenth-century mining as shown in the Kuttenberger Kanzionale. In T. D. Ford and L. Willies (eds.) *Mining before powder*, 81–3. Peak District Mines Historical Society Bulletin 12 (3).

Gale, D. 1995. *Stone tools employed in ancient mining*. Unpublished PhD thesis, University of Bradford.

Gravett, T. and Jowett, H. 1997. *Discovering the Great Orme*. Conwy, Conwy County Borough Council Planning.

Great Orme Mines Ltd. 2004. *Great Orme mines guide book*. Nantwich, Delmar Press.

Haggard, R. 1885. *King Solomon's mines*. London, Cassell and Company.

Hamilton-Dyer, S. 1994. Faunal remains [*Appendix to* Prehistoric copper mining on the Great Orme, Llandudno Gwynedd]. *Proceedings of the Prehistoric Society* 60, 275–9.

Hartley, R. 1994. Tudor miners of Coleorton, Leicestershire. In T. D. Ford and L. Willies (eds.) *Mining before powder*, 93. Peak District Mines Historical Society Bulletin 12 (3).

Humphrey, J., Oleson, J. and Sherwood, A. 1997. *Greek and Roman technology: a sourcebook*. London, Routledge.

Hutton, R. 1991. *The pagan religions of the ancient British Isles: their nature and legacy*. Oxford, Blackwell Publishers.

Insoll, T. 2004. *Archaeology, ritual, religion*. London, Routledge.

James, D. 1990. Prehistoric copper mining on the Great Ormes Head. In P. Crew and S. Crew (eds.) *Plas Tan-y-Bwlch occasional paper* 1, 1–4. Blaenau Ffestiniog, Plas Tan-y-Bwlch.

James, S. 2011. *The economic, social and environmental implications of faunal remains from the Bronze Age copper mines at Great Orme, North Wales*. Unpublished PhD thesis, University of Liverpool.

Lewis, A. 1996. *Prehistoric mining at the Great Orme: criteria for the identification of early mining*. Unpublished MPhil thesis, University of Bangor.

Lynch, F. 1995. *A guide to ancient and historic Wales: Gwynedd*. London, Her Majesty's Stationery Office.

Lynch, F. 2000. Later Neolithic and Earlier Bronze Age. In F. Lynch, S. Aldhouse-Green and J. Davies (eds.) *Prehistoric Wales*, 79–138. Stroud, Sutton Publishing Ltd.

Merrifield, R. 1987. *The archaeology of ritual and magic*. London, Batsford.

O'Brien, W. 1996. *Bronze Age copper mining in Britain and Ireland*. Shire Archaeology 71. Buckinghamshire, Shire Publications Ltd.

O'Brien, W. 2014. *Prehistoric copper mining in Europe: 5500–500 BC*. Oxford, Oxford University Press.

Owain, S. 1988. *Geirfa'r Mwynwyr*. Llyrau 11. Llanwrst, Gwasg Carreg Gwalch.

Palmer, J. 2001. *Animal wisdom*. London, Element.

Pare, C. 2000. Bronze and the Bronze Age. In C. Pare (ed.) *Metals make the world go round. The supply and circulation of metals in Bronze Age Europe*, 1–38. Oxford, Oxbow Books.

Parker Pearson, M. 1993. *Bronze Age Britain*. London, Batsford Ltd.

Pennick, N. 1986. *Skulls, cats and witch bottles*. Cambridge, Nigel Pennick Editions.

Pryor, F. 2003. *Britain BC*. London, Harper Perennial.

Pryor, F. 2006. *Farmers in prehistoric Britain*. Gloucestershire, Tempus Publishing.

Senior, M. 2001. *Portrait of North Wales*. Llanwrst, Gwasg Carreg Gwlach.

Timberlake, S. 1994. Archaeological and circumstantial evidence for early mining in Wales. In T. D. Ford and L. Willies (eds.) *Mining before powder*, 133–43. Peak District Mines Historical Society Bulletin 12 (3).

Timberlake, S. 2003. *Excavations on Copa Hill, Cwmystwyth (1986–1999)*. BAR British Series 348. Oxford, Archaeopress.

Wager, E. 2002. *The character and context of Bronze Age mining on the Great Orme, North Wales, UK*. Unpublished PhD thesis, University of Sheffield.

Watson, A. 2001. The sounds of transformation: acoustics, monuments and ritual in the British Neolithic. In N. Price (ed.) *The archaeology of shamanism*, 178–92. London, Routledge.

Williams, C. 1995. A history of the Great Orme Mines from the Bronze Age to the Victorian Age. *British Mining* 52, 57.

Chapter 8

Between realms: entering the darkness of the *hare paenga* in ancient Rapa Nui (Easter Island)

Sue Hamilton and Colin Richards

Introduction

One of the best known and spectacular feats of prehistoric monumentality is to be found on the small island of Rapa Nui (Easter Island) in the South Pacific. Here, from *c.* AD 1200–1600, over three hundred massive 'stone men' (*moai*) were quarried, dragged and erected on elevated stone platforms known as image *ahu* (Pl. 10); a term used to distinguish *ahu* with statues as opposed to those without (Martinsson-Wallin 1994, 52–3; Van Tilburg 1994, 77). Over two hundred more remain in various states of completion at the great *moai* quarry of Rano Raraku (Skjølsvold 1961). Many other *moai* lie recumbent along the statue roads (*ara moai*) that lead toward Rano Raraku (Richards *et al.* 2011). However, it is the imagery of the *moai* on the *ahu* with their extraordinary topknots (*pukao*) that once adorned their heads that tends to dominate the popular (and archaeological) imagination. In many ways this view is warranted; as Charles Love notes, the 'Easter Island ceremonial centres, collectively called *ahu*, represent one of the most elaborate and complex examples of religious architecture ever developed by Polynesians' (1993, 103). In this quote, Love highlights another important consideration: that despite its physical and supposed cultural isolation, Rapa Nui represents the eastern-most corner of the Polynesian triangle. Therefore, archaeological understandings of the *ahu* have to be situated in a broader Polynesian context, whilst acknowledging the local setting where the monuments directly participated in the constitution of ancient Rapa Nui ritual life.

Both visually and materially the image *ahu* were truly remarkable monumental structures. The beautifully sculpted *moai* with their red scoria cylindrical *pukao* stood in an elevated position on elongated rectangular, sometimes canoe-shaped, platforms. The sea-facing rear wall of the platform was carefully constructed with close-fitting black basalt slabs. The frontage was formed by a sloping ramp surfaced with large rounded beach stones called *poro*, which led down to an open plaza. Behind the *ahu*, crematoria were often positioned adjacent to the ocean.

Today, at the image *ahu* the majority of *moai* lie recumbent, as do the *pukao*, but originally they stood elevated on the platforms facing inland (Pl. 10). Interestingly, during excavations at Ahu Nau Nau, on the north shore of the island, fragments of white coral and disks of red scoria were recovered which together formed eyes for the *moai* (Heyerdahl 1989, 217–9; Van Tilburg 1994, 132–3). Eyes 'were believed to embody the *mana*, life or soul of the individual', noted Handy (1927, 65). Consequently, when the eyes were inserted, the *moai* became animated, and their gaze was inland towards the rising ground beyond the plaza area.

At this point it is worth noting that the *ahu* are not isolated monuments, but form part of broader *ahu* landscapes which incorporate a range of different structures (Hamilton *et al.* 2011). One of the most fascinating components is the canoe-shaped houses, known as *hare paenga*. In this paper we wish to examine the *hare paenga* in terms of the qualities associated with 'being inside and outside' the house. Specifically, we are interested in the experience of passage between the outside world of daylight and into an internalized domain that is constantly cloaked in darkness. We then intend to extend this experience of passage and transgression to bring insight into the broader landscape position of the monumental *ahu*. We argue that to enter the *hare paenga* was homologous to passing beneath the gaze of the *moai* and a journey from the land to the sea. We also argue that the materiality of the *hare paenga* drew on that of the seashore to create analogous experiences of passage between the cosmological domains of *Ao* and *Po*.

An island wrapped in images

The vast majority of *ahu* tend to be constructed in close proximity to the sea (Fig. 8.1). This is an interesting distribution, as not only are the *ahu* situated along the coastline but they really are 'on the edge' in being positioned effectively between land and sea. This situation is precarious as today a substantial number of *ahu* are being severely eroded and undermined by the relentless pounding surf of the Pacific Ocean. Such a pattern of erosion also reveals an unexpected topographic characteristic of the image *ahu*; they are frequently positioned in low-lying areas such as at the base of shallow valleys running down to the sea. Indeed, when travelling along the island's southern coast, it is only as one rounds steep coastal bends that image *ahu* are seen, before falling out of view again. The overall impression of their situation is that the monuments are almost hidden and the vistas to and from the *ahu* are restricted to their immediate valley environs. At first sight it seems paradoxical that such large expressions of monumentality should be built in such unassuming low-lying locations that serve to diminish their overall presence and visual impact (Hamilton 2010).

A resolution to this paradox can be found in a reconsideration of *ahu* architecture. Here, the identification of what is referred to as an *ahu* complex (Martinsson-Wallin 1994, 68) or complex *ahu* (Van Tilburg 1994, 79) is of value. The attribution of such complexity is due to the recognition that *ahu* are frequently composed of a series or grouping of different architectural components (e.g. Love 1993). These include *ahu* platforms, crematoria, plaza areas and paved ramps descending to the ocean. Curiously, in the literature the significance of the paved ramps has been overlooked despite their obvious central position in the overall spatial organization of the *ahu* complex (Fig. 8.2). For example, in her multivariate analysis of *ahu*, Martinsson-Wallin (1994, 54–5) failed to include their presence/absence as a variable.

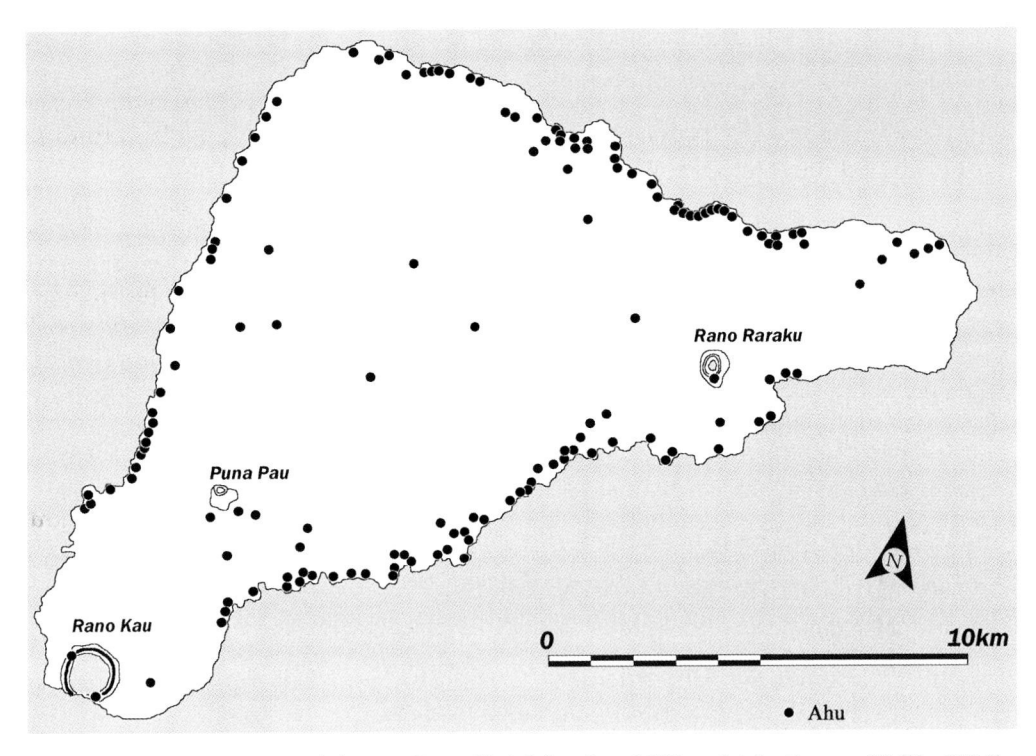

8. Between realms: entering the darkness of the hare paenga

Figure 8.1: Distribution of ahu *on Rapa Nui (after Lee 1992 and Martinsson-Wallin 1994).*

Figure 8.2: The canoe ramp assumes a central position in the ahu *complex at Tahai, on the west coast of Rapa Nui (Adam Stanford).*

The ramps have not always been neglected. In his popular account of the 1955–6 Norwegian expedition, Thor Heyerdahl recalls that, 'in many parts of the island we had seen wide paved roads which disappeared straight down into the sea' (1958, 190). He also noted that they were called *apapa*. However, in attributing function he considered that the ramps were roads upon which topknots (*pukao*) would have been unloaded after they had been transported to the *ahu* by sea: 'one *apapa* ran down to a shallow inlet at the foot of a large temple platform on the south coast. The inlet was full of boulders that the old navigators had had to clear a wide channel to enable craft to come alongside the landing stage' (*ibid.*, 191). Significantly, during its reconstruction Mulloy (1995, 37) effectively reversed this interpretation in identifying the *apapa* structures as canoe ramps at the Tahai *ahu* complex. He emphasized the ramps as, 'necessary solutions to the problem of protection of canoes on an island plagued by continuous high seas and extremely rocky coastlines' (*ibid.*, 37). That the necessary protection for canoes was amongst a massive monumental complex was ignored, as was the significance and *tapu* (ritual prescription and sanctity) attached to launching a canoe throughout Polynesia (e.g. Best 1976 [1925], 164–5).

The centrality of the canoe ramp at Tahai could have important implications. If access to the ocean was an important criterion for the situation of image *ahu*, then their low-lying coastal locations become comprehensible. Perhaps we can go further in suggesting that *ahu* complexes were situated to control *access to the sea* at particular times. There is another consequence of the extensive coastal distribution of *ahu*, and that is the creation of a skin or membrane of monumental architecture that effectively wraps the island. In short, the *ahu* complex on Rapa Nui can be partially understood as a desire to ritually control access to the sea on specific occasions. Instead of the canoe ramps being epiphenomenal architecture, they were in fact a central component of the *ahu* complex.

If canoe ramps were central, it begs the question why such monumentality should be deployed between the land and sea? Secondly, given the architecture of the *ahu*, why should certain journeys from the land to the sea require passage before the eyes of the *moai*? In order to address these questions it is necessary to consider the relational spatial categories that Polynesians employed to differentiate between island topographic zones. For Hawai'i, Malo (1951 [1898], 16–7) identifies a geocentric ordering of island space with the belt of land bordering the sea being called *kahakai* (the mark of the ocean). The division of land and sea also provided a spatially defined frame of reference, as Hyslop notes, 'it is the distinction of landward versus seaward which is salient in the absolute systems of the island residing, seafaring peoples of Oceania' (2002, 51). Reflexively, such an ordering of space in an island world inevitably emphasizes visible and important physical boundaries such as the seashore, allowing an inward–outward directional category to co-exist with concentric layers. Consequently, as François mentions in discussing linguistic categories of directionality in Vanuatu, 'the island is perceived as a container, the outside of which corresponds to the surrounding sea' (2003, 426).

It is also quite clear that in the past Polynesians maintained an ambivalent and ambiguous relationship with the ocean which on the one hand provided food and sustenance in abundance through fishing (e.g. Best 1977 [1929]; Barber 2003), and on the other was home to both supernatural enemies and monsters (Orbell 1985, 137). In the context of voyaging, the Pacific Ocean has been consistently described as a route or roadway (e.g. Gladwin 1970, 33–6; Kirch 2000; Richards 2008). In conceiving the ocean in such a manner, as a route (*ara*) or conduit, it effectively drew disparate places together, thereby potentially fusing widely separated islands and ocean pathways within a single *locale* (cf. Heidegger 1978, 354).

In terms of cosmology, the creation of the Polynesian world occurred with the brief fusion of the complimentary and antagonistic opposites *Po* (darkness, underworld, inner, earth, female) and *Ao* (lightness, upper-world, outer, sky, male) (e.g. Handy 1927, 34–9; Goldman 1970, 37). After the creation of the inhabited world, they remained, 'cosmic principles constituting the dual order of the universe' (Bausch 1978, 175). The manifestation of *Ao* and *Po* is complex. For instance, *Po* is recognized as both sacred and an underworld, and was frequently associated with a locality or place such as *Hawaiki* (Handy 1927, 34–5). Nevertheless, Handy ultimately concludes that *Po* 'should be regarded more properly as signifying a state of existence' (*ibid.*, 69). A corollary of the ocean as a conduit allowed at certain junctures linkage of the inhabited world to the origin island *Hawaiki*. Such a conjunction of places and realms, which could be problematic if not extremely dangerous, clearly required some form of ritual control and sanction.

Because Polynesian cosmology was based on procreation, social reproduction in Polynesia depended on the intermittent conjunction of one realm with the other – the 'irruption' of *Po* into *Ao* (Gell 1993, 126). For this irruption to occur a conduit had to open between the two realms. In the context of the human body, 'orifices were important … because they played a central role in the channelling of *mana* between the realms of *ao* and *po*' (Shore 1989, 147). Childbirth is an obvious example of conjunction between *Po* and *Ao*, and the vagina acted 'like *other* orifices, as a conduit between this world and the other' (Thomas 1990, 70).

Another example of passage between these realms is represented by the journey of the soul on death from the world of the living (*Ao*) to the sacred realm (*Po*). At the end of a person's life it was time for the soul to leave the island world and venture back to *Hiva*, the Rapa Nui equivalent of *Hawaiki*. Access to *Hiva* necessarily involved passing into the realm of *Po* and throughout Polynesia, 'it was generally believed that there was a definite route or path taken by souls of the departed on their way to the next world' (Handy 1927, 71). Access to the ancestral realm *Hawaiki* often involved travelling across an island in a westerly direction to a specific coastal location, where the spirit 'jumped off' into the depths of the ocean to continue the journey westwards and downwards. Spirit roads or paths leading westwards to a 'jumping off' point were present throughout Eastern Polynesia, including Hawai'i where spirits made their way to Keana Point at the north-west tip of Oahu (*ibid.*, 71). A similar belief existed in the Marquesas:

> *The souls of the Marquesans passed along the high mountain ridge that forms the backbone of the main island of their group to the high promontory at the west called Kiukiu … Below the promontory was a rock. When the souls clapped their hands this opened, the sea rolled back, and the soul entered the nether world.* (Handy 1927, 72)

These accounts of the passage taken by the soul back to *Hawaiki* are illuminating. They each involve entering the darkness of the underworld as represented by the ocean and a cave. This journey from lightness to darkness reverses the qualities and necessities of birth, embracing both the transformatory qualities of voyaging to *Hawaiki* and the passage into the sacred subterranean world of *Po*. Under such circumstance, the membrane or skin separating these domains is of crucial importance, as is control over any potential transgression. Here, the idea of the island as a container is useful because under such circumstances the nature and materiality of containment is of crucial ontological concern and anxiety.

The *hare paenga*

The architecture of the canoe-shaped houses (*hare paenga*) of Rapa Nui is unique within the Polynesian triangle. Prehistoric Polynesian houses with rounded ends have been recorded in Samoa, Mo'orea and Hawai'i (Van Tilburg 1994, 71), but none resemble the clear boat-shaped ground plan and profile of the *hare paenga*. A resemblance between the *hare paenga* and the cabin of a model Tuamotuan double-hulled voyaging canoe prompted Edwin Ferdon Jnr (1981, 3–6) to suggest that the initial colonists of Rapa Nui were from the Tuamotu islands. On landing, the cabin would be removed from the voyaging canoe and set up as the first habitation on the island, as was documented for the island of Raraka in the Tuamotu islands (Emory 1975, 58). Accepting multiple landings on Rapa Nui, Ferdon (1981, 5) considered this important, as the *hare paenga* would have represented a material symbol of certain ranking members of a particular immigrant group. Regardless of the origins of the *hare paenga* it does represent a particularly striking form of architecture that is clearly referencing the morphology of a canoe.

Interestingly, in constitution the *hare paenga* combined a range of different materials drawn together from different *locales*. The foundation of the house was formed by a series of partially dressed rectangular basalt slabs (*paenga*) that had holes drilled into their upper surface. These were partially sunk into the ground to create an elliptical house plan with a narrow side entrance passage (Fig. 8.3). The upper frame of the house was fabricated from a combination of timber, rushes, grasses and leaves. A number of thin wooden posts, which acted as rafters, were set in the holes of the *paenga* and drawn together at the top and attached to a ridgepole (*hahanga* or *hakarava*). Some of the larger houses were additionally supported by ridge posts (*pou* or *tuu*). Due to the elliptical setting of the *paenga*, the house gradually narrowed from the centre to its ends and the supporting posts correspondingly decreased in length. This effectively lowered the roof height of the house at either end. Successive layers of rushes, leaves and grasses were then applied to form a thick thatched roof to the house (Routledge 2005 [1919], 215; Metraux 1971 [1940], 197–8). As an outside extension to the house, the entrance porch and 'courtyard' were floored with rounded beach pebbles (*poro*) creating a semi-circular external area (Figs. 8.3 and 8.4).

Landscape associations, particularly with *ahu*, have tended to reinforce the interpretation of the *hare paenga* as a high status dwelling (e.g. Lee 1992, 118; Flenley and Bahn 2002, 94); possibly occupied by 'chiefs and their relatives' (Martinsson-Wallin 1994, 124), or 'high-status priests and chiefs' (Van Tilburg 2003, 237–8). This

8. *Between realms: entering the darkness of the* hare paenga

Figure 8.3: A hare paenga *adjacent to the Akahanga section of the* ara moai. *Note the* poro *pavement extending beyond the entrance (Adam Stanford).*

Figure 8.4: Entrance passage into a hare paenga; *note the entrance passage is also paved with rounded* poro *(Adam Stanford).*

designation is partially derived from Katherine Routledge's recording that Nagaara, an early nineteenth-century chief (*ariki*), only attended the inauguration of dwellings of importance, consequently, 'only houses with stone foundations were thus honoured' (2005 [1919], 243). However, the nature and status of the *hare paenga* appears to have gradually diminished since European contact because she also observes that by the early twentieth century, 'many of the surviving old people were born and brought up in these houses, which are known as "haré paenga" '(*ibid.*, 216).

A broader picture of habitation in pre-contact Rapa Nui can be drawn from the results of a detailed survey of archaeological remains undertaken by Patrick McCoy in 1968 around Rano Kau in the south-west area of the island. During the survey, houses were classified into three 'major types' of thatched dwellings: elliptical, round, and rectangular (McCoy 1976, 37). The identification of a basic elliptical architecture (Type 1) led to the production of a confusing array of sub-types, styles and forms (*ibid.*, 40–53). Essentially, there were three variants of the elliptical thatched house: *hare paenga* (subtype 1a); an 'intermediate' form of elliptical houses without *paenga*; and elliptical houses with *paenga* but without the holes in their upper surface (subtype 1b).

For Metraux, the presence of *paenga* provided a direct index of social differentiation, basically, 'they were the expression of wealth' and 'it was easier and cheaper to stick rafters into the ground' (1971 [1940], 195). McCoy (1976, 40) initially followed this equation of social differentiation based on the presence or absence of *paenga*, but the discovery and excavation of rectangular and circular houses (e.g. McCoy 1973) made such simplistic equations problematic. Nevertheless, within McCoy's survey area, of the 902 recorded elliptical houses, 852 lacked *paenga*. Identification of the majority of houses was only through the presence of external areas of large beach pebbles (*poro*), examples of which were noticeably smaller than those employed in the *hare paenga*.

Apart from the *hare paenga*, there are records of extremely large elliptical structures, known as *hare nui* (Metraux 1971 [1940], 200). These too were directly associated with *ahu*; for instance, an example recorded in La Pérouse's 1797 atlas is thought to have been observed at Ahu Te Peu, on the west coast, where the partial foundations of several enormous structures remain visible today (Pl. 11). The *hare nui* were massive canoe-shapes buildings measuring up to *c.* 100m in length and 3m in width. Their foundation was formed of correspondingly large rectangular *paenga* of up to 3.6m in length. These were extraordinary structures in all respects and Metraux (*ibid.*) notes that this size of structure could accommodate nearly two hundred individuals and was interpreted as a community house (*hare nui*).

Into the darkness of the house: changing realms

Access into the *hare paenga* was along a narrow passage and through a small hole centrally positioned in the side of the house. The passage was formed by two parallel *paenga*, embedded in the ground and projecting at right angles. These foundation *paenga* supported a low, narrow, tunnel-like passage, which was paved with rounded sea-worn pebbles (*poro*). The entrance *poro* maintained a continuation of the larger pebbles forming the external pavement (Fig. 8.4). The passage led to little more than a hole, 'eighteen inches or two feet high' in the side of the house (Forster 2000 [1777], vol. 1, 570).

There is clear evidence that the entrances to *hare nui* were at certain times flanked by small stone or wooden statues (see Metraux 1971 [1940], 201, 262–3) (Fig. 8.5). Likewise, the entrance passages of *hare paenga* also appear to have been periodically externally flanked by stone or wood statues or pillars (Van Tilburg 1994, 68; Flenley and Bahn 2002, 94). Metraux cites Loti describing entry into the house of a chief, 'whose door was guarded by two idols of granite' (1971 [1940], 198) (Pl. 12). Today there remain upright stone pillars flanking the entrance to a *hare paenga* at Ahu Te Peu, confirming McCoy's observation that 'occasionally there were stone pillars on either side of the tunnel-like entrance' of the *hare paenga* (1976, 40). Furthermore, Metraux notes an informant describing how ancient islanders also placed carved wooden images 'on each side of the porches leading to their huts' (1971 [1940], 198). The interesting point here is that just as the eyes of the *moai* could be detached at times when the *ahu* was not in use, so too could the small stone or wooden images be removed from the doorway of the *hare paenga* (Fig. 8.5).

The low, narrow passage constituted a very small space to access the *hare paenga* forcing entry to be 'upon all fours' (Cook 1777, vol. 1, 292) or even prone on the stomach (Eyraud 1866/7 in Metraux 1971 [1940], 199). Apart from the main entrance, Routledge was informed that during the historic period there was a small 'opening near each end by which the food was passed in' (2005 [1919], 216). However, this opening must have been extremely small as it let in little light and 'perfect darkness reigned' (*ibid.*). Indeed, this description of entering into darkness is a consistent feature of early accounts (Metraux 1971 [1940], 199; Van Tilburg 1994, 69). The only beam of light would have come in through the small and narrow entrance, thereby illuminating the large *paenga* often positioned directly opposite. Apart from the darkness, a further feature of the interior was that no form of internal subdivision was present, the interior being described in one case as 'perfectly naked and empty' (Forster 2000 [1777], vol. 1, 570). An appreciation of the material and cosmological qualities of the *hare paenga* as constituting a skin both separating and containing, requires once again focusing on practice.

If we begin to think again about Carsten and Hugh-Jones' contention that, 'the

Figure 8.5: Probable portable house moai *(Mike Seager Thomas, courtesy of Museo Antropologico P. Sebastian Englert).*

relationship of people to houses is one of contained to container' (1995, 42), then the architecture and physical qualities of the *hare paenga* can be appreciated on a broader canvas. The *hare paenga* was a place for sleeping at night, and the presence of stone 'pillows', some decorated, appears common (e.g. Routledge 2005 [1919], 256). Metraux (1971 [1940], 199) quotes Forster in 1777 writing that, 'the natives told us they passed the night in these huts ... they must have been crammed full, unless the generality of people lie in the open air ... or only use them in bad weather'. Metraux (*ibid.*, 199) also quotes Eyraud as writing in 1866/7:

> by night time when you could not find other refuge, you are forced to do as others do. Then everyone takes his place ... The door, being in the centre, determines an axis which divides the hut in two equal parts. The heads facing each other on each side of that axis, leaving enough room between them to let pass those who enter or go.

In sleep, the soul was separated from the body and it was during sleep that other souls and ancestors were encountered (e.g. Best 1954 [1922], 8; Handy 1927, 58–9). Hence, sleeping and dreaming constituted a very important immaterial practice (Best 1898, 125). Even today in Rapa Nui the word *po* relates to night, darkness and sleep (Sorobael Fati pers. comm.). Presumably, ancient Rapa Nui cosmology was typically Polynesian as recounted by Handy (1927, 37):

> the male principle, light, life, occult knowledge, the east and day (Ao), and the strong right side ... while on the negative side were included nature inferior, the common and unsacred, the physical, the passive, receptive female principle, darkness, destructive influences and death, ignorance, the west and night (Po), and the left or weak side.

The main elements to draw out of this not unproblematic dual classificatory scheme are the opposed qualities of night and day, darkness and light, and the domains of *Po* and *Ao* (see Gell 1995). The idea of *Po* being an internalized precinct contained by a membrane or shell from an outer *Ao* is a recurrent theme in Polynesian cosmology.

Returning to the *hare paenga*, it is worth considering the physical requirements of the architecture of entry. Passage entails assuming a prone, virtually prostrate, bodily posture, passing between two stone (or wood) images – before and sanctioned by the gaze of ancestors – over a path of *poro*, through a narrow tunnel (that Van Tilburg (1994, 73) compares to the 'birth canal'). Finally, to pass over the threshold and into the darkness of the interior was to enter a differentiated sacred, secret world. Hence, this architecture constitutes an orifice connecting two worlds, *Ao* and *Po*, and, consequently, to pass between worlds requires clear demarcation and sanction.

The experience of darkness is sometimes simplistically equated by the sighted with a state of absolute blindness, but neither should it be considered as necessarily imageless or total. Actual complete darkness is rare in the natural world, except deep in a cave. Instead, a potent sense of 'pitch black' is often a product of a sudden contrast, such as going from light or illumination quickly into darkness. Architecturally, total darkness can mostly only be achieved in windowless, sealed rooms with no direct exit to light, or in rooms and places where at night there is restricted penetration of any outside illumination. *Hare paenga* were likely permeable to a slight degree of light. The thatch that covered their staked superstructure was of plantain leaves and grasses, and may have allowed a small amount of daytime light to filter in. The entrance to a *hare paenga*, although small in height and narrow with a short covered tunnel in front, would have let in a shaft of daylight or, on occasion, moonlight. Eyraud states of the entrance opening that it lets 'enter enough light to see when you have been inside for a while' (Metraux 1971 [1940], 199). Depending on the time of day and the season, the atmospheric light on Rapa Nui can be very bright due to the intensity of the Pacific sun. On entering and exiting from a *hare paenga* during the day, the contrast between the outside dazzle and inside dimness would have been stark, sudden and 'blackening'.

The visible scale of space and landscape, with potentially open and panoramic seaward vistas, likewise stands in significant contrast to the cramped and limited visual scale of the narrow, low interior of a *hare paenga*. *Hare paenga* are recurrently situated on elevated ground overlooking the ceremonial plaza of an *ahu* with their entrances facing, in the case of the image *ahu*, the eyes of the statues and the sea. Entering a *hare paenga* would have thus involved turning one's back on the sea and the eyes of the *moai*. In most open landscapes at an elevation between 300 and 400m (in daylight), simple sweeping body actions are recognisable at 250m while smaller-scale hand and feet actions becoming clearer between 150 and 190m, and facial expressions from about 10m (Hamilton and Whitehouse 2006). In the restricted daytime dimness of a *hare paenga*, the distance at which information could be discerned with the eyes would have been significantly curtailed. People would only have been able to see outlines or shadows; details of each other, animals and things would only have been visible at close proximity. As described by Pierre Loti in 1871, who entered several *hare paenga* on different daytime occasions, once his eyes adjusted to the darkness it was possible to see proximate things, often in some detail, including, 'cats and rabbits moving around us', 'chickens', and for the inside of one *hare paenga* he states that, 'a thousand items are carefully attached to the walls: little idols made of black wood, which are wrapped in macramé; spears with flaked flint tips; paddles with human faces; feather headdresses' (Loti 2004 [1872], 67, 74). Perception of colour would also have changed. Outside, Rapa Nui's nature's colours vary with the seasons but largely are blacks/greys (volcanic basalt), greens/yellows/reds (vegetation and red volcanic soil) and blues (sky/sea). Inside a *hare paenga*, the dimness or darkness will have turned clothed, painted or tattooed people, structures and objects a darkish monochrome. The sense of touch would have been more active than colour.

The *hare paenga* would have provided some protection against extremes of weather, from sun, wind and rain, and may have had a sensory microclimate of its own. Eyraud describes them as 'rather hot inside' (Metraux 1971 [1940], 199). The enclosed space of a *hare paenga* interior would have created a claustrophobic experience and, at the same time, perhaps a reassuring womb-like enclosure in which other more direct and intimate senses would be heightened as vision was curtailed. Outside, more often than not, only feet are in contact with the ground and the rest of body moves freely. On entering on hands and knees, the sudden loss of light would have triggered an immediate sense of disorientation. The smell and feel of direct bodily contact with the ground and the constraining touch of the sides of the narrow entrance conduit would have constituted primary sensations. The body would have experienced changes in the hardness and texture of the surfaces, from the smooth hardness of the *poro* paved entrance corridor to the interior surface that would have been of a different temperature, humidity, and feel. Inside a *hare paenga* most people would have been sleeping prone or sitting down and in contact with bare volcanic earth, or the straw mats ('carpet of braided reeds') that Loti describes (2004 [1872], 73). When a *hare paenga* was occupied there would have been additional sensory experiences relating to the close proximity of bodies of people and animals buffeting and pressing on one another. This, combined with a lack of fresh air, would all have been intensified by the narrowness and lack of height of the building and its entrance. The touch of skin-on-skin and skin against fur or feathers would all have been potentially experienced in the confines of a *hare paenga*. Loti wrote vividly of the personal intimacy of a peopled *hare paenga* interior: 'inside the hut, which smells like an animal den, it is impossible to see anything, in particular because of the crowd of people milling around and their shadows, it is also impossible to stand up and, after the fresh and invigorating breeze outside, the air is barely breathable' (2005, 129), and 'little by little, I become impregnated with the odor of a wild man and a savage' (2004 [1872], 70).

Inside, external sounds will have been muffled by the thatch superstructure and experienced differently, although likely not wholly obscured. Loti (2004 [1872], 73) mentions waking up alone in a *hare paenga* with a silence, 'that is broken only by the distant sounds of the sea on the coral reefs and, occasionally, by the noise of the reeds of the hut as they rustle in a gust of wind'. Rapa Nui has a constant Pacific breeze and sound is directional; personal experience today suggests that the sounds of the few animals on the island such as cockerels and sea birds can travel far. Within a *hare paenga*, these outside sounds would still be heard, but they would be muted and less directional. Conversely, the activities of the darkened inside would not only have been rendered 'invisible' to those outside, but smells and sounds would have been contained by the thatch and matting, too.

Looking out and emerging from a *hare paenga* would have been a reversed sensory experience to that of darkness, restricted entry and enclosure. Loti describes (2004 [1872], 73) how, 'suddenly a ray of sunshine bursts through the hole that serves as a door, I see the shadow of one of the idols that guards the door'. Emerging from a *hare paenga* involved passing these shadowy guards, into light, to experience the impact of breezes and other weather phenomena on the skin and senses, and more often than not, the clear sounds of the sea, and a renewed colour and olfactory palate. As the body unfolded from prone to upright and the eyes became elevated they would have refocused on distance and landscape vistas. It would also have been a release from the close sensory experiences of an intimate womb-like place.

Potentially, entering a *hare paenga* served as an everyday reminder of the yet more tortuous, extended and heightened sensory experience of entering Rapa Nui's family caves, which were used for burial or dying and the safe-keeping of ancestral objects. Both required difficult entry through narrow 'holes' into voids of reduced height, and caves described as half the height of a man (Heyerdahl 1958). Heyerdahl (*ibid.*) reported that Father Sebastian Englert spoke of how people crawled into caves to die when they knew death was near. Caves were also used, by tradition, to sleep in (Englert 2003 [1936], 117). These transitions that we have discussed, between outside and inside, between upright and prone, between openness, light and multiple sensory experiences, and enclosure, darkness and intimacy, place the *hare paenga* within a conceptual world that was at the core of the island's spinal structure of underground caves and their association with ancestry and death.

Monumental architecture and the *hare paenga*

To finally assess the architecture of the *hare paenga* and relate it to the broader pattern of monumental architecture on Rapa Nui, requires an appreciation of the dominance of the wrapping or containing structuring principle in pre-contact Polynesian life. When Carsten and Hugh-Jones called for an 'alternative language of the house' (1995, 2), the initial area identified for comment was that the house and the body were intrinsically linked. They developed this theme further with the statement that, 'the house is an extension of the person; like an extra skin, carapace or second layer of clothes, it serves as much to reveal and display as it does hide and protect' (Carsten and Hugh-Jones 1995, 2). This characterization elevates its physical constituents as a membrane or skin, and to some degree establishes 'the relationship of people to houses is one of contained to container' (*ibid.*, 42). Islands have also been characterized as containers (e.g. François 2003, 426), and the crucial quality of containers is containment, and the main concern transgression.

Transgression appears to be the dominant theme of architectural elaboration in both the *ahu* and *hare paenga*. To move from the light, everyday world of *Ao* to the sacred realm of darkness *Po* is clearly a transgression of great import that requires strict control; the dominant form of sanction is the image of ancestor or deity. However, more subtle material devices provide a metaphoric and metonymic extension between these different areas of human experience. For example, *poro*, rounded pebbles created by the pounding surf and emblematic of the transitional qualities of the seashore, pave the entrance passage of the *hare paenga* and canoe ramps of the image *ahu*. At one level, the seashore, as a component of landscape, is displaced and redeployed as a symbolic resource in the architecture of the house (see Hamilton *et al.* 2011). At another, its transformatory qualities participate in and 'lubricate' the transition between Ao and Po, from the light into the darkness.

There is, however, an interesting distinction between the monumental *ahu* complex and the comparatively small-scale *hare paenga*. In fact, it is more of a reversal. Although house and island can be portrayed as containers, that which is being contained is different. The *ahu* wrap the island in a ring of monumentality and the island, as a container, is the domain of people: of *Ao*. Conversely, the house contains the darkness and sacred darkness of *Po*. Interestingly, in both cases the ancestral beings embodied in stone images face outwards from the sacred domain towards the place of humanity.

To conclude, we argue that in ancient Rapa Nui an architectural homology was embodied in both *ahu* and *hare paenga*. In short, to enter the dark interior of the *hare paenga* was to pass from the everyday realm of *Ao* to the sacred realm of *Po* and transgress the skin or membrane separating these cosmological opposites. Such transgression can also be recognized in the formalized passage from land to sea, again associated with the dual realms of *Po* and *Ao*. The *moai* gaze inwards towards the land and to pass from the everyday (*Ao*) to the ocean – a conduit to *Hawaiki* (*Po*), or rather *Hiva* on Rapa Nui – is to pass through the monumental wrapping separating two domains. In both cases, transgression involves passing before the eyes of the ancestors and over *poro*. Just as Gell notes, the maintenance of differentiation (and passage between differentiation) was, 'the source of certain ontological anxieties that played an enormous part in Polynesian life' (1995, 23). Such anxieties and their alleviation were realized as much in the architecture and materiality of the house as in the monumental architecture that fames Rapa Nui to this very day.

Acknowledgements

This paper was given at the 'Into the earth: the archaeology of darkness' conference at I.T. Sligo in 2012, and Marion and Robert cannot be thanked enough for organizing such an excellent conference. We would also like to thank them for their editorial comments and patience with this paper.

Explorations into the ideas of wrapping and the material manifestations of the membrane or skin separating the domains of *Po* and *Ao* have formed part of the Rapa Nui (Easter Island) Landscapes of Construction Project, which is currently supported by AHRC funding. We would particularly like to thank team members Jane Downes, Mike Seager Thomas, Kate Welham and Ruth Whitehouse for broader discussions of *hare paenga*. We also appreciate the critical comments of Rosemary Joyce and Susan Kus following a presentation of a version of this contribution at the 'Holy Houses' session of the 2012 SAA conference in Memphis, Tennessee.

Mike Seager Thomas researched and identified possible examples of 'house idols' both in the Museo Antropológico Padre Sebastián Englert (MAPSE) store and in other museums outside Rapa Nui. Rapa Nui (Easter Island) Landscapes of Construction Project is based at University College London (S. Hamilton), University of Manchester (C. Richards) and Bournemouth University (K. Welham).

References

Barber, I. 2003. Sea, land and fish: spatial relationships and the archaeology of South Island Maori fishing. *World Archaeology* 35 (3), 434–48.

Bausch, C. 1978. Po and Ao, analysis of an ideological conflict in Polynesia. *Journal de la Société des Océanistes* 34 (61), 169–85.

Best, E. 1898. Omens and superstitious beliefs of the Maori. *Journal of the Polynesian Society* 7 (3), 119–36.

Best, E. 1954 [1922]. *Spiritual and mental concepts of the Maori*. Dominion Museum Monograph. Wellington, R. E. Owen.

Best, E. 1976 [1925]. *The Maori canoe*. Dominion Museum Bulletin 7. Wellington, Government Printer.

Best, E. 1977 [1929]. *Fishing methods and devices of the Maori*. Dominion Museum Bulletin 12. Wellington, Government Printer.

Carsten, J. and Hugh-Jones, S. 1995. Introduction, about the house – Lévi-Strauss and beyond. In J. Carsten and S. Hugh-Jones (eds.) *About the house: Lévi-Strauss and beyond*, 1–46. Cambridge, Cambridge University Press.

Cook, J. 1777. *A voyage towards the South Pole and round the world (1772–75), Volume 1* (2nd edition). London, W. Strahan & T. Cadell.

Emory, K. P. 1975. *Material culture of the Tuamotu archipelago*. Pacific Anthropological Records 22. Honolulu, Bernice P. Bishop Museum.

Englert, S. 2003 [1936]. *Legends of Easter Island*. Rapa Nui, Rapa Nui Press.

Ferdon, E. N. 1981. A possible source of origin of the Easter Island boat-shaped house. *Asian Perspectives* 22 (1), 1–8.

Flenley, J. R. and Bahn, P. 2002. *The enigma of Easter Island*. Oxford, Oxford University Press.

Forster, G. 2000 [1777]. *A voyage round the world in H. M. B.'s Sloop Resolution, commanded by Captain James Cook during the years 1772–1775*. London, B. White.

François, A. 2003. Of men, hills and winds: space directionals in Mwotlap. *Oceanic Linguistics* 42 (2), 407–37.

Gell, A. 1993. *Wrapping in images: tattooing in Polynesia*. Oxford, Clarendon Press.

Gell, A. 1995. Closure and multiplication: an essay on Polynesian cosmology and ritual. In D. de Coppet and A. Iteanu (eds.) *Cosmos and society in Oceania*, 21–56. Oxford, Berg.

Gladwin, T. 1970. *East is a big bird: navigation and logic on Puluwat Atoll*. Cambridge MA, Harvard University Press.

Goldman, I. 1970. *Ancient Polynesian society*. Chicago, University of Chicago Press.

Hamilton, S. 2010. Back to the sea: Rapa Nui's *ahu* seascapes. In P. Wallin and H. Martinsson-Wallin (eds.) *Migration, identity and culture*, 167–82. Gotland, Gotland University Press.

Hamilton, S., Seager Thomas, M. and Whitehouse, R. 2011. Say it with stone: constructing with stones on Easter Island. *World Archaeology* 43 (2), 167–90.

Hamilton, S. and Whitehouse, R. 2006. Phenomenology in practice: towards a methodology for a 'subjective' approach. *European Journal of Archaeology* 9, 31–71.

Handy, E. S. C. 1927. *Polynesian religion*. Honolulu, Bernice P. Bishop Museum Bulletin 34.

Heidegger, M. 1978. *Basic writings* (D. F. Krell ed.). London, Routledge & Kegan Paul.

Heyerdahl, T. 1958. *Aku-Aku: the secret of Easter Island*. London, George Allen & Unwin Ltd.

Heyerdahl, T. 1989. *Easter Island: the mystery solved*. New York, Random House.

Heyerdahl, T. and Ferdon, E. N. (eds.) 1961. *Reports of the Norwegian archaeological expedition to Easter Island and the east Pacific Vol. 1: the archaeology of Easter Island*. London, Allen & Unwin.

Hyslop, C. 2002. Hiding behind trees on Ambae: spatial reference in an Oceanic language of Vanuatu. In G. Bennardo (ed.) *Representing space in Oceania: culture in language and mind*, 47–76. Canberra, Pacific Linguistics, Research School of Pacific and Asian Studies, Australian National University.

Kirch, P. V. 2000. *On the Road of the Winds: an archaeological history of the Pacific Islands*. Cambridge, Cambridge University Press.

Lee, G. 1992. *The rock art of Easter Island: symbols of power, prayers to the gods*. Los Osos, Institute of Archaeology, University of California.

Loti, P. (*alias* Julien Viaud) 2004 [1872]. Diary of a cadet on the warship *La Flore*. In A. M. Altman (trans.) *Easter Island 1864–1877, the reports of Eugene Eyraud, Hippolyte Roussel, Pierre Loti, and Alphonse Pinart*. Los Osos, Easter Island Foundation.

Loti, P. (*alias* Julien Viaud) 2005. Diary of a cadet on the warship *La Flore* – 1872 (trans. Ann M. Altman). *Rapa Nui Journal* 19 (2), 127–39.

Love, C. M. 1993. Easter Island *ahu* revisited. In S. R. Fisher (ed.) *Easter Island studies*, 103–11. Oxbow Monograph 32. Oxford, Oxbow Books.

Malo, D. 1951 [1898]. *Hawaiian antiquities*. Honolulu, Bernice P. Bishop Museum Special Publication 2.

Martinsson-Wallin, H. 1994. *Ahu – the ceremonial stone structures of Easter Island*. Uppsala, Societas Archaeologica Upsaliensis.

McCoy, P. 1973. Excavation of a rectangular house on the east rim of Rano Kau, Easter Island. *Archaeology and Physical Anthropology in Oceania* 8 (1), 51–67.

McCoy, P. C. 1976. *Easter Island settlement patterns in the late prehistoric and protohistoric periods*. Bulletin 5. New York, Easter Island Committee, International Fund for Monuments Inc.

Metraux, A. 1971 [1940]. *Ethnology of Easter Island*. Honolulu, Bernice P. Bishop Museum Bulletin 160.

Mulloy, W. 1995. *The Easter Island bulletins of William Mulloy to the World Monuments Fund, New York*. Houston, Easter Island Foundation.

Orbell, M. 1985. *The natural world of the Maori*. Auckland, David Bateman Ltd.

Richards, C. 2008. The substance of Polynesian voyaging. *World Archaeology* 40 (2), 206–23.

Richards, C., Croucher, K., Paoa, T., Parish, T., Tucki, E. and Welham, K. 2011. Road my body goes: re-creating ancestors from stone at the great moai quarry of Rano Raraku, Rapa Nui (Easter Island). *World Archaeology* 43 (2), 191–210.

Routledge, K. 2005 [1919]. *The mystery of Easter Island*. Rapa Nui, Museum Press.

Shore, B. 1989. Mana and tapu. In A. Howard and R. Borofsky (eds.) *Developments in Polynesian ethnology*, 137–74. Honolulu, University of Hawaii Press.

Skjølsvold, A. 1961. The stone statues and quarries of Rano Raraku. In T. Heyerdahl and E. Ferdon Jnr (eds.) *Reports of the Norwegian Archaeological Expedition to Easter Island and the East Pacific. Volume 1: the archaeology of Easter Island*, 339–79. London, Allen & Unwin.

Thomas, W. 1990. *Marquesan societies: inequality and political transformation in Eastern Polynesia*. Oxford, Clarendon Press.

Van Tilburg, J. A. 1994. *Easter Island: archaeology, ecology and culture*. London, British Museum Press.

Van Tilburg, J. A. 2003. *Among stone giants: the life of Katherine Routledge and her remarkable expedition to Easter Island*. New York, Scribner.

Chapter 9

Dark places and supernatural light in early Ireland

John Carey

What do you see when you cannot see? You cannot know unless you try; and again and again down through the ages men and women have embarked on journeys into darkness in the search for vision. In an Irish context, we hear the voice of one such searcher speaking to us in a poem, composed perhaps about a thousand years ago. The poet has been set the task of describing various hills in the vicinity of Dublin; but, instead of going out to look at them, he retreats into his room and lies down in the dark:

> *Though it be dark to me in my bed ... every great plain, every mighty fortress, is clearly visible ... When I would be occupied with the most eminent of the grave mounds ... the deeds of every troop [would be set] in order, so that they are all illuminated* (Pl. 13).

It is in the dark that all of the landmarks which he wishes to celebrate are manifest to the poet, 'clearly visible' (*imréil*), 'all illuminated' (*imshuilsi*). Returning to this theme at the very end of his poem, he says that the mountain of Sliab Lecga appears to him although he does not see it: 'to my probing eye, [even] without looking, it is not dark' (Gwynn 1991 [1903/35], iii. 110–8; all translations are my own). The mind's gaze sees in a different kind of light; and in order to experience this light the glare of day must be shut out.

This poet was referring to ideas and to practices by no means peculiar to himself. Accounts of Gaelic poetic schools written hundreds of years later still speak of how apprentice poets had rooms with 'no windows to let in the day', and describe how they would lie shut away from the light composing their verses (O'Sullevane 1744 [1722], cvii–cix in Bergin 1970, 6-8); 'and indeed they furnish such a style from this dark cell, as is understood by very few' (Martin 1884 [1716], 116 in Bergin 1970, 8–9). As the old order was crumbling, around the beginning of the seventeenth century, the poet Fear Flatha Ó Gnímh criticized a rival for presuming to compose verse in the open air, 'without a dark hut, without difficulty ... a poem without secrecy, without darkness' (*dán gan diamhoir gan dorchacht*).

> *If I should make a poem myself, I like – so that error may be the less – an obstacle to keep the sunbeam from entering, [and] secret beds protecting us. If I did not close my eyelids between myself and the pure rays, as a sheltering thatch against the day, my skill would be spoiled* (Bergin 1970, 118–19).

This kind of vision was not cultivated by Irish poets merely to enhance their art: it was a thing essential to their identity. The Irish word for an elite professional poet, *fili*, originally meant 'one who sees' – and when a poet is defined in terms of sight, it is not physical eyesight that is being referred to. This is made still more evident by the synonymous term *éices*, with an etymology meaning 'one who looks inward'. When early Irish legal texts such as the Old Irish introduction to the legal collection *Senchas Már* speak of the qualifications of the 'sage' or master poet, they insist that he must possess a clairvoyant faculty called *imbas for-osnai*, the 'great knowledge that illuminates' – again, he must be able to see what others cannot see, lit up in a radiance which is invisible to other eyes (discussion in Carey 1997).

In terms of 'The Archaeology of Darkness', do we have any physical traces of this poetic brooding in the dark? So far as I know, no remains of the windowless cubicles of the traditional poetic schools have yet been identified, and perhaps they never will. But even if we are obliged to confine ourselves to a sort of 'virtual archaeology', delving into the verbal landscape that is revealed to us by examining ancient texts, there is much that we can learn. This is the path that I shall be pursuing in what follows – and it is, indeed, that for which my own training best qualifies me.

We can, for instance, look more closely at the mysterious *imbas for-osnai*, the 'great knowledge that illuminates'. How did one go about obtaining it? One remarkable passage, from a glossary written around the year AD 900, purports to describe the ritual that was used:

> [*Imbas for-osnai*] *discloses whatever thing the* fili *wishes, and whatever it pleases him to reveal. This is how it is done. The* fili *chews a piece of the red meat of a pig or a dog or a cat; and after that it is put on a stone behind the door. And he chants an incantation over it, and offers it to pagan gods, and summons them to him; and he does not depart from it on the next day. And then he chants over his two palms, and summons pagan gods to him so that his sleep may not be disturbed, and sets his two palms on his two cheeks, and sleeps. And watch is kept, lest anyone turn him or disturb him; and after that the thing of which he had been in search is shown to him – at the end of three days, or twice or three times that much, depending on how long or short a time he allotted to the offering* (Meyer 1912, 64 §756).

The references to a door, and to the *fili* lying down to sleep, suggest that these ceremonies were carried out in the poet's own room. To this extent, we are reminded of the accounts of inspiration in darkness which we have already been considering; and indeed I believe that this passage belongs to the same strand of tradition. It is evident, though, that even more is involved: offerings and prayers to pagan gods, and a magical prophetic sleep which must not be disturbed. It is no surprise when the text goes on to tell us that '[Saint] *Patrick prohibited that ... and gave his word that whoever performed it should have neither heaven nor earth, for it is a denial of baptism*' (ibid.).

Can we really accept this as evidence that non-Christian rites were still being performed in medieval Ireland, in the search for supernatural illumination? Different experts will give different answers, determined largely by their broader assumptions; and ultimately we cannot know for sure. But what we can be sure of, because the texts are there to tell us so, is that ideas about such things were current.

Another example, of a rather different kind, is afforded by *The Tale of Tuán son of Cairell*, written *c.* AD 900 or perhaps somewhat earlier. This story's premise is that Tuán, a hermit interviewed by a saint in the sixth century, had been alive in Ireland ever since humans first settled here, regenerating himself age after age by changing into the shapes of different animals, and at last being reborn as a human (Carey 1984). All of this is fascinating, and intriguingly reminiscent of what ancient Greek and Roman writers have to tell us concerning a druidic belief in reincarnation: for summaries of the evidence see, for example, Kendrick (1927, 104–13), Chadwick (1966, 55) and Carey (2006). But the most interesting thing about Tuán's narrative with respect to our immediate concern is that he too seems to describe a ritual associated with his transformations – and also, significantly, with his all-encompassing memory. When old age weighed heavy upon him, he would go to a cave (*úam*) – always to the same place. There he would fast for a fixed period – probably nine days, although the terminology is ambiguous – after which he would sleep. It is in this sleep that he regained memory of all of his previous existences, and also the ability to change into another shape. Again, then, we have the basic pattern of retiring to a dark place, ritual behaviour, and supernatural knowledge revealed in sleep.

These are exciting hints, to say the least, and our thinking about their significance can draw upon a vast body of comparable material from other times and places, extending from the hallucinations induced by sensory deprivation experiments in our own time, back through such oracles as the underground sanctum of Trophonius in ancient Greece, to speculations that the cave art of the Palaeolithic may reflect visions experienced in the deep chambers where it is found. In any case, I want to keep my focus on Ireland and on the evidence afforded by medieval literature.

Even with this focus, there is far more to be considered than I can even mention here. However brief the treatment, there is one topic that must be touched upon: the *síde*, or 'fairy mounds'. It is a constant of Irish supernatural belief that the immortals, the old gods, have their habitation within heights of land – in natural hills or mountains, or in ancient burial mounds. These are not the only places where they were thought to dwell: stories describe them as existing under lakes, or beyond the sea, or – in a more mysterious, and perhaps more essential way – outside the whole framework of our time and space (some discussion in Carey 1982 and 1987). But it was with the *síde* that they were associated and identified, to such an extent that even the inhabitants of an underwater or overseas Otherworld could be described as living 'in the *síde*'. The palaces of the gods were subterranean chambers: whether actual, like those within the Neolithic mounds of Newgrange and Knowth; or imagined dwellings inside such mountain heights as Slievenamon or the Paps or Ben Bulben.

There is something peculiarly Gaelic here. The etymology of *día*, the Irish word for 'god', tells us that the gods of the ancient Celts were originally associated, like those of the other Indo-European peoples, with the radiance of the open heavens (Pokorny 1959, 183–7; a more concise treatment in Watkins 2000, *s.v. dyeu-*). What led the Irish gods to go beneath the earth? Here we can only guess. What seems evident, however, is the effect of this momentous change upon the mental landscape. The gods, and the whole supernatural realm of which they are rulers, are underground. The sun shines on the surfaces of land and water; but the ancient powers of the world are behind and beneath those surfaces, in the dark.

This is a powerful symbol; and symbols too have the capacity to take us past the surface, into depths of meaning beyond the reach of eyesight. In this tradition, the curtain of earth which divides us from the underground is less of an obstruction than is the veil of 'concealment', a blindness somehow inherent in our state of consciousness, which renders the inhabitants of the *síde* invisible to us. When barriers between the worlds are removed, these are barriers of *perception*. Samain or Hallowe'en, the night on which the Otherworld lies open, is the time when, in the words of the tale *The Boyhood Deeds of Finn*, 'there is no concealment upon the *síde*' (Meyer 1881/3, 202 §21). And it is our own fallen condition which causes this concealment. In the tale of *The Wooing of Étaín*, a visitor from the immortal country says that it is 'the darkness of Adam's sin' which hides his people from our awareness (Bergin and Best 1934/8, 180–1 §10).

Whenever you get close to a mystery, you will find your path blocked by a paradox; and there is a paradox here. What we experience as vision, as the unreflective, unproblematical world of daylight, appears to the people of the *síde* as darkness: we are the walking blind. We can only escape from our blindness by turning our backs on the only light we know: the only way out of darkness leads into darkness. It may be this idea which lies behind a curious scene in *The Wooing of Étaín*: a king, repeatedly thwarted in his attempts to dig up a *síd* mound, is only successful when he leaves blind puppies and blind cats at the site of the digging (Bergin and Best 1934/8, 184–5 §16). Something similar may underlie an even more troubling text concerning the death of Cú Chulainn, the beginning of which survives only in fragments: these seem to describe children being blinded in one eye so that they would gain magical powers (Kimpton 2009, 11, 35; discussion in Borsje 2012, 128–39).

Often, those who find their way into the Otherworld do so only by losing it in this one. King Conn, and his attendant druids and poets, are surrounded by a *'great mist ... so that they did not know whither they were going because of the greatness of the darkness* (dorcha) *which had come upon them'*. Conn fears that he is being conveyed 'into an unknown land'; and indeed he soon finds himself in the magnificent feasting-hall of the god Lug. It is the darkness of the mist, rather than any obstacle of physical distance, which lies between the worlds; and when Conn returns to his mortal realm he does so again by going into darkness, in this case described as Lug's own shadow (*foscad*) (Murray 2004). The same idea, this time within an explicitly Christian frame of reference, is fundamental to the story of *The Voyage of Saint Brendan*. The island which Brendan seeks is not remote beyond the ocean, but just off the coast of Donegal: what divides it from us are great 'clouds' (*nebule*) or 'darkness' (*caligo*), such that voyagers passing through can barely see one another, or the prow or stern of their own boat. Beyond that barrier, though, the earthly paradise lies bathed in 'a mighty light' (*lux ingens*) (Selmer 1959, 5, 78–9).

In medieval Ireland a complicated symbolism associated the supernatural inspiration of the poets, the *imbas for-osnai*, with water, and with certain famous rivers especially: the Boyne, and also the Shannon and the Bush. These rivers were variously imagined to flow from a spring in the realm of the *síde* (O'Rahilly 1946, 318–23; Carey 1991, 165–72). Not only is the source of inspiration hidden in the subterranean realm of the immortals: it comes up out of a spring. The vehicle of illumination rises from the darkness of the earth. And the mysterious source itself lies beyond the range of normal vision. One story tells us that it was forbidden for anyone to look into the spring or well save its divine guardian and his three servants: if any defied this prohibition, their eyes would burst on the spot (versions of this story in Stokes 1892, 500, 1894, 315–16; Gwynn 1914, 1991, iii. 28–30; van Hamel 1933, 37–8; Vendryes 1953, 3; with discussion of the mythological background in Dumézil 1963; and Carey 1983).

We have had plenty of darkness, but not much archaeology. Are there no further indications of a material dimension to what we find in the medieval texts? The *Annals of Tigernach* give us one tantalising hint: under the year 1084 there is a reference to a prophecy revealed by Oengus Óc, the immortal ruler of the *síd* of Newgrange, to one 'Gilla Lugán, who used to visit the *síd* every year on the night of Samain' (Stokes 1993 [1895/7], ii. 308–9). At the end of the eleventh century, then, people were still visiting the sunless houses of the gods in the search for knowledge; that Gilla Lugán may have been following a well-established custom is suggested by the tale *Airne Fíngein*, which speaks of a king conversing every Samain with a woman of the *síd* in order to learn, 'what there was of mysteries and of wonders in the royal strongholds of Ireland, and in its *síd*-troops' (Vendryes 1953, 1). Is it only a coincidence that Newgrange itself was so constructed that its inner darkness should be pierced by light on the shortest day of the year (cf. Carey 1993)? Or is coincidence even a meaningful concept, so close to the bedrock of consciousness?

References

Bergin, O. J. 1970. *Irish bardic poetry*. Dublin, Dublin Institute for Advanced Studies.
Bergin, O. J. and Best, R. I. 1934/8. Tochmarc Étaíne. *Ériu* 12, 137–96.
Borsje, J. 2012. *The Celtic evil eye and related mythological motifs in medieval Ireland*. Leuven, Peeters.
Carey, J. 1982. The location of the Otherworld in Irish tradition. *Éigse* 19.1, 36–43.
Carey, J. 1983. Irish parallels to the myth of Odin's eye. *Folklore* 94, 214–8.
Carey, J. 1984. Scél Tuáin meic Chairill. *Ériu* 35, 93–111.
Carey, J. 1987. Time, space, and the Otherworld. *Proceedings of the Harvard Celtic Colloquium* 7, 1–27.
Carey, J. 1991. The waters of vision and the gods of skill. *Alexandria* 1, 163–85.
Carey, J. 1993. Time, memory, and the Boyne necropolis. *Proceedings of the Harvard Celtic Colloquium* 10, 24–30.
Carey, J. 1997. The three things required of a poet. *Ériu* 48, 41–58.
Carey, J. 2006. Reincarnation and shapeshifting. In J. T. Koch (ed.) *Celtic culture: a historical encyclopedia*, volume iv, 1484–6. Santa Barbara, Denver and Oxford, ABC-Clio.
Chadwick, N. K. 1966. *The druids*. Cardiff, University of Wales Press.
Dumézil, G. 1963. Le puits de Nechtan. *Celtica* 6, 50–61.
Gwynn, E. J. 1991 [1903/35]. *The Metrical Dindshenchas*, 5 volumes. Dublin, Dublin Institute for Advanced Studies.
Gwynn, L. 1914. Cináed úa Hartacáin's poem on Bruigh na Bóinne. *Ériu* 7, 210–38.
Hamel, A. G. van 1933. *Compert Con Culainn and other stories*. Dublin, Dublin Institute for Advanced Studies.
Kendrick, T. D. 1927. *The druids*. London, Methuen and Co.
Kimpton, B. 2009. *The death of Cú Chulainn: a critical edition of the earliest version of Brislech Mór Maige Muirthemni*. Maynooth, School of Celtic Studies.
Martin, M. 1884 [1716]. *Description of the Western Islands of Scotland circa 1695*. Glasgow, T. D. Morison.
Meyer, K. 1881/3. Macgnimartha Find. *Revue celtique* 5, 195–204.

Meyer, K. 1912. *Sanas Cormaic: an Old-Irish glossary compiled by Cormac úa Cuilennáin*. Anecdota from Irish Manuscripts 4. Halle, Max Niemeyer.

Murray, K. 2004. *Baile in Scáil: 'The Phantom's Frenzy'*. Irish Texts Society 58. Dublin, Irish Texts Society.

O'Rahilly, T. F. 1946. *Early Irish history and mythology*. Dublin, Dublin Institute for Advanced Studies.

O'Sullevane, T. 1744 [1722]. Introduction. *Memoirs of the Right Honourable the Marquis of Clanricarde*. Dublin, S. Powell.

Pokorny, J. 1959. *Indogermanisches etymologisches Wörterbuch*. Bern, A. Francke.

Selmer, C. 1959. *Navigatio Sancti Brendani Abbatis*. Notre Dame, University of Notre Dame Press.

Stokes, W. 1892. The Bodleian Dinnshenchas. *Folk-Lore* 3, 467–516.

Stokes, W. 1894. The prose tales in the Rennes Dindsenchas. *Revue celtique* 15, 273–336 and 418–84.

Stokes, W. 1993 [1895/7]. *The Annals of Tigernach*, 2 volumes. Felinfach, Llanerch.

Vendryes, J. 1953. *Airne Fíngein*. Dublin, Dublin Institute for Advanced Studies.

Watkins, C. 2000. *The American heritage dictionary of Indo-European roots* (2nd edition). Boston and New York, Houghton Mifflin.

Chapter 10

Enfolded by the long winter's night

Charlotte Damm

'Night was man's first necessary evil, our oldest and most haunting terror.' This is the introductory sentence to a recent book on night-time (Ekirch 2005). Darkness is often attributed negative connotations such as danger, death and evil. But is the dark really universally associated with such fears? Is this a biological given from when our ancestors fled and hid from predators, or are the fears and myths to a much greater extent part of cultural repertoires and symbolization, employing natural phenomena and dichotomies such as light and warmth – often celebrated through the sun – and, on the other hand, darkness, the epitome of evil? Perhaps we are blinded by our modern preferences for sedentary lifestyles, large houses with central heating, and plenty of electric light, unable to see some of the positive aspects of the dark. Living north of the Arctic Circle in pre-modern times meant that each winter was one long dark night. This presented some particular challenges of cold and darkness, but ethnographic and historic evidence suggest that it was not necessarily associated with fear.

Arctic living

Holidays to regions north of the Arctic Circle are becoming increasing popular, partly due to natural phenomena such as the Midnight Sun and the Northern Lights. When you live there, however, you find that one of the most common questions asked is: how do you cope with the darkness? Because while the summers are light, the winters are dark. In Tromsø, Northern Norway, at a latitude of 69.6° north, the sun doesn't set for almost two months every summer. On the other hand, in midwinter it does not rise above the horizon for two months. Thus from November 21st until January 20th it is not possible to see the sun directly. This is known as 'the dark season'. Similarly, in the Nunavut territory in Canada the local Inuit population call this period 'Tauvikjuag', the *Great Darkness* (MacDonald 1998, 101). Some people get more easily depressed and tired during this period, and experts advise treatment with special bright-light lamps. However, many people do not seem to be particularly affected by this dark period.

As someone who has lived within the Arctic Circle for about twenty years, I greatly appreciate the seasonal changes one experiences here. During the summer there is always hectic activity. This is when people work on their houses; this is when you pick mushrooms and berries and conserve them for the winter; this is when you go fishing in the middle of the night. Come autumn, it is time to fill the freezer with grouse, reindeer, elk and lamb. In the dark season, things are quieter; larders are well stocked, and it is time to sit back, consume, and enjoy. November, December and early January is therefore a good time to socialize with friends and family. When the sun returns in January there is usually a good deal of snow; rivers and lakes are frozen and it is time for new outdoor activities such as skiing or ice fishing. In late spring there is a burst of new life: birds return, you may feast on eggs, and soon the Midnight Sun encourages rapid growth of grasses and flowers. In this wider context, the dark season has its own place in the yearly cycle of activities and events.

My experience of the winter within the Arctic Circle is set in a modern world with plenty of electric light and central heating, but how did the long dark winter affect people living in these areas in the past?

How dark is the dark?

The disappearance of the sun within the circumpolar region can last anywhere from a few days at the Arctic Circle at the northern latitude of 66° 33', to about two months at a latitude of 70° (Northern Norway, Disco Bay in Greenland, the north coast of Alaska), and three and a half months at around 78° north (Longyearbyen on Svalbard, areas north of Baffin Bay in north-eastern Canada and Greenland, and the Taymyr region in Siberia). In these latter areas the polar night – when the sun is more than 6° below the horizon – lasts from mid-November until the end of January.

While the sun never rises above the horizon during the dark season, this does not in fact mean that there is complete darkness twenty-four hours a day. Even though the sun doesn't rise, in many areas it is just below the horizon, allowing several hours of twilight or dusk around midday. In areas with polar night, however, there is not even twilight during the darkest period. In addition to these hours of twilight, other circumstances have significant impact on this winter darkness. Snow and ice provide some light in themselves, but in addition they reflect light from the moon and stars on cold and clear nights. The Aurora Borealis, the Northern Lights, is another natural phenomenon that breaks the darkness on clear nights.

While the first snow may fall early in the autumn, it does not necessarily mean a permanent snow cover from this time onwards. In the Tromsø region the snow cover is most stable from January until April. On a seasonal cycle, this means that the period from October through to early January is the darkest. The day is significantly shorter, and the snow cover has not yet stabilized, making this period generally the darkest of the year. The combination of the returning light with a more stable snow cover make the period shortly after midwinter significantly brighter.

Living in the dark and the cold

The exact time for the snow and ice to stabilize and melt varies somewhat from region to region. However, some overall similarities in seasonal cycles may be established. It is important to emphasize that the annual cycle of activities in the Arctic is influenced not only by the seasonal availability of resources and the amount of light, but also very much by technology and historical and cultural circumstances.

Travel

In pre-modern times much travel in the Arctic would have been by boat. In some areas, such as along the Norwegian coast as far as Murmansk on the Kola Peninsula, sea travel would have been possible all year round, as the warm Gulf Stream prevents the sea from freezing. However, in many other Arctic regions sea ice covers vast areas. Similarly, lakes and rivers freeze everywhere. It does, however, take a while for the ice to stabilize and reach a thickness that allows humans to traverse it. During this period, sub-zero temperatures, storms and increasing ice prevent seafaring (Burch 2006, 52), while also preventing other kinds of travel across the sea, rivers and lakes. This period generally occurs during the late autumn and early winter, with a similar situation again during the late spring as the ice melts.

In other words, the darkest period before the actual dark season is also the most hazardous with regard to travel. The darkness makes navigation on sea or land more difficult. The ice is insecure. Walking on uneven terrain in the dark is hard going. Orientating oneself is another challenge. Interestingly, many of the Inuit appear not to have used the stars to any significant extent (Collignon 2006, 66). This may be partly due to the fact that they are not visible during the summer with twenty-four hour daylight, but may equally be attributed to the important fact that visibility in the Arctic is affected not only by darkness, but also by snowstorms or fog. Instead, other types of knowledge were used, including techniques based on the sense of touch, hearing and smell (*ibid.*, 66).

As a result of darkness and other climatic and environmental factors, travel in the past was restricted for a shorter or longer period during the late autumn and early winter. In many Inuit societies communities would gather on the coast after the autumn terrestrial hunting to wait for the ice to settle (Burch 2006; Collignon 2006, 33). Once the ice had thickened (typically in December), camps were moved out onto the ice where igloos were built. The waiting was over and a stable period of winter activities set in.

Once stabilized, ice and snow are no obstacles for travel if the appropriate technology is available. In fair weather it is quite possible to travel at night during winter, even if at a somewhat slower pace (Burch 2006, 56). Most Arctic communities would have had some form of specialized winter transportation. Dog sledges are well known from many areas and periods in the high Arctic (e.g. *ibid.*, 252; Petersen 2003). In historic times, sledges pulled by reindeer were a widespread mode of transport in northern Eurasia, and there are some indications that sledges may have been an ancient technology in this area too (Kuokkanen 2000). Similar to boats, sledges allow transportation of bulk goods, and enable the old, fragile, and young children to travel long distances. Snowshoes and skis (Burch 2006, 254; Naskali 1999) are other technologies that improve mobility and travel during the winter. Since most of the objects involved in transportation were made of organic material, the evidence from prehistoric periods is sparse and fragmented. However, boats are very numerous on rock art in Northern Fennoscandia dating back to the fifth millennium BC, and both snowshoes and skis are represented there too (Helskog 2014). To the best of my knowledge, there are no images of sledges depicted in northern prehistoric art, but several sledge runners from Fennoscandia are radiocarbon dated to the fourth millennium BC (Kuokkanen 2000). In Greenland, sledge runners made of whale bone are documented from the first millennium BC (Jensen 2004, 155).

Heat and artificial light

While the lack of direct sunlight did not prevent all outdoor activities, many hours must have been spent inside dwellings during the dark season. Dwellings differed between regions and through time. Tents of various forms were common, but also sod houses and, in some regions, igloos (Odgaard 2003). The winter temperature varies tremendously in the Arctic, from quite mild along the coast of Fennoscandia where the temperature rarely drops below -10°C, to extremely cold in high Arctic and inland areas with temperatures regularly at and even below -30°C. But in all areas one had to deal with not only the dark, but also the cold. This means that technology was required to provide heating, light and cooking facilities.

In most Arctic regions firewood is very limited. In some areas and periods driftwood would have provided an important and welcome resource for fuel, but also as material for dwelling structures and for essential objects such as boat frames and sledges (Grønnow 1996; Odgaard 2003; Petersen 2003). Other available fuel would have been animal bones and dung, but perhaps especially blubber and oil from marine mammals (seal, walrus, whale), or other types of fat. Oil lamps, often made from soapstone or similar materials, are known from a number of regions. However, in Greenland they appear to be a late phenomenon, and lamps are not known at all from Northern Fennoscandia. From Alaska, there are reports that a single oil lamp was able to maintain an indoor temperature of 10–15°C in a sod house, while two lamps provided enough light to read and write (Burch 2006, 225). This suggests that even a single lamp or equivalent allowed people to work on handicrafts.

Ulla Odgaard (2003; 2007) has conducted experiments with different types of hearths from Arctic prehistory. One very successful method involved using a stone-lined box-shaped hearth as a lamp, and burning fat with a moss wicker. Her estimation is that this would heat a dome-shaped tent, measuring 4m in diameter and covered by two layers of caribou skins, to over 8°C even when the outside temperature was -30° (2003, 358). The amount of fat needed for two months was estimated at 175kg, or twelve seals. Eight degrees and limited light may not be considered acceptable living conditions by most modern western Europeans, but should keep you reasonably warm if wearing skin clothing. The reindeer skin clothing familiar to many Arctic societies is remarkably warm, as the hollow hairs have a particularly insulating effect.

That such lamps were effective is also evidenced in a report from a communal house in an Alaskan settlement:

> *The interior was really clean and cheerful, a spacious room 20 feet [6m] square, with brilliant lights in troughs of seal oil, the wicks formed of moss placed in a row at the edge and fed by a piece of blubber hanging within reach of the flame; the light was excellent* (Trollope 1855 in Burch 2006, 221).

In the same text, Trollope comments on how warm the interior was despite the very low temperature outside.

Another common method for heating dwellings is the use of movable stones (Odgaard 2003). Here, stones are heated in a fire. When the fire dies out, the heat from the hot stones sustains the temperature for some time. Similarly, a stone-set hearth without movable stones will transmit heat for some time after the open fire is exhausted. In some cases, the stones may have been heated outside and brought into the dwelling for heating without smoke. This method is well known in the archaeological record from the piles of fire-cracked stones found in the vicinity of dwelling structures in Fennoscandia and elsewhere. Once the fire was extinguished there would be no light emanating from the hearth, leaving the dwelling in darkness.

Heat would also be needed for melting and cooking. The 8°C mentioned above is sufficient to melt ice for drinking water (Odgaard 2003). And the heat from a lamp would help dry meat or clothes hung over it (Odgaard 2007, 12). The hot rocks warming a dwelling would also assist in drying meat. Amongst the Iñupiat in Alaska there was usually only one cooked meal a day, and a fire was built only for the preparation of this (Burch 2006, 226). A lot of food was eaten dried, frozen or fermented (*ibid.*, 212). Some roasting over open fires took place, but otherwise boiling was the prevalent method of cooking. If stone or ceramic vessels were available these could be utilized, but in many cases hot rocks were used to bring water in an organic container to the boil (for illustration, see Odgaard 2007). Cooking pits where hot rocks were put into a pit with meat and then covered are also known from prehistory.

The possibilities for light, heating and cooking were overall better in northern Fennoscandia as firewood would have been readily available from the Middle Mesolithic onwards, as birch and even pine rapidly colonized areas all the way to the Barents Sea. This would have allowed more extensive use of open fires and/or of heating rocks for a warm but smoke-free interior. It would also have provided opportunities for varied ways of cooking. As outlined here, oil lamps or open fires may have lit up dwellings. But usually the lamps would be quenched at some point and the heat possibly maintained through heated stones. This would have left the interior in the dark. However, it did not necessarily prevent people from chatting, singing or telling stories (Burch 2006, 55).

Dark season activities

Having established the time and length of the dark season in the Arctic, as well as the possibilities for artificial light and heating, we must now turn to the actual activities that took place during this part of the year. A combination of darkness and difficult hunting and travelling conditions occurs in all Arctic regions for a shorter or longer period. Earlier scholars have interpreted this period in rather negative terms:

during the 2½ months of darkness, the hunter families must have been tempted to pass a lethargic indoor existence living on stocks like several of the four-legged creatures of the Musk-ox way: bears, ermine and lemming (Knuth 1967, 194);

They must have lived through the dark period in a kind of torpor. The women were unable to sow, the men could not work up flint articles (ibid., 201).

This rather grim perspective is thoroughly contradicted by ethnographic and historical information. In fact, 'most Eskimos look forward to the winter darkness more than to any other period' (Stefansson 1944 in Burch 2006, 51). Similarly, Malaurie (2002, 376) argues that the Inuit love the long winter's night and he describes it as a motherly embrace. Burch's investigations of the Iñupiaq Nations in Alaska revealed variations in the annual cycles for each group, but one common element was a holiday season in the short days between late November and early January (2006, 51; see also MacDonald 1998, 108). New clothing was prepared for this event so everyone looked their very best. This was an occasion for enjoyment filled with dancing and singing. Some see this as linked to the return of the sun, but the emphasis on this aspect seems to vary (*ibid.*, 109).

In some regions, the winter solstice period was also a time for extensive travel, to spend the festive period with friends and relatives elsewhere. As noted above, short days did not prevent travelling. Although these trips sometimes only took a few days, others travelled hundreds of miles and journeys took several weeks (Burch 2006, 56). Visitors brought gifts and contributions to hosts. Festivities could include ceremonies and other formal events, but also dancing, singing, feasts and games. While some games may have taken place outdoors, others, such as string games where different images are made with one *circa* 1m long loop of string (Pl. 14), were well-suited even for confined indoor space (MacDonald 1998, 125; Malaurie 2002, 373). Several such activities were either restricted to, or at least predominantly performed, during the dark season.

In seventeenth- and eighteenth-century Greenland, Inuit would travel all the way from southern Greenland to west Greenland. The journey was about 1,000km long and involved visitors spending the winter in the west staying in a communal house before returning home the following summer (Gulløv 2004, 332). Perhaps such long distance visits wintering in other communities were practices also found in other Arctic regions in the past? Similarly, we know of trade fairs in northern Fennoscandia from the 1500s onwards. From this point in time, we have records confirming that these places were frequented by traders and tax collectors, and in the 1600s several were institutionalized by Nordic monarchs (e.g. the markets in Jokkmokk and Arjeplog in Swedish Lappland). Some of these took place in winter. The market in Varanger in the far north, for instance, was reported in 1530 to be a regular event, taking place just after Christmas (Hansen and Olsen 2004, 241). It is unknown whether such events built on older traditions.

It is clear, however, that there has been significant cultural and historical variation with regard to winter activities and journeying. For the Inuinnait in the eastern Canadian Arctic, Collignon observed that the 'time of the ice-sheet' was traditionally the time of community life and long evenings spent in the igloo (Collignon 2006, 34). In the past, the Great Darkness was associated with relative inactivity (MacDonald 1998, 101). Story-telling appears to have been a popular activity on long dark winter nights. For non-literate societies in general, and perhaps particularly for areas with a sparse and low density population, story-telling must have been a very important way of transmitting knowledge. Through narratives, new generations acquired traditional religious and historical information (Damm 2005), but also learned about living and surviving, and information about distant areas could be exchanged with visitors. While many of the stories told by the Inuinnait are concerned with myths and cosmogonic tales, many also provide more local and regional information about the landscape, the habits of animals, and the best way to cope with the environment in various situations (Collignon 2006, 75). In other words, these long dark nights of story-telling were closely linked to the transmission of local knowledge and essential to continued survival in the Arctic landscape. Burch (2005, 51) notes that many Iñupiaq stories are very long, taking several hours a night for days or even weeks to complete. The long evenings, possibly with a storm outside but with full larders close by, must have made this time of year perfect for long narratives. Obviously not all winter was spent socialising or confined to dwellings. Hunting and fishing would have continued on days with fair weather. In the evenings, and during bad weather, lamps or open fires would have provided enough light for mending clothes and other handicrafts.

Arctic hysteria

The winter also caused anxiety, however, as survival over long northern winters should not be taken for granted (MacDonald 1998, 101). The Arctic climate is harsh, larders may run empty, and accidents happen. A phenomenon referred to as 'Arctic hysteria' or 'Pibloktoq' has at times been linked to the darkness of the Arctic winter (MacDonald 1998, 103; Malaurie 2002, 273). It was first observed, and the phrase coined, by the Peary's around 1900 (Dick 1995, 3). It refers to an emotional state where the individual will begin to scream or cry, perhaps tear off their clothes, and walk or jump about aimlessly. It has generally been described as a mental disorder. Initially this was linked to what was perceived to be childish behaviour, not unexpected in 'inferior' cultures, and in addition was associated predominantly with women (*ibid.*, 4). It was soon argued to be related to the onset of the dark season. As one scholar expressed, the '*long winter darkness and the loneliness and silence of a hunter's life make the Arctic peoples more susceptible to this disorder than the rest of the human race*' (Jenness 1928 in Dick 1995, 5). Later, some researchers linked the behaviour to dietary deficiencies, but the phenomenon seems to have been mainly disregarded since around 1970.

Dick's review (1995) of the observed cases suggests that the 'disorder' was predominantly an emotional response to particular circumstances, including separation of the family and migration to remote areas, but also fear of starvation and death. In many instances this was caused by explorers wintering in the area, and hiring the best hunters to journey with them. This caused great anxiety, not only for the families who had to make do without them, but also for the hunters worrying about those left behind. In some cases the perceived fits may have related to increased shamanic activities. It seems clear that 'Arctic hysteria' was not caused by darkness and isolation. It was, to a certain extent, a result of misconceptions of an unfamiliar culture by the explorers, and partly induced by European demands and behaviour.

More recently, another disorder linked to the dark season has emerged – winter depression, or Seasonal Affective Disorder (SAD). Many people feel tired and down during late autumn and winter, and the recommendation is to get out in daylight as much as possible, and to invest in special bright-light therapy lamps. First of all, it has been pointed out that what is popularly called a dark season depression should not in general be confused with a mental diagnosis (Hansen *et al.* 2008). Mostly, the condition is associated with lack of sleep and disturbed sleep patterns, as well as a loss of energy, possibly linked to abnormal variations in melatonin, and vitamin D deficiency (Johnsson and Moan 2006). Furthermore, a recent study comparing Norwegian and Italian students showed that there was no significant difference in the occurrence of depression between the two countries. In other words, the hypothesis that SAD is linked to the amount of environmental light and latitude was not supported (Brancaleoni *et al.* 2009). While there is some disagreement as to the extent to which diet and lack of daylight impact upon well-being during the winter, some studies argue that it is not the darkness itself that affects us, but psychosocial factors and negative connotations of the dark season. In other words, there is a cultural expectation of depression caused by the dark season, which may in itself have a negative impact on an individual's well-being. This of course does not make the experience any less real, but the direct causal effect of darkness appears to have been exaggerated (Hansen *et al.* 2008).

Returning to the pre-modern period, there is consequently no reason to expect any mental disorders as a direct result of the dark season. However, this does not exclude all effects of long nights. We have seen that while light would have been available through lamps or open fires, darkness was probably prolonged in many dwellings. Darkness need not have prevented all activities, but perhaps sleep was extended during the winter period. It has been pointed out that before the modern era, Western Europeans commonly segmented their night into two periods of sleep separated by a period of activity (Ekirch 2005, 300). A similar pattern can be found in many other societies (*ibid.*, 303). When awake, people would talk, pray, eat or even do housework before going back to sleep (Koslofsky 2011, 6). In the same way that summer activities in the Arctic are not restricted to any particular time of the day due to the Midnight Sun, mid-winter activities or sleep is unlikely to have been dependent on the time of day; sleep cycles may have floated round the clock and indeed been longer than during the summer.

Conclusion

While darkness is most certainly very widely associated with danger, fear and death, the perception of darkness would still seem to be linked to regional particularities, and historical and economic circumstances. In the above I have emphasized ethnographic and historical information that does not link the dark season to hardship or anxiety. I am aware, however, that other examples pointing to different perceptions can be found. To me, this suggests that the darkness of winter and the environmental challenges during that period of the year varied regionally, but perhaps in particular were addressed and dealt with in historically and culturally distinctive ways.

References

Brancaleoni, G., Nikitenkova, E., Grassi, L. and Hansen, V. 2009. Seasonal affective disorder and latitude of living. *Epidemiologia e psichiatria sociale* 18 (4), 336–43.
Burch, E. S. Jr. 2005. *Alliance and conflict. The world system of the Iñupiaq Eskimos*. Lincoln, University of Nebraska Press.
Burch, E. S. Jr. 2006. *Social life in northwest Alaska. The structure of Iñupiaq Eskimo Nations*. Fairbanks, University of Alaska Press.
Collignon, B. 2006. *Knowing places. The Inuinnait, landscapes, and the environment*. Circumpolar Research Series 10. Edmonton, Canadian Circumpolar Institute Press.
Damm, C. 2005. Archaeology, ethnohistory and oral traditions: approaches to the indigenous past. *Norwegian Archaeological Review* 38 (2), 73–87.
Dick, L. 1995. 'Pibloktoq' (Arctic Hysteria): a construction of European-Inuit relations? *Arctic Anthropology* 32 (2), 1–42.
Ekirch, A. R. 2005. *At day's close. A history of nighttime*. London, Weidenfeld & Nicolson.
Grønnow, B. 1996. Driftwood and Saqqaq culture woodworking in West Greenland. In B. Jakobsen and C. Andreasen (eds.) *Cultural and social research in Greenland 95/96. Essays in honour of Robert Petersen*, 73–89. Nuuk, Ilisimatusarfik/Atuakkiorfik.
Gulløv, H. C. 2004. Nunarput, Vort Land – Thulekulturen 1200–1900 e.v.t. In H. C. Gulløv (ed.) *Grønlands forhistorie*, 281–342. Copenhagen, Gyldendal.
Hansen, L. I. and Olsen, B. 2004. *Samenes historie fram til 1750*. Oslo, Cappelen Akademisk forlag.
Hansen, V., Skre, I. and Lund, E. 2008. What is this thing called 'SAD'? A critique of the concept of seasonal disorder. *Epidemiologia e psichiatria sociale* 17 (2), 120–7.
Helskog, K. 2014. *Communicating with the world of beings: the World Heritage rock art sites in Alta, Arctic Norway*. Oxford, Oxbow Books.
Jenness, D. 1928. *The people of the twilight*. Chicago, University of Chicago Press.
Jensen, J. 2004. Dorsetkulturen. In H. C. Gulløv (ed.) *Grønlands forhistorie*, 142–72. Copenhagen, Gyldendal.
Johnsson, A. and Moan, J. 2006. Rytmer, depresjon og lys. *Tidsskrift for den Norske legeforeningen* 126 (8), 1044–7.
Knuth, E. 1967. The ruins of the Musk-Ox Way. *Folk* 8–9, 191–219.
Koslofsky, C. 2011. *Evening's empire. A history of the night in early modern Europe*. Cambridge, Cambridge University Press.
Kuokkanen, T. 2000. Stone Age sledges of Central-Grooved type: Finnish reconstructions. *Fennoscandia Archaeologica* XVI, 37–56.
MacDonald, J. 1998. *The Arctic sky. Inuit astronomy, star lore and legend*. Toronto, Royal Ontario Museum and Nunavut Research Institute.
Malaurie, J. 2002. *Thule. Det yderste land*. Copenhagen, Gyldendal.
Naskali, E. 1999. On ancient skis. In M. Huurre (ed.) *Dig it all. Papers dedicated to Ari Siiriäinen*, 295–306. Helsinki, The Finnish Antiquarian Society, The Archaeological Society of Finland.
Odgaard, U. 2003. Hearth and home of the Palaeo-Eskimos. *Etudes/Inuit/Studies* 27 (1–2), 349–74.

Odgaard, U. 2007. Hearth, heat and meat. In D. Gheorghiu (ed.) *Fire as an instrument. The archaeology of pyrotechnologies*, 7–18. BAR International Series 1619. Oxford, Archaeopress.

Petersen, R. 2003. *Settlements, kinship and hunting ground in traditional Greenland*. Meddelelser fra Grønland, Man and Society 27. Copenhagen, Danish Polar Center.

Stefansson, W. 1944. *The friendly Arctic: the story of five years in the polar regions*. New York, MacMillan.

Trollope, H. 1855. *Journal kept by Commander Henry Trollope during a trip from H. M. sloop Rattlesnake in Port Clarence to King-a-Ghee, a village four or five miles round Cape Prince of Wales, January 9, 1854–January 27, 1854*. House of Commons, United Kingdom, Sessional Papers, 1854–5; Accounts and papers 35 (1989), 868–79.

Chapter 11

'The outer darkness of madness' – the Edwardian Winter Garden at Purdysburn public asylum for the insane

Gillian Allmond

The Victorian/Edwardian lunatic asylum or mental hospital, often still a physical presence in British and Irish towns, tends to be understood today as a place of darkness. The inhabitants of such a place, particularly those inhabiting it in the past, are frequently cast as the pitiable victims of an uncaring or actively abusive regime. There is much academic support for a view of the asylum as grim and forbidding. Andrew Scull, perhaps the leading historian of the Victorian asylum, has maintained that, although the reforming intentions of the asylum movement may have been good, by the closing decades of the nineteenth century the ever-increasing numbers of patients had led to a tendency to 'warehouse' the insane in huge hospital complexes, with asylum buildings becoming 'increasingly monotonous, drearily functional, prison-like' (Scull 1993, 167).

And yet, contemporary literature advising on the nature of mental illness and on the proper construction of institutions for those diagnosed as insane suggests that, at the end of the nineteenth century, asylums were deliberately constructed as places of light which were intended to act therapeutically on patients and assist their recovery. Primary sources indicate that light and darkness were perceived to strongly affect mental and physical health and the material evidence confirms that these values were expressed, explicitly and implicitly, in the architecture and interior spaces of institutions for the mentally ill. Furthermore, the asylum of this period was materially constituted as a direct counterpoint to the prison and light played a critical part in this discursive positioning. This chapter will examine the cultural context relating to ideas of darkness and light and analyze the physical nature of an early twentieth-century structure known as the Winter Garden which was built at Purdysburn asylum for the insane near Belfast. By bringing together the material evidence and an analysis of contemporary published materials, the Edwardian institution for the mentally ill will be situated within medical discourses of the period.

Victorian/Edwardian discourses of darkness and light

A substantial corpus of contemporary literature relating to hospital and asylum environments, mental and physical health, and hygiene allow us to reconstruct

Edwardian attitudes towards darkness and light and their relationship to mental illness. Strong themes emerge from these texts which can be grouped into the following categories:

1. *Darkness is madness: light is sanity.* Medical discourses made a continual correlation between madness and darkness. For example, the asylum superintendents' publication, the *Journal of Mental Science,* speaks of 'the outer darkness of madness and the broad daylight of rational intelligence' and of 'the importance of abundance of light to dispel mental darkness' (*JMS* 12 1867, 551; *JMS* 31 1886, 486). This latter comment illustrates a continual elision in the literature between metaphorical and literal understandings, the 'abundance of light' here being literal while the 'mental darkness' is figurative but felt to be nonetheless susceptible to *actual* daylight. Many accounts of the dissection of deceased patients refer to 'dark' structures or fluids within the brain, suggesting that discourses of darkness affected the way that the pathology of madness was perceived and that patients were seen to bear the physical imprint of their metaphorical 'dark affliction' (e.g. *JMS* 5 1859, 587; *JMS* 18 1872, 165–6).

2. *Darkness is barbaric: light is humane.* The asylum movement represented itself as an enlightenment project that had swept away the misguided and often brutal treatment of the insane in the past, replacing it with the humane regime of the modern asylum. Key to this narrative, as continually replayed in the pages of the *Journal of Mental Science*, was the understanding that the insane were, before the era of the public asylum, kept in dark, prison-like cells and physically restrained and/or beaten (e.g. *JMS* 19 1873, 329). The light-filled rooms of the asylum were therefore a literal and metaphorical counterpoint to the inhumane treatment of the past. Asylums in Britain, Ireland and around the world were discursively policed and lauded or condemned to a large degree on the basis of how light or dark were their dormitories and dayrooms. The provision of light was so powerful a marker of humane treatment that it was maintained that fastening the door on a patient 'whether for bodily illness, for observation, or for mental excitement' in a room that was well-lit was a valuable strategy, while shutting patients in a dark room was worthy of the Lunacy Commissioners' criticism (*JMS* 20 1874, 332).

3. *Darkness promotes disease: light prevents disease.* Darkness was seen as directly responsible for causing specific diseases or conditions. For example, idiocy/cretinism, which at this period was considered to be related to mental illness and would have been treated in an asylum in the same way, was thought to be caused or exacerbated by an upbringing in dark dwellings and by a lack of sun and air. The dark and damp valleys of the Alps were particularly notorious in this regard (*JMS* 2 1855, 114; Nightingale 1860, 49; *JMS* 19 1873, 171; *JMS* 51 1905, 126). Florence Nightingale held that insufficient light promoted scrofula (a form of TB) among children, and from 1890 following Robert Koch's discoveries in Germany that light could kill the TB bacillus, sunlight began to be understood as a specific curative for TB. However, discourses relating to asylum construction had stressed from a much earlier stage that

light was 'amongst the foremost sanitary requirements' for these buildings (*JMS* 2 1856, 273). Nightingale's highly influential works on nursing and hospitals reinforced this understanding, stating that light had a 'purifying effect' on the air of a room, removing odours and disease-causing agents, and that therefore hospital rooms must be orientated so as to be 'sunned' at some point during the day (Nightingale 1860, 16–8).

4. *Darkness is tranquilising: light is stimulating.* Keeping patients in the dark was usually understood as inhumane, but light was also seen to possess stimulating qualities and manic, excitable patients had to be protected from over-exposure with seclusion in a dark room sometimes being used as a means of reducing stimulation (*JMS* 48 1902, 684). Winslow (1867, 231) recommended that light was excluded completely from the bedrooms of the insane 'in order to tranquilize them and cause sleep'. The idea of light as stimulating is related to a pervasive understanding in medical and wider discourses of the period that there was a correlation between human beings and plants. A popular American work on hygiene published in 1863 summarizes the thinking of this period, pointing out that light is essential to the development of plants and animals, which both become blanched and stunted without it (Hammond 1863, 206–10). Human beings could not develop properly in the dark and would become thin, deformed and etiolated. Etiolation, a term usually applied to plants grown in the dark and which become spindly, pale and weak, is here used to describe human beings who were characterized by watery blood, pale skin, rapid pulse, underweight, lack of energy and susceptibility to illness. Light is described as a 'most healthful stimulant, both to the nervous and physical systems … The delirium and weakness which are by no means seldom met with in convalescents kept in darkness, disappear like magic when the rays of the sun are allowed to enter the chamber' (*ibid.*, 206–10). Winslow suggests that the etiolation which takes place in human beings when the 'vital stimulus of light' is withdrawn is not only physical but also 'moral and mental' leading to intellectual deterioration and crime as well as bodily deformity, disease and death (1867, 5).

5. *Darkness depresses: light elevates.* Darkness was seen as having a depressing effect on mood and Winslow (1867, 5–6) compares the 'nervous depression' of the urban labouring poor who lived and worked in relative darkness, with the 'bright, ruddy, happy faces and buoyant spirits' of rural folk 'on whom the sun is generally shining'. Consistent reference is made to 'cheerfulness' as a quality associated with light (*JMS* 2 1856, 376) and light is one aspect of the therapeutic influence of environment which is expected to operate on the mentally ill by elevating mood. However, darkness was also undesirable because it made 'illusions of the imagination … much more liable to be mistaken for realities' (*JMS* 11 1866, 529) and even the sane could be prone to 'the process of dissolution' that happens in darkness (*JMS* 36 1890, 302), so that those confined alone in 'dark cells' sometimes became unhinged (*JMS* 41 1895, 368). Bibby (1895, 97–8) cautions against ornamental work in the design of the asylum that is 'grotesque' or casts 'undesirable shadows' so that there may be 'as little as possible for the disordered mind of the patient to dwell upon'.

6. Darkness is unhygienic: light is hygienic. The provision of light and elimination of darkness in the asylum environment was part of a wider discourse on hygiene which saw an 'intimate connection' between bodily and mental functions (*JMS* 7 1861, 319). The medical superintendent of Purdysburn asylum, William Graham, who had worked closely with his architects to produce the final asylum designs (Allmond 2012, 22–3), was not untypical among his peers in his conviction that 'insanity is as much a physical disorder as is consumption or smallpox'. Graham further believed that although heredity was largely to blame for insanity, the inherited susceptibility to madness could be circumvented by attention to proper hygiene. He asserted that: 'half the existing insanity could be banished or contracted to inconsiderable limits, were the hygienic conditions in the home, the school and the factory what they ought to be' (*Belfast District Lunatic Asylum Annual Report 1902*, 11). Hygiene had much wider associations in this period than it has today. Burdett, an influential writer on asylum design, stated that medical superintendents in charge of asylums needed to be experts in 'hygienic treatment' including light and atmosphere, furnishing and decoration, diet and clothing, and occupations and amusements (1891, 187). It follows from the correlation between mind and body that a 'hygienic' environment which was physically healthy was also considered to be mentally healthy and, indeed, therapeutic.

The Winter Garden at Purdysburn – exterior

Purdysburn was an asylum for the mentally ill built in a rural area outside Belfast on a 'colony' plan as a series of dispersed villas sited near communal buildings such as a hospital, recreation hall, administration block, laundry and churches. The two Winter Gardens at Purdysburn were constructed as part of the hospital building which housed patients who were too unwell, mentally or physically, to be placed in separate villa accommodation.

The hospital building was designed by prominent English asylum architect George Thomas Hine and built between 1909 and 1912. The building comprises a three-storey central block with single-storey wings on either side, the west wing for males and the east, identical, wing for females. The building is orientated roughly west to east and open verandahs originally ran along the length of both wings, facing southwards where patients could be exposed to air and sunlight during fine weather (Fig. 11.1). Classical architectural theory, which correlates constructed forms with the proportions of the human form, allows us to view the low wings either side of the tall central block of the hospital as resembling articulated limbs, curving forwards in a gesture that is embracing/confining. The Winter Gardens are situated in the position of the 'palm of the hand' on both male and female wings of the building with adjoining dorms and annexes forming 'fingers' (Fig. 11.2). The three dormitories of each hospital wing all open onto the Winter Garden as does the service annexe for each wing (kitchens) and the sanitary annexe (baths, wash basins and WCs). The Winter Garden, therefore, provided a panoptic hub for each wing of the hospital, with all dormitories visible and accessible

11. 'The outer darkness of madness' – the Edwardian Winter Garden at Purdysburn   121

Figure 11.1: Exterior of male wing of the hospital showing Winter Garden roof lantern (Belfast Mental Hospital 1924: PRONI HOS32/1/9).

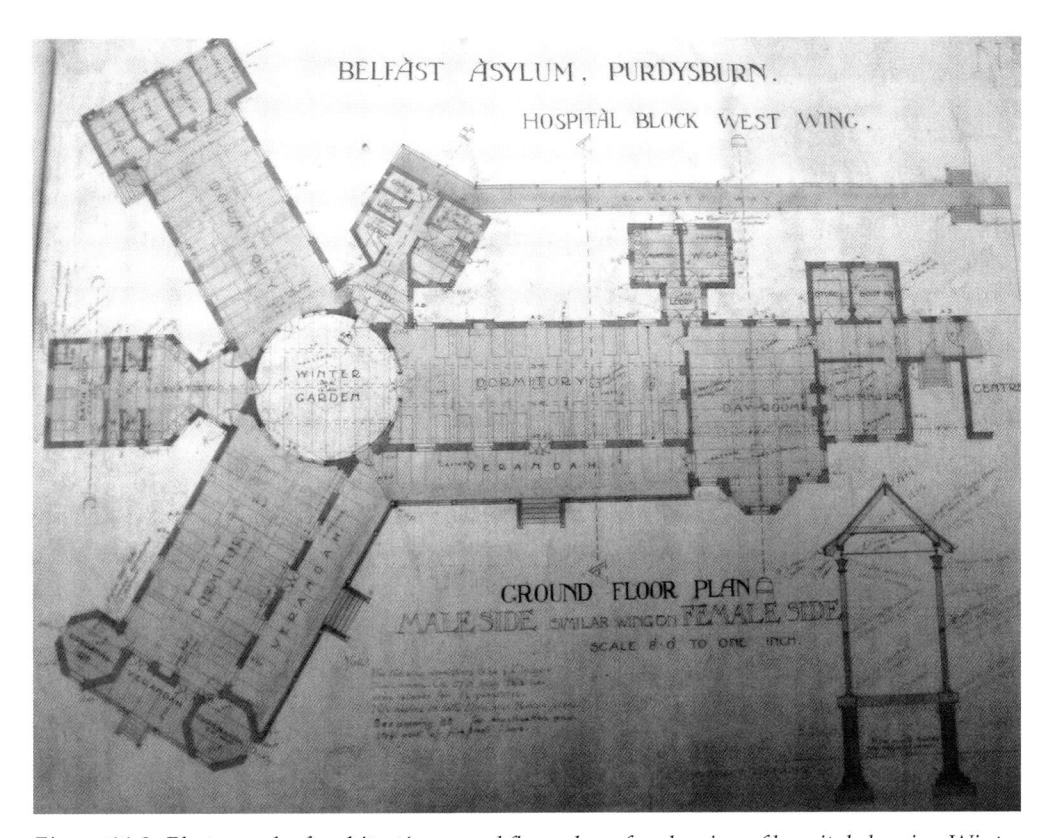

Figure 11.2: Photograph of architect's ground floor plan of male wing of hospital showing Winter Garden, c. 1910 (Gillian Allmond).

from it. However, while the Winter Garden was certainly intended to provide good visibility into areas occupied by patients, another primary function was its construction as a light-filled space that acted as a funnel feeding light into the Winter Garden itself and the adjoining dormitories.

In the closing decades of the nineteenth century, a winter garden was an indispensable addition to the facilities of hotels, health resorts and spas and was associated with health, leisure, and freedom from the stresses and constraints of modern living (Koppelkamm 1981, 45–6). Winter gardens were usually on a grander scale than the domestic conservatory and commonly featured masonry or brick walls with large windows. The earliest winter gardens were built with tiled or slated roofs, in a style that echoed early orangeries, but the early nineteenth century saw a change to glazed roofs arising out of an increasing understanding of the importance of overhead or perpendicular light to the growth of plants. John Claudius Loudon, one of the most prominent horticultural writers of this era (Grant 2013, 25), observed that: 'the summits of all bodies in the free atmosphere receive more light than their sides; and hence the trees in dense forests … continue to grow and thrive though they receive little benefit from light, except from that which strikes on the tops of the plants. Hence the great importance of perpendicular light to plants under glass' (Loudon 1842, 91).

Although overhead light in summer was thought essential for the ripening of fruit, Loudon considered that a glass roof was also important for a 'greenhouse in which no fruit is ripened but in which the abundance of light is required all the year'. He recommended that such a greenhouse should have, 'perpendicular glass to receive a maximum of light during winter and a sloping roof of glass at an angle of 45°, which is found favourable for the admission of light at every season' (Loudon 1842, 91). Loudon's ideal for a greenhouse was based on the understanding that when rays of light hit glass at an angle of between 90° and 40°, more than 85% of the light passes through the glass. However, at angles lower than this, the amount of light transmitted through the glass rapidly begins to fall off until, at a 10° angle, more light is lost than passes through (Lawrence 1963, 107–9). Given that the altitude of the sun does not rise above 40° for several months of the year in northern latitudes, the glass surface of a greenhouse or winter garden must approach the vertical on at least some portion of the structure in order to capture a maximum amount of light during the cooler seasons.

The original two stage lantern roof of the Winter Garden at Purdysburn was hexagonal, the lower stage a vertical glazed plinth with windows that opened on three sides and a roof of fixed panes at an approximate pitch of 35–45° (Fig. 11.3). This was surmounted by an identical smaller scale lantern of vertical fixed panes and an angled roof, and the whole was finished with a tall iron finial. The roof lantern presents a substantial surface of vertical glass to lower angles of the sun in the early and late hours of the day and through the winter months. The design also captures the overhead sunlight which was deemed so important to the development and health of plants, and a large glass surface is available to catch diffused light from all directions, particularly on fully overcast days when the distribution of light is symmetrical about the zenith (Hopkinson *et al.* 1966, 23).

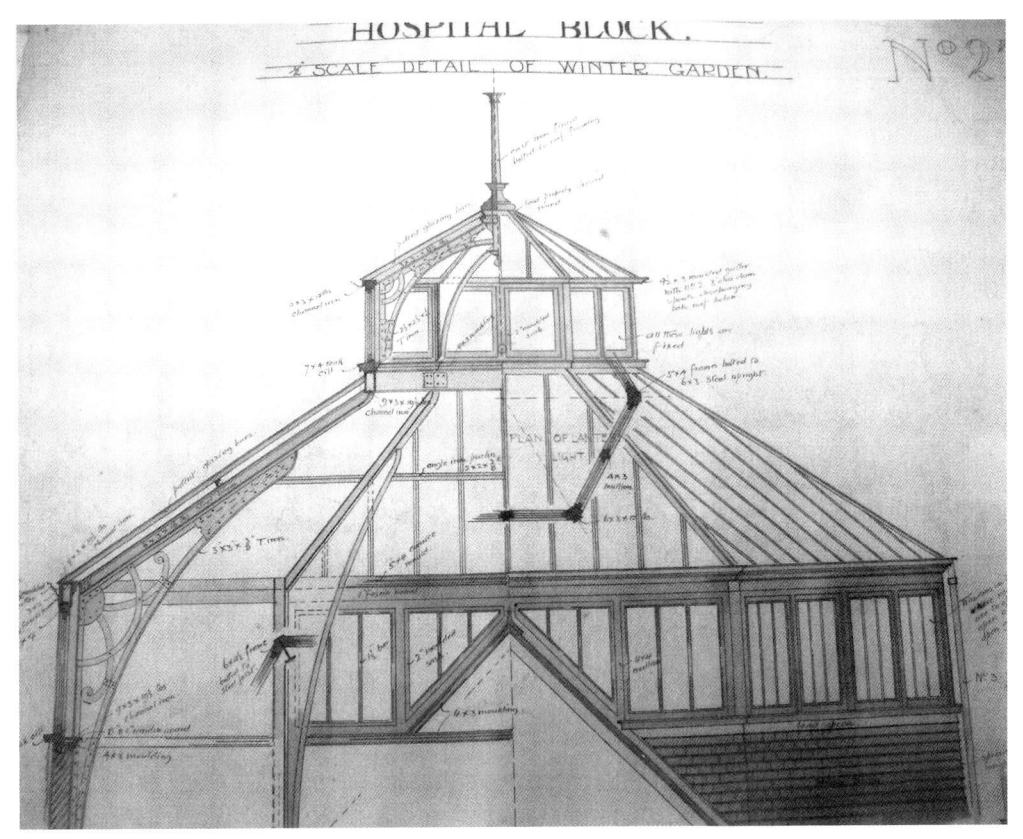

11. 'The outer darkness of madness' – the Edwardian Winter Garden at Purdysburn

Figure 11.3: Photograph of architect's drawing, c. 1910, of the Winter Garden roof lantern at Purdysburn public asylum (Gillian Allmond).

The Winter Garden at Purdysburn – interior

An image, taken from a Belfast District Lunatic Asylum annual report, which was captured within a few years of the hospital's opening in 1912, depicts the Winter Garden on the female side of the hospital and can be interpreted as a deliberate discursive construction of the asylum as a place of light (Fig. 11.4). The room is dominated by a large and verdant tropical plant whose great size, dark leaves and vigorous growth give a strong impression of an environment of optimum health. The presence of the plant implies that the room is light-filled but the light is also made visible within the lofty room by the pale colours of the floor and walls and the glazed surfaces of the wall tiles. Half-glazed doors, set in a glazed screen, marked the entrances between the Winter Garden and the dormitories. The glazed screens are brought into the picture showing how the light from the Winter Garden feeds into the other areas of the hospital. The only visible shadows are those cast by the elegant tables on which books are placed.

These cultural objects are balanced with the natural object, the plant, and occupy a discursive position that would have been occupied by statues or works of art in a public winter garden.

The patients are shown enjoying rest and recuperation in a genteel bourgeois context, with the emphasis on humane treatment in an ambience which is suggestive of a hotel or spa rather than the spartan working class homes from which they are likely to have come, and which contemporary discourses reviled as dark, dirty and airless (Mearns 1883, 4–5; Booth 1890, 166). The scene speaks of the beneficial effect this environment is having on the patients. They are sedate and composed, there is no agitation and apparently no noise, all the patients appear to be silent. They are sedentary, but well enough not to be lying in their hospital beds which are seen vacant in the background. This space would be understood by contemporaries as one where the patients could obtain exercise by walking around the room, perhaps stopping to look at the pictures or words laid out on the tables, rather as promenaders would use a public winter garden, pausing to view the works of art while sheltered from inclement conditions outdoors.

Figure 11.4: Winter Garden interior dating from c. 1914 (Belfast District Lunatic Asylum Annual Report 1922).

Discussion and conclusion

The Winter Garden at Purdysburn asylum was constructed to offer patients the benefit of the therapeutic qualities that light was thought to possess. A Winter Garden, with its cultural associations of health and freedom from the stresses of modern living, was provided for the more fragile patients as a means of allowing them to be outdoors while indoors, and thus avail of the many benefits that exercise in the open air could afford including bathing in the overhead light that the roof lantern was carefully designed to capture, without being exposed to the cold and wet. The design of the roof ensured that the Winter Garden was filled with light, whenever light was in the sky, with its vertical panes angled to catch light in the cooler seasons and the sloping roof able to capture beneficial perpendicular rays and diffused light from all directions.

We cannot understand a structure such as the Winter Garden at Purdysburn without understanding contemporary cultural values attached to darkness and light. Although almost every text relating to asylum building or mental health at this time stresses the importance of light, these references can be rather cursory and a full appreciation of the Victorian and Edwardian attitude to light requires some excavation from the literature. Together with the evidence of the buildings themselves, which goes beyond the textual in making a material commitment to an ideology of light, a strong case is made that we take seriously claims of therapeutic care and the desire to heal and cure. The Winter Garden as a place of light is also a place of health and hygiene, where the sunlight streaming into the room could destroy disease-causing agents and purify the atmosphere. The perceived continuum between physical and mental disease during this period meant that there was often no clear division between treatment for psychiatric disorders and bodily ones. Providing a physically healthy and hygienic environment including well-lit accommodation was part of a regime that was intended to promote recovery in the insane.

However, there were some ways in which light and the absence of darkness were understood to specifically address states of mind. Access to light and its 'cheerfulness' and avoidance of darkness was known to be important in dispelling gloom, for example, in cases of melancholia, which was particularly prevalent among the female patients at Purdysburn (*Census of Ireland 1911*). Patients with more complex cases involving hallucinations and visions were to be protected from the dark shadows and corners of ill-lit rooms. The hexagonal roof lantern of the Winter Garden which admits light from all directions, and the circular form of the lower part of the room, reduce shadows for such vulnerable patients.

The explicit meaning of the Winter Garden as light-filled space often overlaps with more indirect and symbolic resonances. A Winter Garden is ostensibly a space for the cultivation and display of tender tropical plants and the plant that was placed at the centre of the room is shown as thriving within this environment, with large, strong leaves of a deep colour and exuberant growth reaching above head height. The plant stands in vivid contrast to the blanched and spindly specimens that would be grown in a less healthy and darker environment. The mentally fragile patients are implicitly correlated with tender and fragile tropical plants and the light that benefits plants is perceived as also engendering vitality, energy and vigour in the patients, extending to their weak and disordered minds which could be properly nurtured within the asylum and encouraged to heal.

We have seen that mental illness, in this period, was frequently metaphorically cast as a 'dark affliction' and that there was a continual elision between metaphorical and literal understandings in relation to the heavily resonant concepts of darkness and light. The correlation between darkness and madness often extends beyond its use as a figure of speech. Light, with its overtones of health, sanity and well-being, is invoked as a weapon that can be used quite literally against darkness/madness. The symbolic force of light seemingly accounts for some of the quasi-scientific beliefs in its medical efficacy, while the symbolic force of darkness allows it to be co-opted as a means of giving (im)material expression to the fear, horror and distress surrounding the idea of mental disease.

This chapter began with the observation that the Victorian/Edwardian asylum is often perceived today as a place of darkness. Medical professionals working in the psychiatric field in the nineteenth and early twentieth centuries also felt that asylums were 'stigmatized as dark places' (*JMS* 20 1874, 340) and were conscious of the need to present asylums as places of healing to a public that was fearful, sceptical and at times outraged by tales of wrongful confinement (Wise 2013). Light was conceptually equated with knowledge and humane treatment, and darkness with ignorance and barbarism. Light allowed the proper authorities to uncover the wrongdoing and abuses that were concealed by darkness, while providing the environmental conditions for health and vitality.

As an enlightenment project, asylum buildings were not only places of light, but also had to be seen to be so, and thus hygienic, healthy and able to promote mental healing. Central to this was the need to discursively position the asylum in opposition to the prison. Where the prison had bars, locks and single cells, the asylum had open doors, unbarred windows and shared dormitories, correlating it with the forms and practices of a hospital environment. But most crucially of all, where the prison was dark, or perceived to be so, the asylum was filled with light. Through the provision of light-filled spaces the asylum authorities attempted to demonstrate the provision of an environment that was not only sane and healthy but also humane and compassionate. The Winter Garden at Purdysburn must be seen as carrying its own symbolic resonances in an attempt to defeat the expectation of the asylum as a dark place. The juxtaposition of 'winter' with 'garden' suggests that even in the midst of the darkness of madness there was a hope that sanity might be recovered. In the prelapsarian 'paradise' of the asylum Winter Garden, that hope is given material form.

Acknowledgements

I would like to thank Marion Dowd and Robert Hensey for their helpful comments on an earlier draft and Raymond Hamilton and Stephen Larmour of Knockbracken Healthcare Park for facilitating access to the Purdysburn estate and its archives. My thanks to the Deputy Keeper of Records at the Public Records Office, Northern Ireland, for permission to reproduce Fig. 11.1 and to Richard Fallis of the Medical Library at Queen's University Belfast for assistance with Fig 11.4.. This project has been funded by the Department for Employment and Learning (Northern Ireland).

References

Allmond, G. 2012. *Domesticating the asylum: light and darkness at the Purdysburn villa colony.* Unpublished MSc dissertation, Queen's University Belfast.
Belfast District Lunatic Asylum Annual Report 1902.
Bibby, G. H. 1895. *The housing of pauper lunatics.* London, B. T. Batsford and Bibby.
Booth, W. 1890. *In darkest England, and the way out.* London, the Salvation Army.
Burdett, S. H. C. 1891. *Hospitals and asylums of the world. Volume I. Asylums – history and administration.* London, J. & A. Churchill.
Census of Ireland 1911. (Available at www.census.nationalarchives.ie) [Accessed 19-01-2015].
Grant, F. 2013. *Glasshouses.* Oxford, Shire Publications.
Hammond, W. A. 1863. *A treatise on hygiene, with special reference to the military service.* Philadelphia, J. B. Lipincott & Co.
Hopkinson, R. G., Petherbridge, P. and Longmore, J. 1966. *Daylighting.* London, Heinemann.
JMS: Journal of Mental Science 1855–1914, Volumes 1–59.
Koppelkamm, S. 1981. *Glasshouses and winter gardens of the nineteenth century.* London, Granada.
Lawrence, W. J. C. 1963. *Science and the glasshouse.* Edinburgh and London, Oliver and Boyd.
Loudon, J. C. 1842. *The suburban horticulturalist or an attempt to teach the science and practice of the culture and management of the kitchen, fruit and forcing garden to those who have had no previous knowledge or practice in these departments of gardening.* London, William Smith.
Mearns, A. 1883. *The bitter cry of outcast London: an inquiry into the condition of the abject poor.* London, James Clarke & Company.
Nightingale, F. 1860. *Notes on nursing: what it is, and what it is not.* London, Harrison.
Scull, A. 1993. *The most solitary of afflictions: madness and society 1700–1900.* New Haven and London, Yale University Press.
Winslow, F. 1867. *Light: its influence on life and health.* London, Longmans, Green, Reader & Dyer.
Wise, S. 2013. *Inconvenient people: lunacy, liberty and the mad-doctors in Victorian England.* London, Vintage.

Chapter 12

Descent into darkness

Tim O'Connell

I am prepared to admit that this man-serpent game, with its prospects of having to lie, sometimes for hours, on nasty cold rock, in mud or icy water, rubbing the skin off elbows, knees, and all parts of the body is not everyone's idea of enjoyment ... Is there not enough beauty under the vault of heaven? (Casteret 1947)

Caves and caving

Cavers rarely spend time in complete darkness. On occasions where you are waiting alone for any period of time, you turn off your light. Perhaps because you are waiting for someone to arrive, sounds like lapping water turn into gurgling voices; distant repetitive noises like dripping turn into approaching footsteps; and the darkness can begin to have a solidity or weight about it. Usually, though, cavers live in a dim pool of light as generated by their headlamps and those of other cavers, surrounded by shadows and darkness. When I tell people I go caving the most common response is, 'I wouldn't like that, I'm claustrophobic' or, more simply 'Why?' Writing this paper has been a way of answering that question to my own satisfaction.

Caves can be defined loosely as underground spaces large enough for a person to enter, the most common of which are cavities formed in limestone rock (Fig. 12.1). Limestone caves are formed by the erosion and chemical dissolution of rock by slightly acidic water over thousands of years or longer (Jackson 2005). Karst landscapes (such as in the Burren, Co. Clare) – the type of landscape where caves form – cover approximately a quarter of the earth's land surface (Margat 2013). As such, caves in some shape or form are found in most countries of the world (Walker 2007).

Caves come in an astounding variety of negative spaces, dynamically sculpted by the waters which create them. The world's longest cave is Mammoth Cave in Kentucky, USA. It truly merits the name at 628km in length (Walker 2007). At 2,191m, the deepest known cave is Krubera-Voronya Cave in Abkhazia (Macnamara 2011). There is great potential to find more caves in every part of the world. They remain one of the mysteries of our planet, with superlative records like 'deepest', 'biggest' and 'longest' frequently broken. In 2012, three kilometres of additional passages were added to the longest cave in the world, and the second deepest cave in the world was discovered to be deeper

Figure 12.1: The author on a caving trip in Poll na Grai, Co. Clare (Colin Bunce).

than previously thought (www.nps.gov). These explorations, as well as many more modest local discoveries, create an atmosphere of potentiality and excitement.

History and statistics

Modern recreational caving began in the Alps and Pyrenees with Édouard Martel's descent into potholes during the late nineteenth century (Walker 2007). Martel visited and archived thousands of caves across Europe, including Ireland and the UK. He introduced the concept of speleology as a distinct area of study, establishing the Federation of French Speleologists (Gunn 2004). The University of Bristol Speleological Society (UBSS) is the oldest caving society in the British Isles, established in 1919. The UBSS have been active in Ireland since the 1920s, focusing on Clare from the 1940s (Mullan 2003). Caving became somewhat popular with university clubs in Dublin and Belfast from then onwards. The Speleological Society of Ireland, since renamed the Speleological Union of Ireland (SUI), was established in 1964 and the Irish Cave Rescue Organisation (ICRO) in 1951 (www.caving.ie).

In 2012 there were over 12,000 people and 135 clubs insured by Mountaineering

Ireland for climbing, walking, rambling and scrambling (www.mountaineering.ie). By contrast, 138 people were insured by the Speleological Union of Ireland in 2013, with far fewer caving on a monthly basis. The best known and most visited caves in Ireland are those in Clare and Fermanagh. There are nearly one hundred kilometres of mapped cave passage in Clare (Mullan 2003). Caves in Clare are predominantly horizontal – longer than they are deep. Fermanagh caves are the opposite, with more deep, vertical cave systems and less horizontal passages (Fogg and Fogg 2001). There are plenty of other caving regions, but these are the most popular.

Caving has a reputation for danger. Despite this reputation, caving is not inherently dangerous. Statistically, in the UK there is one non-fatal accident per 153 caver years (Mohr 2000). If you prefer, by caving five hours a week, an individual can hope for eight decades of accident-free caving. The main dangers and injuries are caused by cold and water. Hypothermia is the greatest statistical danger for cavers. Other risks involve being caught in a flooding system, falling from a height or getting stuck in a small constriction (*ibid.*).

Skills, equipment and safety: the Irish context

A caving trip, in the modern sense, comprises variously walking, squeezing, shimmying, crawling, contorting, traversing small canyons, wading, climbing and descending on both ladders and ropes, digging, occasional swimming and using explosives (though not at the same time!). For safety, cavers use a helmet, light, belt, robust warm clothes and carry food, basic first aid and spare batteries. In Ireland and the UK, trips typically vary from a short one-hour underground walk, to anything from twelve to sixteen hours on digging trips where a cave's limits are being explored. Longer trips are usually for exploration. It is unusual for a caver to travel any distance alone, with anywhere from three to seven people being the usual group size, dependant on the nature of the cave.

The skills involved start with knowing the previously mapped survey of the system and reading up on any known risks: whether the cave is prone to flooding, whether the group size is appropriate, what equipment is needed (such as rope or other equipment), what the weather will be like (particularly the quantity of rain over previous weeks and days, and the forecast while you are underground), as well as accident and contingency planning. Cavers always leave details such as group size, planned route and expected return time with a person on the surface. Failure to make contact soon after the expected return time means that the Irish Cave Rescue Organisation is called out via the emergency services.

Why go caving?

Caving is exciting. One of the many rewards of caving is the pleasure of viewing the formations: calcite shapes in infinite variety, from the ridiculous to the sublime, moving beyond the beautiful yet humble stalagmite and stalactite. It is a sensory feast in a unique environment. This is a total, immersive experience for all the senses, moving from outside to inside. The term 'caving' covers a broad range of activities, so there is of course no simple answer as to why an individual ventures underground. The commonality shared by anyone going caving is curiosity. This takes many forms: the joy of photographing a strange environment, the excitement and possibility of discovering a new cave, or simply of overcoming the physical and mental challenges of the underground environment. People suspend belief on their first caving trip; there is a shared 'anything can happen, the rules are not the same' feeling. You might sometimes find yourself looking at an expanse of rock which forms the roof of a cavern, marvelling that there is an unimaginably heavy burden of rock over your head, resting on nothing. You can feel the weight of all that rock, and the soil and sky above it.

Caving represents a diverse range of activities in an alternative space. Boundaries are not the same as above ground, you can explore and play and discover new aspects to skills and pastimes you have in your 'above ground' life. It is also a fun, healthful and relatively safe alternative to the clean, bright and tidy environment of everyday life. It can occasionally be nothing more than a thinly veiled excuse to wallow in mud and blow-up rocks. A big part of the appeal of caving is that it offers an opportunity to be 'one of the few', even the first, to see something, to be somewhere. There are underground places in Ireland you can get to within an hour of leaving the comfort of your car, without possessing any particular ability beyond reasonable fitness and a willingness to crawl in damp darkness; and in these places, perhaps only four or five people have been before you. If you poke around behind that pile of rocks, or push down that little tunnel, who knows what you might discover? Perhaps caving is one of the last opportunities to explore for those on a modest income.

Being able to contort and squeeze through small, difficult passages, being able to get through narrow constrictions, is a real rite of passage in the caving community. You know you are talking to someone bitten by the bug when they happily describe getting into a passage so small that it meant having to exhale all the air from their lungs to decrease the size of their ribcage, wriggle forward a few inches, stop to breathe, then wriggle forward again. The rewards of doing this are a feeling of remoteness, perhaps to see some pristine formations, or to discover a never-before-seen passage opening into a large cavern. For some, there is simply an inherent thrill in pushing comfort zones.

Vertical caving

Most cavers are skilled at climbing and descending a rope to access deeper parts of a cave. This involves rigging deep, sheer, vertical pits underground and is a truly thrilling aspect of the sport. The deepest cave in the British Isles is Ogof Ffnnon Ddu in Wales, at 308m total depth (Walker 2007). Sitting on a harness and clipped into a rope, on the lip of an empty space, the echoing depthless blackness below has a hypnotic quality, one which you must ignore or master if you are to concentrate on getting safely to the bottom (Pl. 15). There is an element of trust involved: trust that the equipment is safe and that the person who has rigged the knots has done it safely and correctly. In a very short length of time the immediacy of this decision to trust another builds a strong bond between people caving together. You must be competent enough not to be a burden or danger to others in the group. In the dark, you lose your individuality and become a caver amongst cavers, identically clad in helmet and shapeless clothes, faceless in the glare of the headlamp.

My experience in Krubera, Abkhazia

One of the most memorable occasions in my life came in late 2009, near the village of Carron. After fifteen digging trips with other members of the Clare Caving Club, following a draft of air emanating from a short cave (a sure sign that there is substantial cave beyond), the last boulder was pulled out revealing a space half a kilometre long and 80m in depth, which we called Poll Gonzo. The first trip into Poll Gonzo was incredible. A beautiful, pristine, never-before-seen cave which we had discovered, together. The feeling for those few hours is indescribable. We were one big overflowing vessel of wonder, almost beyond using meaningful language in our joy. It was all we could do to be safe, so absorbed in our surroundings were we. A shared first view of a thundering waterfall, vertical drops, block-strewn chambers and calcite formations were the fruits of our labour.

And so, when the opportunity arose a few months later to join the expedition to Krubera-Voronja, the deepest cave in the world, I jumped at the chance. I knew a long, multi-week caving trip like Krubera would be physically and mentally draining. A climbing friend who has been on many difficult and long expeditions in the past mentioned that when you do an expedition like that, the masks come off and you see what you are really like, an idea which appealed to me in an abstract kind of way. Krubera is the only cave in the world to exceed 2km in depth (Macnamara 2011).

Buoyed up from the experience at Poll Gonzo, and confident in my skills, I booked flights to Abkhazia, a breakaway republic in the north of Georgia. I joined Stephen Macnamara, Krubera veteran, and experienced caver/climbers Eoghan Mullan and Niall Tobin, as the Irish contingent on the Lithuanian-led six-week 'Call of the Abyss' expedition in July and August 2010. I realized I had made a mistake at the very first team meeting. The unassuming French gentleman beside me mentioned returning, 'from China, where I advised them on establishing their national cave rescue organisation'.

Without going into the specifics of the trip, I found it really, really challenging and earned myself the moniker 'the weakest link' due to my rudimentary skills. I managed to damage my descending device on the first drop of the descent on an acclimatisation trip, much to the bemusement of the more experienced cavers – which is to say nearly everyone on the expedition.

There are usually two types of expedition. The first is called 'Alpine style' and involves travelling light and fast with as few people and as little equipment as possible. The second is called 'siegeing' where large numbers of people with large quantities of supplies and equipment methodically work towards a particular goal (Fig. 12.2). Our expedition involved laying siege to the cave. The goal was to gather scientific data and support cave divers who were pushing into the deepest, flooded section of the cave. As part of this siege, our team spent nine nights underground, ferrying large numbers of bags loaded with SCUBA equipment for the divers, as well as food and fuel. The Irish team's aim was to install data logging devices to monitor the water levels of the cave. There were three camps in the system, one necessitating a free dive through a short flooded passage into the oxygen starved area below (Macnamara 2011). In the cave there are broad pitches 150m deep, of a scale I had not encountered before. Looking below on one occasion, I could see two cavers on the rope 30m and 60m in depth beneath me. Their lights dimly lit a flake of rock so large it was like the prow of some cave-bound cruise ship. Most of the cave was not so dauntingly vast.

I have already described the closeness and trust which can build up from shared time with other cavers on a rope. It reached new heights with the Irish team in Krubera. Most of the time, when not edging up a rope, was spent giggling uncontrollably over the most banal, ridiculous things. Saying 'pass the cheese' turned into an elaborate pantomime of sniggering and constant, silly tangents and riffs. This, and a lot of cursing through gritted teeth. Each person had only a small amount of clean water to drink. We moved with one, two or even three weighty bags (8–12 kilos each) dangling beneath.

Figure 12.2: Niall Tobin and Eoghan Mullan with their caving gear, 500m deep into Krubera (Niall Tobin).

This was something I was not prepared for, or experienced before. We quickly fell out of a circadian rhythm. Days became longer – perhaps sixteen hours on the go, twelve hours sleeping (dreaming all the while of rope, rope, rope), and wearing the same clothes for nine sweaty days.

Shuffling up and down a rope for ten to twelve hours a day, perhaps with a person way above you and out of reach for conversation, did not lend itself to much reflection beyond asking, constantly, 'What on earth am I doing here?' On occasion, as I was slow on the rope, I was the last person in the cave, everyone above me on the journey out. The oppressive and crushing feeling this generated, the weight of the darkness behind, was like a living thing. It was more than just feeling low; psychologically, anybody who ended up being last for a while on the way out experienced this all-consuming feeling.

As the days wore on, I found my mind making strange little loops; tiny phrases, remembered conversations, gestures and moments playing on a monotonous repeat, way beyond my control. All day. For example, I would see a vivid image of my sister talking about the board game 'Ludo', and the four colours of a Ludo board would flash in front of my eyes as I huffed up a rope. And then it would keep re-playing that same ludicrous short scene all day, and I only a helpless viewer.

I remember one particularly low day, one of the last. Alone all day on the rope, no-one in sight above or below for a full fourteen hours. I was mildly imagining ghostly white faces which flashed and flickered on my right hand side, but I was used to this at that stage. For the first half of the day I moved pretty quickly up the rope, thinking the two cavers below me were hot on my heels and I didn't want to slow them up. After a short sleep on a ledge I realized that there was still no-one behind me. I waited for my team-mates for what seemed like an age, then slowly started to climb. I went slowly, thinking they would catch up with me, and started to feel that low, oppressive feeling again. It is the worst I have ever felt, face pressed against a rock, hanging on a rope which seemed never-ending, an awful song stuck in my head. Slow, slow movement upwards. Finally, a warmly lit tent ahead.

Returning to the surface

The following night we exited Krubera – relieved, dehydrated and very tired (Fig. 12.3). I remember the air becoming clearer as we approached the surface, and then the smell of burnt plastic at minus 200m (the Russian camp often used plastic wrapping to start their fires). We four kept our pace and slowly worked our way up the gnarled rope. I remember the passage slowly turn from bare rock to seeing mossy clumps, then tiny ferns and, eventually, a star overhead. I can't remember who got out first, but I do remember all of us sitting in silence, looking at the moon for a long while. Then we changed our clothes and ate some cheese.

When one first comes back outside after a long trip, the intense variety of textures and colours of the world become apparent, the infinite variety of colours and the unbelievably crisp outlines of a tree set against the sky. Smells are sharper, sounds are noticeably different. The feeling returning to the surface – with light, air, odours and

Figure 12.3: Back outside: after eleven days in the world's deepest cave (Niall Tobin).

wind – is a wonderful, sweet relief.

And so, to return to my original question, 'Why is caving worthwhile?' Maybe it is because it *isn't* purposeful. Without meaning to be flippant, perhaps the value is intrinsic, and recognized by few of us strange creatures. If the idea of crawling in damp darkness is pointless, that is okay. It is one of those activities where work and its usual opposite – pleasure – are cheerfully avoided and replaced with something else. It offers the possibility of experiencing the kind of 'joyful anguish' spoken about by Mark Rowlands (2013, 199) in relation to running.

Architect Antoin Gaudi supposedly once said that he tried to create a balance between light and dark in his architecture, as extremes of either can blind. Sometimes we have far too much light in this world. By caving you encounter the dark on its own terms. Your lamp is not strong enough to blind you, it's just about enough to guide you.

Acknowledgements

I would like to thank Stephen Macnamara, Terry Casserly, Eoghan Mullan, Colin Bunce, Niall Tobin and particularly Joanne Finnegan for their encouragement both over and underground. I would like to thank Colin Bunce, Axel Hack and Niall Tobin for permission to use their photographs.

References

Casteret, N. 1947. *My caves*. London, J. M. Dent & Sons.

Fogg, T. and Fogg, P. 2001. *Beneath our feet; the caves and limestone scenery of the north of Ireland*. Belfast, Environment and Heritage Service.

Gunn, J. 2004. *Encyclopaedia of caves and karst science*. New York, Taylor & Francis.

Jackson, J. A. 2005. *Glossary of geology* (5th edition). Berlin, Springer Science & Business Media.

Macnamara, S. 2011. *Report of the Irish members of the international expedition to Krubera Voronja Cave 2010*. Bell Harbour, Speleological Union of Ireland.

Margat, J. 2013. *Groundwater around the world: a geographic synopsis*. London, CRC Press.

Mohr, P. 2000. Gauging the risk. *Descent* 153 (1), 20–3.

Mullan, G. 2003. *Caves of County Clare and South Galway*. Bristol, University of Bristol Speleological Society.

Rowlands, M. 2013. *Running with the pack*. London, Granta Publications.

Walker, S. M. 2007. *Caves*. Minneapolis, Lerner Publications.

www.caving.ie: *http://www.caving.ie/icro/50-years-of-icro/* [Accessed 15-01-2016].

www.mountaineering.ie: *http://www.mountaineering.ie/_files/Reportpdf2012.pdf* [Accessed 15-01-2016].

www.nps.gov: *http://www.nps.gov/maca/parknews/mammoth-cave-400-miles.htm* [Accessed 15-01-2016].

Chapter 13

Coming in and out of the dark

Gabriel Cooney

Illuminating darkness

There are occasions when you attend a conference and you know that you have had the privilege of being at a special event. Such events inform us about the human condition and the particular contribution that archaeologists and colleagues working in related fields make to understanding human life. That was what I brought away from the 'Into the earth: the archaeology of darkness' conference held at the Institute of Technology, Sligo in October 2012. The organizers, Marion Dowd and Robert Hensey, brought together an inspiring and diverse range of speakers to address this fascinating topic. It is reflected in, and was brought back to me while, reading the papers in this volume. I think all the contributors to the conference and the audience would acknowledge that a very special element of the event was Brian Keenan's reflections on darkness and its impact in the context of the four and a half years he was held as a hostage in the Lebanon during the 1980s.

As organizers of the conference and editors and drivers of this volume, Marion and Robert come to the topic of darkness from two different perspectives captured in two recently published volumes. Marion is the leading archaeological researcher on caves in Ireland and has produced a major synthesis of that research (Dowd 2015). Robert's primary research interest is in the Irish passage tomb tradition and his book contextualizing the best known monument of that tradition, Newgrange, is an important contribution to Neolithic studies (Hensey 2015). These interests demonstrate that archaeologists have to understand the role of darkness in the human use of the exterior, the open air, and the interior of natural places like caves and built structures such as tombs – a theme that runs through the papers in the volume. This point is returned to below but it is worth emphasizing here that the human experience of darkness is socially mediated and historically contingent, or to put it another way, people experience darkness in different ways depending on how, where and when they live.

The challenge for the archaeologist, historian or anthropologist in understanding how darkness was experienced and perceived in other societies is to be reflexive and to remember that our understanding of darkness is grounded in our upbringing and social surroundings. Several of the contributors (Paul Pettitt, Ruth Whitehouse, Robin Skeates, Marion Dowd and Tim O'Connell) focus on caves. We might assume that the human encounter with darkness in caves would be oblivious to cultural context, but the reality is that modern researchers bring a very different sensibility about darkness to our experience of place. As Hensey points out, we live in a world very different to that of even the recent past in the sense that darkness has retreated, particularly for the majority who live in urban spaces. Such is the impact of artificial light and sky glow on the night sky that there is increasing concern to protect the dark night sky, for example through dark sky reserves (e.g. Prendergast 2015). So, we need to be aware of transferring our twenty-first-century sensibilities to our research. This is nicely illustrated by Charlotte Damm in pointing out that it was perceptions of darkness brought by European explorers which caused them to link 'Arctic hysteria' in indigenous people to the supposed negative impact of the prolonged darkness of the Arctic winter.

Light and dark

While the focus of this volume is on darkness, a key point to emphasize is that darkness and light are complementary. After all, I could not write and you could not read about darkness without light. This interplay between light and dark, lightness and darkness, underpins all the papers. The lived comparison of states of light and dark is a powerful and constant aspect of the human experience. This is why, as Ruth Whitehouse discusses, darkness has such widespread, complex and culturally varied metaphorical meanings. The alternation of light and dark happens on a daily basis as day turns into night, and on a seasonal basis through the annual cycle of spring, summer, autumn and winter. Most of the papers are set in temperate Europe but the contributions from Charlotte Damm (Arctic) and Sue Hamilton and Colin Richards (Rapa Nui (Easter Island)) remind us that daily and seasonal rhythms are geographically varied and distinct, as are notions of dawn and dusk: the transition points between day and night.

Recognising the widespread cultural variability in the interpretation of darkness and the need to be wary of any simple binary division of light and dark, there is a pervasive tendency to contrast them as states of awakeness and sleep, life and death, this world and the supernatural, our world and the spirit world. As John Carey points out, connections are made between key turning points in the relationship between the daily and seasonal patterns of light and dark, such as the Celtic festival of Samain; marking the beginning of winter, the shortest days of the years and the longest nights, and changes in the relationship between this world and the next. At Samain the boundaries between the living and dead are seen as being more porous, and the dead are more likely to be seen in the dark.

If the spirits of the dead or other creatures are one type of illumination of the dark there are others that serve to show the complex and necessary interplay of night and dark. The star compass concept used by Pacific Island navigators is a sophisticated application of the use of stars for human orientation at night and as direction indicators (Huth 2013, chapter 7). But this only becomes useful when it is sufficiently dark for stars to shine. The mix and interplay of the dark and light provides the environment in which most of us live our lives most of the time. It is against this human background, as Paul

Pettitt puts it, that 'impenetrable and inexplicable' darkness is difficult to experience and understand.

For archaeologists the opportunity to think about these key issues is when we have definite evidence for human activity in settings or contexts in which darkness would have been an integral feature. For example, Richard Bradley explores earlier prehistoric monuments in Ireland and Britain from the outside. He examines their orientation in relation to the light and the dark, sunrise and sunset, arguing that after 3000 BC we can see a polarization. From that time there is an increasingly powerful link between domestic structures and sunrise, while in the case of stone monuments associated with the bones of the dead there is an emphasis on orientation towards the setting sun; the dark sky. Caves are the context of human encounters with the dark that is most widely explored in this volume; from the modern caver's experience (O'Connell), the particular use of caves in Late Bronze Age Ireland (Dowd), the evidence from caves in Italy (Whitehouse) and Sardinia (Skeates) focusing on the Neolithic period, to the experience of caves in Upper Palaeolithic Europe (Pettitt). We return to caves below but it is worth bearing in mind here what Marion Dowd (2015, 2–3) has described as the unique and liminal environment of caves involving a descent into darkness, and a transition from the daylight zone near entrances to the twilight and dark zones of deeper parts of caves. These zones provide the setting for different kinds of activities, at least in part predicated on the degree of darkness, with occupation related to the brighter areas and ritual performance in the darker ones.

That contrast between light and dark also applies to houses, to paraphrase the title of a Seamus Heaney (2010) poem, the door may be open but the house may be dark. Houses are built to live in but to fulfil that purpose light and heat are required. Sue Hamilton and Colin Richards explore the role of the house, the *hare paenga* in ancient Rapa Nui, while Charlotte Damm discusses the role of the house in the Arctic, particularly during the winter darkness. A house, even if it is in darkness, conjures images of family, of home, of where people want to be. By contrast, contact with the dark may at least in part arise out of force and/or necessity, as with mining. One way of thinking about underground mines is as humanly constructed caves for the extraction of particular materials. In the case of the Great Orme mines in North Wales discussed by Sian James, copper mining was carried out in the Bronze Age and post-medieval periods and she suggests that it may have been children who were the miners. And in a nice play on the ideas of the light and dark, Gillian Allmond situates the Edwardian Winter Garden at the Purdysburn asylum near Belfast in the context of asylums being constructed as places of light intended to aid confined patients in their recovery.

In his consideration of dark places and supernatural light in early Ireland, John Carey makes the key point that it is in darkness that the Irish poet or *fili* sought illumination, knowledge and vision. He is one of several authors who set out schema of symbolic and metaphoric comparison between light and dark and recognizes their complementary character and paradoxical relationship. For example, there is the widespread association of darkness with the underworld or otherworld (e.g. Hensey, Bradley, Dowd, Hamilton and Richards). Linkages are made between the idea of the light of life contrasting with the darkness of the container of the womb, tomb and cave (e.g. Whitehouse, Hamilton and Richards), and the need to consider light and dark working together (e.g. Pettitt and Skeates). In this context, not surprisingly there is a focus on ideas of transition, of liminality, of being betwixt and between; whether it is light or dark, living or dead, this world or the next.

The experience of darkness

Returning to an archaeological perspective, a striking strength of this volume is the focus on caves. The record of the use of caves not only covers the history of *Homo sapiens sapiens*, but extends back to earlier hominin species. And as Paul Pettitt points out, from at least the Upper Palaeolithic period onwards people ventured into the deep and dark parts of caves, beyond the lit areas of cave entrances and adjacent areas, to carry out ritual performances. They created Palaeolithic and Neolithic cave art (Pettitt and Skeates), made deposits focused on particular parts of caves and features such as niches, speleothems and water features (Whitehouse and Skeates), and used caves for burial, for example going into the deepest and darkest parts of caves during the Late Bronze Age in Ireland for this purpose (Dowd). Robin Skeates, in a memorable phrase in his paper, refers to the particular effects of light and darkness mediating between people's bodies, cave architecture and cultural objects.

While I suspect not all the contributors would agree, one broad framework within which to place all these experiences and practices is that put forward by Lewis-Williams and Pearce (2005, 25–8). They argue that there are three interlocking dimensions of religion: experience, beliefs and practices. The latter lead people into religious experiences and demonstrate belief. This approach can be combined with another well-known definition of religion by Clifford Geertz (1966) as a set of symbols which acts to formulate ideas of a general order of existence. This religious dimension would explain why people had the belief and felt the necessity to experience the dark – the other world. It would also explain the rich variety of symbols and practices that were undertaken by people with specific sets of beliefs in the quest for a religious experience and as an expression of those religious beliefs. For example, as Hamilton and Richards discuss, the Polynesian cosmology based on the complementarity of the realms of *Ao* and *Po* is woven through and given physical, material expression in the different elements of the cultural landscape of Rapa Nui.

Of course as Ruth Whitehouse points out, we cannot assume in all cases that people were present in dark places by choice as part of religious practice. This applies even more strongly to users of the dark such as the prehistoric and post-medieval miners at Great Orme (James), or the confined patients of the Edwardian era asylum at Purdysburn (Allmond). On the other hand as Sian James points out, both the Bronze Age and post-medieval miners appear to have left offerings to appease the spirits who lived in the mines. This belief in knockers or mine spirits can be linked to the folklore of Sardinia where fairies are believed to live in caves (Skeates) and to the discussion by John Carey of the inhabitants of the *síde* or fairy mounds in Ireland. Here the folk belief was that the place of the gods and the supernatural realm was underground, for examples within mounds like Newgrange and Knowth.

Hence cosmological beliefs provide us with a powerful framework for understanding human encounters with the dark. John Carey goes on to explain why in the particular cultural tradition of the early Irish poet or *fili* (one who sees) real wisdom and knowledge comes to those who can see in the dark. As I mentioned earlier, the most engaging and thought-provoking contribution to the conference was that of Brian Keenan and the wisdom of the human condition he emerged with from his long journey of incarceration in Beirut, 'the vertigo of the night' as he describes it in his poem *Nightmare* (Keenan 1992). Linking in with Carey's contribution, Brian Keenan describes how he was visited in captivity by the presence of Turlough O'Carolan, a blind seventeenth-century Irish harper who was very much in the *fili* tradition, living a creative life shaped by the dark. Keenan (2000) went on to write the novel Turlough, based on O'Carolan's life. In the novel's acknowledgements he refers to a woman from Alaska who had written to him, convinced that O'Carolan had blindsightness (some who inhabits dreams, who sees in their dreams). Brian Keenan (2004, 314–8) describes meeting this woman, Debra Chesnut, a shaman, in Alaska and she acted as his guide to the spirit world. His reflection on that encounter is also a useful way of thinking about the richness and diversity of views about darkness contained in this book; 'the best of guides don't only show the way, they help you when you stumble'.

References

Dowd, M. 2015. *The archaeology of caves in Ireland*. Oxford, Oxbow Books.
Geertz, C. 1966. Religion as a cultural system. In M. Banton (ed.) *Anthropological approaches to the study of religion*, 1–46. London, Tavistock.
Heaney, S. 2010. *Human chain*. London, Faber and Faber.
Hensey, R. 2015. *First light: the origins of Newgrange*. Oxford, Oxbow Books.
Huth, J. E. 2013. *The lost art of finding our way*. Cambridge, MA, Belknap Press of Harvard University Press.
Keenan, B. 1992. *An evil cradling*. London, Hutchinson.
Keenan, B. 2000. *Turlough*. London, Jonathan Cape.
Keenan, B. 2004. *Four quarters of light: an Alaskan journey*. London, Doubleday.
Lewis-Williams, D. and Pearce, D. 2005. *Inside the Neolithic mind*. London, Thames and Hudson.
Prendergast, F. 2015. The Great Stone Circle (B) at Grange, Co. Limerick: a ceremonial space for all seasons? *Journal of Skyscape Archaeology* 1 (1), 65–92.